To Jane, for putting up with me, and Robyn, for being my daughter.

Contents

YEMEN
Gulf of Aden
Cape Gardafui
Bossaso
DJIBOUTI
Ras Harfun
SOMALILAND
Hargeisa
PUNTLAND
Eyl
ETHIOPIA
Hobyo
SOMALIA
Harardhere
Baidoa
Indian Ocean
Mogadishu
Kismaayo
200 miles

Foreword

Not long after my release from captivity, when I first thought of writing a book on Somalia, my opening piece of research was to go to Stanfords bookshop in Covent Garden to check out the competition. Opened in the 1850s, Stanfords is probably the most famous travel book and map shop in the world, having supplied such historical luminaries as Dr Livingstone, Florence Nightingale and Cecil Rhodes. Even Sherlock Holmes was said to have bought a map of Dartmoor here before heading off to Baskerville Hall. To this day, Stanfords still prides itself on covering every country under the sun, and yet when I scoured the 'Africa' shelves for offerings on Somalia, there was hardly anything on events in the past decade.

'No, we've seen nothing much recently,' agreed the shop assistant. 'Somalia's covered in the maps section, but even then we only have one.'

'Why is there so little?' I asked.

He looked at me, slightly surprised.

'Well, frankly, I don't think many publishers would want to risk the life of a writer by sending them there.'

Having already done the hard part – and having proven how right the shop assistant was – I headed home and started typing. What has resulted is, I hope, not one story, but three. The first is my own tale of being kidnapped. The second is the wider story of the Somali pirates, whose activities I had originally gone to Somalia report on. And the third is the story of Somalia itself, and why it has fallen into such a state of anarchy that such outlaws can thrive in the first place.

This book does not claim to be an exhaustive account of either Somalia's piracy or its politics. It is intended more as a snapshot of what remains a complex, disputed and ever-changing picture. This is partly due to the ongoing difficulties of reporting on the ground. Somalia remains as dangerous for foreigners as ever, and pirates, like most people in organised crime, do not generally welcome scrutiny of their activities.

I have also focused on those parts of the country of which I have some direct experience; inevitably, this means ignoring others. This book does not for example, discuss the rather happier picture in Somaliland, the breakaway region of north-west Somalia that has now been largely peaceful for two decades, and which wants its independence recognised by the outside world. Nor, contrary to the practice of many outsiders who write books on Africa, is this a book that tries to highlight the 'good side' – the virtues, decency, and courage-under-fire of the vast majority of the country's inhabitants. Instead, it is about the villainous minority, the bandits, crooks and warlords who have so often enjoyed the upper hand in recent years. On which note, I should point out that for legal reasons, the names of a few of the people I have come across have been changed.

Finally, a few acknowledgements. It is common for authors to use the phrase 'without whom this book would never have been written' when thanking those who have helped them. In this case, that is quite literally true. Were it not for the help of the *Sunday Telegraph* staff and many other people, I would quite possibly still be languishing in a cave, or worse. They are too numerous to mention, and some prefer their role to remain secret, but here are a few.

At the *Sunday Telegraph* itself, the foreign desk team of Adrian Michaels, David Wastell and Nick Meo worked day and night to help get my fellow captive José Cendon and me released. All were acutely aware that the longer we were held, the greater the chance was of something going horribly wrong – a deadline far more stressful than any in a newsroom. The same goes for Ian MacGregor, the *Sunday Telegraph's* editor, who had the small matter of running a national newspaper to worry about as well.

Others who played a key role were Abbie Sanderson, the foreign desk manager, whose administrative skills ensured that the few things that could run smoothly did so, and Annabelle Whitestone, the *Sunday Telegraph* foreign picture editor, whose fluent Spanish was vital in liaising with the authorities and José's family in Spain. David, Adrian and Nick's absence from normal foreign desk duties also meant that the likes of Will Kinnaird, Peter Hutchison, Joe Jenkins, Damien

McElroy, David Blair, Sally Peck and Angus McDowall had to work countless extra shifts over the Christmas period (my apologies, folks, for being kidnapped over the festive season). Big efforts were also made in the newspaper's personnel, legal and PR departments, not least by Fiona MacDonald, who had the unenviable task of dealing with round-the-clock calls about the kidnapping from outside media.

Others contributed from further afield. Fellow journalists Ian Evans and Mike Pflanz roped in their contacts in South Africa and Kenya respectively. Spain's ambassador to Nairobi, Nicolas Martin, and his staff gave us VIP treatment at his personal residence.

Perhaps the greatest heroes of all, though, were those much closer to home – namely my family and Jane, who coped with the whole thing far better than I had any right to expect. On which note, a mention also to the charity Hostage UK, whose advice to Jane gave vital reassurance during some of the darker moments.

Finally, thanks to Dan Collins at Monday Books for showing faith in the project, and friends Neil Chandler, Oliver Poole, Adam Lusher and Phil Perrins for proof reading the earlier versions. Roger Middleton, piracy expert at the think tank Chatham House, and Nuradin Dirie, independent Somali analyst, also provided useful perspectives on Puntland, as did countless other knowledgeable people who generously spared their time.

And very last of all, thanks also to my fellow hostage José Cendon, whose cheer and good company made it far more bearable than it might otherwise have been.

London, April 2011

Introduction

The cave must stretch about a hundred yards into the mountain. Its mouth, which catches the sun from mid-morning to late afternoon, is as wide as a house, while its innards taper into a narrow passageway that plunges downwards into pitch darkness – a meandering, cobwebbed tunnel that grows danker and gloomier with every step. A few days ago, on a particularly idle afternoon, the Old Bastard and some of the other guards went exploring; they must be the only potholing team in the world to carry AK47s, but no helmets or ropes. They found an exit on the far side of the mountain and walked back up the valley, triumphant, hours later. I did not share their excitement. I'd hoped never to see them again.

Forgive my malice. Plotting unpleasant ends for my captors is one of the few ways to pass the time in this grim place, where every minute seems like an hour – except for those when I'm savouring one of my precious cigarettes. Since the Old Bastard began threatening me a few days ago, I've had him bitten by a poisonous scorpion, struck by lightning, murdered by his own men, and eaten alive by the baboon pack down in the valley. If a rescue mission was to shoot him dead, that would be good too.

Sadly, I don't believe that armed rescue missions are on the agenda. We are being held in a mountain range on the pirate coast of northern Somalia, stashed away like buried treasure, but without the map where 'X' marks the spot. Northern Somalia is one of the remotest, emptiest places on the planet, and even on Google Earth it comes up as little more than a beige smear. I've barely seen a village, road or other human landmark since the day we were kidnapped. Besides, even if someone did know where we were, I don't fancy the prospect of another shoot-out in the cave. As we learned last week, solid stone walls are terribly prone to ricochets.

My stomach is feeling queasy. Probably the result of last night's goat stew, or possibly our drinking water, which comes out of an old diesel can. Caveman's Belly is one of the drawbacks of modern Stone

Age life, not something they ever mentioned in *The Flintstones*. I can't understand how they could have left it out: with so little else to do, answering the call of nature is one of the big events of the day round here.

So, the drill: first I grab my shoes, checking for spiders, scorpions or other poisonous vermin that might have climbed in. Then, stand up, with care. Lying on a thin mattress all day, you often get dizzy when you first get to your feet. Now, off to the bathroom, or at least the spot at the back of the cave that is reserved for that kind of thing. Thankfully, we still have a few tissues. The gang has told us that we will soon have to start using sticks and rocks.

On the way back, I pause halfway down the tunnel, where a section of the rock wall runs flat and smooth. If I were a caveman living here thousands of years ago, this is where I'd paint a picture of my clan out hunting an antelope. I pick up a shard of rock. I too am going to leave my mark here, something more permanent than a few cigarette butts. What shall I draw? A matchstick-men version of the kidnappers, with José and me as the quarry? Sadly, that will take a while, and if I linger here, the gang will think I have tried to flee down the pothole. Instead, I settle for some bog-standard graffiti:

'CF was here, 18/12/2008'.

I stagger back to the mattress, and tell José what I have done. A good move: we manage to squeeze at least ten minutes' worth of conversation out of it. This is the longest we've talked for a while. Perhaps some archaeologist will discover my scrawl here in thousands of years' time, I say. Or perhaps some other poor hostages will be dragged up here in years to come, and add their name to mine. Or, maybe, in ten or twenty years' time, if Somalia becomes a safe place to visit again, I will be able to come back, hire someone to help me find this cave, and see it for myself.

If I ever get free, that is.

1: Land of lotus eaters

'If a fit and proper person volunteer to travel in the Somali Country, he goes as a private traveller, the Government giving no more protection to him than they would to an individual totally unconnected with the service.'
(The Court of Directors of the Honourable East India Company, 1849)

AS WOULD HAVE seemed entirely reasonable to anyone suffering drug-induced paranoia, the man in the next hotel room had spent the whole night with a gun at his side. He stepped out into the corridor mid-morning, one hand rubbing a pair of bloodshot, sleep-deprived eyes, the other cradling a Kalashnikov that swung in the folds of his robes. He had been living a comfortable expatriate life in Belgium, and the stress of returning to his native Somalia had clearly taken its toll.

In fact, he'd fallen prey to the routine that all too many of his countrymen adopted in times of stress. Chew a lot of qhat, the amphetamine-filled plant of which Somalis are so fond. Grab an assault rifle. Prepare for the very, very worst.

'I heard yesterday evening that we are in danger here in this hotel,' he whispered, mouth foaming with green qhat cud, pupils swivelling up and down the corridor. Through the furred-up mosquito gauze on the window at one end, glints of morning sunshine were piercing through, signalling the start of another hot day. 'An attack is perhaps being planned. I made one of the hotel guards give me his gun. I have had it by my bed all night.'

'Who's after us?' I asked.

He smiled, shaking a balding, close-cropped head. 'That I cannot tell you. I do not know myself.'

With that he disappeared back into his room, leaving me to ponder our unseen foes. Here in Bossaso, a ramshackle Somali fishing port with sidelines in piracy and people trafficking, there was no shortage of people who might have grudges against the few foreigners in town. The Somalia section of Britain's Foreign Office travel advice website, which I'd read before coming here, had abandoned all sense of restraint in its efforts to urge caution. Warlords, Islamic terrorists and insurgent gangs were all out there, waiting to kidnap, kill and carbomb. There was also something called 'general internal insecurity', a kind of bucket-clause for any other unforeseen hazards. Who, after all, would have predicted that pirates would ever be back in business, having not troubled the average international traveller for several centuries? The Foreign Office said that if you were thinking of going to Somalia, you probably shouldn't, and if you were there already, you'd better leave at once.

The other possibility, of course, was that my excited neighbour was just high as a kite, a theory backed up by the trail of qhat twigs that littered his room. Qhat is the narcotic shrub that is chewed all over the Horn of Africa, with much the same disregard for moderation that the British have for alcohol. Its leaves contain cathinone, a natural amphetamine which yields a high somewhere between ten cups of strong coffee and half a tab of Ecstasy, depending on who you ask. Somalis are deeply fond of grazing on this psychedelic spinach, despite doctors' advice that it weakens their minds, wrecks their marriages and will ultimately destroy what is left of their country. Sir Richard Burton, who explored northern Somalia in the mid-19th century, thought it was the inspiration for the mythical lotus plant, mentioned in Homer's *Odyssey* as a narcotic which ensnares all who indulge into an agreeable stupor. The problem is that, if chewed non-stop for several days, qhat tends to induce psychosis, a condition ill-suited to a country where an assault rifle is seldom far from reach.

My neighbour had been on just such a bender. He'd spent the past week chewing day and night with other Somalis in the hotel lounge, excess leaves gathering on the floor around them like a newly-trimmed privet bush, jabbering with ever more urgency and ever less sense. It was tempting to conclude that he was now just in the grip of qhat paranoia, and that the only real threat to our safety was that someone had lent him a gun when he was stoned off his head.

And he was supposed to be one of the good guys. When not sitting around chewing qhat, he was working as the fixer for the two French television journalists further down the corridor. Along with my photographer José and I, and a bearded South African businessman who seemed to spend most of his time holed up in his room, we were the only other foreigners in the hotel, which, as it was the only one in Bossaso deemed safe for us to stay in, meant we were probably the only other Westerners in the whole of town.

I was in Bossaso on behalf of my newspaper, the *Sunday Telegraph*. José and I were hunting pirates, just as the French journalists and their fixer were. Unlike terrorists, warlords and drug barons, pirates were not a breed of outlaw that – until recently – the modern foreign correspondent had expected to report on. They'd provided plenty of lurid, racy copy for my predecessors in the 1700s, back when they wrote of 'pyrate terror', but they belonged to a time when the world was a much bigger, less conquered place. Back then, there were pirates in Penzance, never mind the West Indies or Madagascar. Today, more than three centuries later, very few parts of the world remain ungoverned enough to offer pirates a safe haven.

Somalia, though, was the glaring exception that proved the rule. Ever since its government collapsed in 1991, it has been in almost complete anarchy, a mosaic of clan factions who fight and pillage each other with a ferocity that defies all attempts at mediation. Much of it goes unreported by the outside world, especially compared to other trouble spots like Iraq or Afghanistan. The risks are too high, and the land too bereft of oil, minerals or other valued things to merit much news space beyond the 'African basket case' sector of our minds and newspapers; it only really grabs attention is when its own problems become a threat to the outside world. Which was why, when the pirate attacks started escalating in autumn of 2008, the qhat-chewing fixer and I ended up as neighbours.

*****

As they do, the pirates had sailed into my life uninvited, during the middle of an assignment in Pakistan about forced marriages. Part of the fun of being a London-based foreign correspondent is the sheer unpredictability of it. A military coup in Chad, pro-democracy protests in Burma, Germany's unfathomable cult worship of the folk singer Roger Whittaker; there is no telling what or where the focus of the working week will be, or whether it may switch mid-way through. I'd just got back to my lodgings in Islamabad when my mobile rang. It was the foreign editor, David Wastell. Kidnapped brides in Pakistan were about to be shunted down the news agenda by kidnapped sailors on the Indian Ocean.

'A tanker's been hijacked by Somali pirates.' he said. 'It's called the *Sirius Star* and it has $100 million worth of oil on it, plus two Brits among the crew. It would be good to do a big number on Somali piracy for this weekend; if you can manage it. Weren't you talking about going there a few months ago?'

He was right, I'd been researching the Somali pirate story for a while, trying to work out various options for reporting on the ground. And then, constantly, finding reasons to put it off. As foreign assignments go, Somalia was arguably trickier than anywhere else in the world at the time.

In Iraq and Afghanistan, there were at least Western armies running around trying to patch things up. The last time the Americans tried that in Somalia resulted in US soldiers' corpses being dragged through the streets of Mogadishu, events later dramatised in the film *Black Hawk Down*. US soldiers I'd met in Iraq used to watch *Black Hawk Down* on DVD to remind themselves that things could be worse. Somalia has no Baghdad-style Green Zone that provides foreign visitors with an oasis of safety. The nearest British and American embassies are 1,500 miles away in Nairobi. If you get into trouble, you might as well be on another planet.

Still, if you don't get a slight kick out of being in dangerous places, becoming a foreign correspondent isn't a great idea. For all the high-minded talk of 'bearing witness' and so on, old-fashioned thrill seeking plays a part as well, at least it did for me. Unlike some,

I hadn't got into foreign reporting because I wanted to change the world, but because I wanted to change my own life. In my previous incarnation I'd been a lower-rung reporter on the *London Evening Standard*, where I seemed to spend most of my time writing about roadworks, train delays, and the odd bit of celebrity gossip. When the US invasion of Iraq loomed, I realised that rather than being out covering the biggest story of my generation, I was likely to be writing about disruptive cable-laying programmes on the North Circular road through Catford. And so it was that on Christmas Eve 2002, bored and hungover while doorstepping the ex-wife of the TV entertainer Michael Barrymore, I had an idea. I'd say goodbye to my job, my flat and a relationship that was going nowhere, and head to cover the war in Iraq as a freelance.

The plan was not without its critics, who pointed out that I had no experience of war zones, no travel insurance, no contacts, and no work lined up. But by holing up in a $5-a-night hotel in Baghdad, hiring an ex-Iraqi tank commander as a translator, and freelancing for everyone from the *San Francisco Chronicle* through to *Laundry & Cleaning Today*, I'd managed to earn a living. Then in 2005, I'd landed a staff job as a foreign correspondent with the *Sunday Telegraph*. If that sounds slightly smug, forgive me, but when you've spent as much of your life writing about roadworks as I have, it's hard not to feel self-satisfied at leaving it all behind.

*****

One thing you notice when flying to Somalia is that no airline risks spending much on the plane that takes you there. Daallo Airlines, which flies in from neighbouring Djibouti, lays on a rusting propeller-driven Antonov, a Soviet-era relic custom-made for the world's less accommodating airports. The Antonov's rugged engines need no sophisticated ground maintenance staff, yet have sufficient lift to flea-hop on and off very short airstrips, which made it ideal for ferrying arms and mercenaries around during the Cold War. Sure enough, our own craft was being piloted by an unshaven Russian in a white suit and sunglasses, who looked like the Man from Del Monte gone to seed. Inside, everything except the plywood toilet cubicle was upholstered in a leopardskin pattern. Combined with the pilot's 1980s-style aviator shades, it felt like clambering into the airborne equivalent of a Ford Capri.

Even getting this far was something of a triumph. Following the phone call from my boss about the *Sirius Star*, I'd spent the last 36 hours booking a complex chain of last-minute flights to Bossaso via Islamabad, Karachi, Dubai and Djibouti, and touring various money wire offices to withdraw $6,000 in cash – the paper trail I left would have resembled that of some terrorist on a major suicide mission.

Sat alongside me in Air Leopardskin was a Spanish freelance photographer called José Cendon. An East Africa specialist, he was based in Ethiopia and had come recommended by another correspondent on the foreign desk. All I knew about him was that he was aged 34, had black hair and a beard, and travelled under a Spanish passport number 823345 – the details he'd supplied to the office in case he wound up dead or missing during our trip. It's not unusual to go on foreign assignments with photographers you've never met before. You just have to hope that you will get on well, or failing that, can work together without getting on each other's nerves too much. Over the cups of tepid water that passed as the in-flight hospitality, we made each other's acquaintance. To my relief, José spoke perfect English. More importantly, he'd been to Somalia several times before. It wasn't the sort of place you wanted to go with a novice, not that I was exactly an old Somali hand. I'd been just once before, to Mogadishu in 2006, although that alone was enough to qualify me as the office expert.

As the Antonov droned over the flat desert of Djibouti, I opened my laptop and ploughed through a file of hastily-downloaded cuttings on the piracy situation, reading up as if swotting for some exam. Geography has not done Somalia many favours – its harsh, sun-scorched scrubland offers precious little natural resources, animal, vegetable or mineral. What it does offer, however, is plenty of prime locations for piracy, its coastline of 1,900 miles being the longest in Africa. Particularly well-placed is the northern region known as Puntland, which forms the lower lip of the Gulf of Aden, the channel of water that leads to Egypt's Suez Canal and links Asia with Europe. More than 20,000 vessels push through the Gulf every year, carrying 20 per cent of the world's trade. Seen from a plane, the sea is flecked with vessels: sleek Arab dhows; quarter-mile-long oil tankers; Chinese and Indian freighters; the odd luxury yacht. Seen from a pirate skiff, crewed by men from one of the poorest and most desperate nations in the world, it must seem a rich and almost limitless hunting ground.

Piracy had been a problem in these waters ever since the early 1990s, when Somalia's government had first collapsed. But since 2005 it had become much more organised, and in autumn 2008, the number of attacks had rocketed. There'd been 70 attempted hijacks between August and November alone, compared to just 30 for the previous year. Nobody really had a good explanation as to why; it just seemed that word had spread that piracy was an easy game to get into. Apart from a couple of motor launches, all that you needed was a few Kalashnikovs, a rocket-propelled grenade launcher and maybe a heavy machine gun, and you were in business. These were items easily available in a country still awash with Cold War weaponry. Even the sailing expertise required was limited. These days, the pirates could steer themselves not by the stars, but by hand-held mobile GPS systems. The nautical answer to the satnav, these meant they could range hundreds of miles out to sea without getting lost.

There was, however, one important difference between the pyrates of old and the pirates of new. Whereas the storybook buccaneers of my youth would steal a ship's treasure and make its crew walk the plank, today it was the opposite way around. Somali pirates weren't really interested in the ship's cargo. A 50,000-tonne consignment of cement or mineral ore was impossible to ship ashore in their small launches, never mind to find buyers for. Instead, they were after the ship's crew, whom they would take as hostages for ransom. That effectively made the pirates professional kidnappers rather than robbers, and, for obvious reasons, therefore a risky interview prospect.

Our aim was to try to meet one, and tell the story from his point of view. That point of view might be, though, that a pair of Western journalists would make far better hostages than a few Filipino deckhands.

*****

'A safe and friendly place for visitors from abroad'
(Website of the government of Puntland State of Somalia)

Beneath the window, through the blur of the Antonov's propellers, the Puntland coastline peeled past. The Gulf of Aden rippled into white breakers that spilled onto a flat, unbroken shoreline. Inland, expanses of rocky desert stretched away into a range of ochre mountains, the terrain almost devoid of roads, houses or other signs of habitation.

Like most of Somalia, Puntland was not known as a particularly welcoming place for foreigners. José and I would not be the first people heading here against the official British wisdom of the day. Ever since the early years of the British Empire, when a colony had been built at Aden to protect spice ships from India, the 'Somali country' to the south side of the Gulf had been seen as a no-go zone, a land of wild tribesmen reputed to be the fiercest in Africa. When the Victorian explorer Captain John Hanning Speke arrived at Aden in 1854 and announced his intentions to make a ground-breaking exploration of the northern Somali interior – partly, it seems, to bag a few more specimens for his private museum of stuffed animals – the political resident at Aden, Sir James Outram, had been horrified.

'He said he would not only withhold his influence, but would prohibit my going there at all,' Speke later recorded in his *Journal of Adventures in Somali Land.* 'The countries opposite to Aden were so extremely dangerous for any foreigners to travel in, that he considered it his duty as a Christian to prevent, as far as he was able, anybody from hazarding his life there.'

Sir James knew a thing or two about dangerous places, having spent part of Britain's first colonial war in Afghanistan wandering through hostile tribal areas in disguise. But like most British explorers of that era, Speke was not the kind to be deterred by warnings that his mission was foolhardy in the extreme. A former officer himself, he was the living embodiment of every cliché of the imperial adventurer class: possessed of a huge bushy beard, fond of blasting at every living thing with his rifle, and prone to describing his exploits among the 'simple-minded negroes of Africa' in language that is a little too robust for modern history books. His description of the Somalis he met in Aden, for example, pulls no punches.

'They are at once easily recognised by the overland traveller by their singular appearance and boisterous manner, as well as by their cheating and lying propensities, for which they are peculiarly notorious; indeed, success in fraud is more agreeable to them than any other mode of gaining a livelihood.'

Today, Speke is barely remembered compared to other famous explorers of his time, like David Livingstone and Henry Morton Stanley. An obelisk is dedicated to him in a corner of London's Kensington Gardens, and credits him with identifying Lake Victoria as the source of the Nile. But it makes no mention of his two less glorious adventures in Somalia, the first alone, the second with his more celebrated travelling companion, Sir Richard Burton, who became famous for translating the *Kama Sutra* into English. That second trip, made in 1855, proved that Sir James Outram's misgivings had been right all along.

On the night of April 18, while travelling through Berbera on the northern Somali coast, Speke and Burton's camp was attacked and nearly wiped out by a spear-wielding mob of clansmen. One British officer was killed, while Burton got a spear blade through his cheek and Speke suffered multiple stab wounds, his trusty Dean & Adams revolver having jammed at the critical moment. The pair finally managed to escape, cursing their local Somali guards, who had failed to put up any kind of fight against the raiders. When they arrived back at Aden, British officials added insult to their many injuries by giving them a severe dressing down. British expeditions were supposed to be roadshows for imperial strength, not weakness. As Speke remarked in his usual bluff fashion in his journal: 'I had nothing to show but eleven artificial holes in my body.'

A century and a half on from that ill-fated expedition, some of the protocols for visiting Puntland as a foreigner hadn't changed. Now, as then, the only way to secure safe passage was by the gun. Unlike Speke, I was not in the habit of carrying a pistol and sword around with me on my travels. Packing guns goes against most normal codes of conduct for journalists; like priests or members of the Red Cross, we are supposed to be 'neutral'. These days, though, you can no longer rely on any kind of Queensberry rules about who is and isn't a target, so we'd be using local armed guards, hired for us by two Somali fixers that José had engaged ahead of our arrival. In Somalia, every foreigner uses them: businessmen, aid workers, even the BBC.

*****

The Antonov descended into Bossaso airport, a long expanse of concrete that hugged the coastline, with a few whitewashed buildings at one end. The Somali passengers, men in business suits and robes, and women in *niqabs* leaving just a slit for the eyes, grabbed their bags, eager to escape the swarm of flies that had boarded the plane along with us in Djibouti. Near the terminal, a large crowd had gathered, including a TV crew.

'There are presidential elections for Puntland in January,' explained an English-speaking Somali who'd been sat near us. 'The man who was sat just behind you is a candidate. Those are his supporters, waiting to meet him.'

Unlike the rest of Somalia, Puntland was not entirely devoid of government. It was semi-independent of the rest of the country, having seceded in 1998 in a bid to disentangle itself from the chaos elsewhere, and now had both a parliament and a police force. None of its institutions, though, were more than semi-functional, and the man behind me in Row 27 had not struck me as much of a president-in-waiting. I vaguely recalled an elderly Somali in an ill-fitting suit, his VIP style cramped somewhat by travelling cattle class on Air Leopardskin. Through the window, though, I could now see him launching into an impromptu press conference before the TV cameras, promising to set his people's many wrongs to right. It is often the way in tiny African statelets like this: political leaders and senior officials are not distant, anonymous figures, but people you sit next to in economy class, see drinking in a hotel bar, or hear name-dropped by others as cousins or pals.

José and I clambered off the plane, into a gathering crowd of Somali faces. Airports like these have none of the strict airside access policies enforced in the West. It is therefore hard to be sure who is who. The man officiously issuing you with a chit and taking your luggage away may be a helpful airport attendant; equally, he may just be an enterprising thief. On a visit to Nigeria, the fraud capital of the continent, I was warned to be suspicious even of people holding up a card with your name. Miscreants had been known to check the flight list for your details, pose as a courtesy taxi driver sent by a hotel, and then politely lead you to a car full of waiting robbers.

To minimise the chances of such mishaps, José had lined up a pair of local fixers in Bossaso to look after us. Nearly all newspapers use fixers to help them negotiate the world's trickier corners. They're usually local interpreters or journalists, who top up their earnings by acting as guides to visiting reporters. A good fixer will get you interviews with the right people, take you where you're not supposed to go, and above all keep you safe, knowing when to charm and when to bully. They are the unsung heroes of the frontline news business, often the key to a hard-to-get interview, yet generally only mentioned to the outside world when killed in the line of duty. In really dysfunctional countries, they are all the more essential, and, unfortunately, all the harder to find. It's then that you are more likely to encounter the bad ones, who are only in it for the money. At best, an encounter with a bad fixer will end up in a blazing row; at worst, they can actually land you in serious trouble. Unfortunately, they are your eyes, ears and voice, and you are entirely dependent on them. Even the formidable Captain Speke, who had a pistol at his side and the might of the British empire behind him, complained of being at their mercy. As he writes in his *Journal of Adventures*: 'It rests entirely on the (fixer's) honesty whether his client can succeed in doing anything in the country he takes him through.'

I can vouch for that view, having dealt with every variety of fixer over the years. Some have become good friends, and one saved my life from a mob of militiamen in Iraq. Others have threatened to kill me after I have sacked them for incompetence, or have simply never turned up at the airport in the first place.

To our relief, our two Somali fixers, Ahmed and Mustapha, were waiting at the bottom of the plane's gangway. They were both about 30, dressed in Western slacks and shirts. They came without any prior recommendations, although that wasn't unusual in very out-of-the way spots. If they weren't up to scratch, part of your job was to just make do with the limited talent on offer. Ahmed, a soft-spoken chap with a wiry build and the high, domed forehead typical of Somalis, introduced himself as the translator. Mustapha, a stocky, boyish-faced figure, was the 'fixer'. This division of labour, it turned out, was because Ahmed was the only one who spoke English. Which meant all our conversations would have to be relayed back in turn to Mustapha – an inconvenience, to say the least, although a relatively minor one by global fixer standards. At least they'd showed up.

We exchanged a few pleasantries, and headed to the terminal under a dazzling bright sun, as if some hole in the ozone layer had opened up right above us. The VIP welcome that the presidential candidate had received did not extend to us. We were directed into a bare, whitewashed side room, where a man in paramilitary fatigues sat listlessly at an unvarnished wooden desk. There was no sign above the door, but if there had been, I think it would have read: 'Dept of Visa Hassle'. A minor inquisition by local officialdom is one of the rituals of arriving at airports like this, as much as breathing in the new air while coming down the gangplank.

'What is your business here?'

'Do you have a letter of invitation from a minister?'

'Why has it not been faxed to airport immigration?'

'Where is your certificate of employment and taxation status?'

'What do you mean, nobody told you about any of this in advance?'

If lucky, you can get away with offering to pay a 'fine' – in other words, a bribe – of a few dollars. If unlucky, you come up against someone honest, who may actually put you back on the plane home again.

Mustapha and Ahmed began a long discussion in Somali with the man in fatigues. Other people entered the room and joined in, some official-looking, others apparently just enthusiastic passers-by who felt they had something to contribute. After about half an hour, I asked Ahmed what was going on. He had a slight stutter, and a habit of prefixing almost everything he said with the phrase 'Understand one thing'.

'Understand one t-thing,' he said. 'The airport p-people say you must get permission to come here before you arrive.'

'But you'd already asked them for it on our behalf, hadn't you?' said José. 'You said it would all be fine.'

'Understand one thing. We did, but there is just s-some small problem. Do not w-worry.'

This was not an encouraging start. Either Ahmed had forgotten to do the permits, and was lying, or he had indeed got them, and was getting hassle nonetheless. That shouldn't be happening. A good fixer always made sure he had airport people on his side.

The discussions rambled on. José and I got permission to leave the room so he could have a smoke. Outside we met a Kenyan-Somali researcher from the International Crisis Group, a human rights NGO. He was likewise getting grief because of reports he'd written that the Puntland government hadn't liked. Three cigarettes later, we were called back inside.

'The Security Minister is going to make things OK,' said Ahmed. 'He is on his w-way.'

Sure enough, ten minutes later, a rotund man in a collarless khaki bush suit appeared. He had thick spectacles and silver hair, which spilled out from under a white skullcap. I was assuming that Ahmed had mistranslated when he said 'the security minister'. He meant, presumably, someone from the security ministry. Surely, whoever was in charge of law and order in Puntland – no easy portfolio, presumably – wouldn't be on hand just to sort out the visa problems of various foreigners.

'I am Abdullahi Said Samatar, Minister of Security for Puntland State,' announced the man in chirpy English, shooing the official away from the wooden desk and taking up residency there himself.

I was impressed. This was the equivalent of having Britain's Home Secretary turn up to sort out a paperwork foul-up at Heathrow. Either Ahmed's fixing skills were better than we thought, or Puntland really was a very small world. Yet it did not appear that the top man was on our side.

'You have entered the country illegally,' Samatar declared. 'You should have got permission before you came. You will go back to Djibouti on the next plane.'

'We were told we could get the visa on arrival,' I protested. 'Our fixer has done all the paperwork already.'

'You should have got the visa at an embassy in your own country.'

'But Somalia has no government. There are no embassies abroad.'

'What do you expect me to do? Break the law for you? Would I expect to get into your country, Britain, without a visa?'

'So is there any way around this problem?' I asked, cursing inwardly for not offering to pay a bribe earlier. The sensible tactic with bribery was to pay the first official who gave you trouble, on the basis that they would be cheaper to buy off than their superiors. Here, though, we'd gone straight to cabinet level. God knew how much a ministerial backhander might be.

'There is one thing you can do. You can write a letter to me now, asking for permission.'

'What, right here?'

'Yes, right here. Where else?'

I pulled some *Telegraph* headed notepaper out of my bag, stashed specially for this kind of bureaucratic arselicking. 'What does it have to say?'

'It needs to be addressed to me, and to say: 'I would like to apply for permission to enter Puntland State of Somalia'.'

'Okay.'

'And it should also say that 'I apologise for the inconvenience caused by my failure to obtain a visa beforehand'.'

'Fine. Anything else?'

'I am not dictating it! You must write it yourself!'

I scribbled away, the minister watching from his desk like a headmaster disciplining two unruly schoolboys. When I'd finished, he took the letter and pored over it. Just as I thought he was about to make me to write 500 lines saying *'I must not come to Somalia without a visa',* he decreed we could stay. The man from the NGO was put back on the plane.

*****

Ahmed and Mustapha took us to a battered chrome-and-blue four-wheel-drive. In a white Toyota pick-up next to us was our armed escort, four ruffianly men dressed in green and brown fatigues and clutching Kalashnikovs. Like most Somalis they had skinny, wiry frames, on which their uniforms hung off them like scarecrows. The youngest looked only about 17, and sported big, mirrored shades. The eldest looked like he could have been the 17-year-old's grandpa, with a grinful of gold teeth under a floppy camouflage hat.

'Aren't we supposed to have eight of them?' I asked Ahmed.

'Understand one thing,' he said. 'This is just for the d-drive to the hotel. It will take only ten minutes. We will have all eight tomorrow.'

I didn't bother arguing. I never had that much in faith in bodyguards anyway. It was one thing if they were ex-SAS men, like the ones that the *Sunday Telegraph* had used when Baghdad had got particularly rough. Those you could reasonably expect to put up a fight on your behalf, especially given that they charged about £2,000 per day. Using 'local nationals', as they were known in bodyguard-speak, was different. Gold Tooth and co were on the going rate of $20 a day each – good by Somali standards, but unlikely to be enough for them to lay their lives down on our behalf. Scarecrows, indeed, was all they were. They might have had some military training, or they might just be Ahmed's cousins, holding a gun for the first time in their lives. Equally, one of them might be some psychotic ex-civil war veteran, who'd blow someone's head off at the slightest provocation. Their suitability for close-protection work was not really the point, though. In Somalia, you weren't paying people to protect you from kidnappers, as much as you paid them not to kidnap you themselves. It was the same principle as the 'mind-your-car-for-you-mister' scam practised by street urchins outside football grounds in Britain, only with rather higher stakes.

We headed out of the airport, looking like the convoy of some tinpot African dictator, plunging into a maze of tumbledown shacks and rubbish heaps. I'd assumed Bossaso airport was some way from Bossaso proper, because we hadn't seen any built-up area from the runway. Now I realised that Bossaso just didn't have any built-up area at all. Most buildings were just one-storey shacks, scattered amid stretches of stony ground, rubble and white sand. There were no proper roads, only grooved, bumpy tracks. Either side of us, goats and seagulls foraged among piles of rubbish and abandoned cars, so old they'd finally exhausted the African ingenuity for keeping them on the road. On the breeze, sea air and sewage tussled for supremacy. The only brightness was the hand-painted adverts on the whitewashed shop fronts, depicting household items like washing powder and soft drinks with childish simplicity.

Yet this was a city in boom, apparently. People fleeing the chaos in Mogadishu and the south had flocked here over the past decade, Ahmed explained, expanding Bossaso's population from around 50,000 to 250,000. It was 19th century San Francisco without the gold, modern-day Dubai without the skyscrapers, new arrivals squatting refugee-style in thatched lean-tos that nestled among the proper buildings. Among Somalis, Bossaso's nickname was the Land of Opportunity, a USA for people who'd never see the real thing.

I knew little else about the place. Puntland was such an unvisited corner of the world that even the internet, which can normally spout limitless data about anywhere on the planet, seemed somewhat stumped, yielding only a few random, gloomy facts. Bossaso had very little industry, apparently, other than the export of a few hardy goats, camels and sheep. Its best-known trade, though, was in livestock of the human variety. The port was one of the biggest people trafficking centres in the whole of East Africa, according to the UN. Thousands of desperate Somalis, Ethiopians, and Kenyans flocked here every year, paying $50 for a place in an overloaded skiff that would ferry them across the Gulf of Aden to Yemen. Assuming they were lucky enough not to drown *en route*, they might find a marginally better life as an illegal immigrant labourer in one of the Gulf Arab states, or make their way to Europe. At dawn, would-be passengers would huddle on the beaches out of town, waiting for the traffickers' skiffs to arrive. Sometimes local Somali aid workers would turn up, trying to persuade them not to take the risk by showing them photos of the drowned, bloated corpses of people whose boats had sunk. But such shock tactics had limited effect; many of those on the beaches had already spent money and risked arrest just to get this far. Having dumped their cargoes off in Yemen, the people traffickers would return to Bossaso with smuggled weapons, drugs and other contraband. The whole place, in effect, was already steeped in maritime criminality, with piracy merely the latest addition to the portfolio.

The International Village Hotel – 'Bossaso's Sheraton', said Ahmed – loomed through a turning. A sprawling, faux-colonial two-storey villa, it hid behind a ten-foot high wall topped with barbed wire. A head-high steel gate operated by two armed guards opened up to reveal a garden restaurant and a yard patrolled by a large and belligerent ostrich, which snapped irritably at anyone who came too close. Why it was there was not clear, although it did look more on the ball than the security guards. I thought back to my old hotel compound in Baghdad, with its concrete anti-blast walls, and dozens of armed sentries, braced for suicide bombers coming at them both by car and on foot. If anybody wanted to storm this place, it would be a comparatively easy task.

Otherwise, it looked pleasant enough, which was just as well, given that we'd be confined here whenever our armed guards weren't around. As we unloaded our bags, I was reminded yet again of what a small world Puntland was. A Somali I'd been chatting to on the plane, who now lived in Ealing in west London, wandered over.

'You are staying here also,' he beamed. 'You said you were a journalist, yes? Would you like to interview the Interior Minister? I am his friend.'

'Well, yes, that would be great,' I said. 'Do we make an appointment through his office?'

'Why, no,' he said. 'He's just over there.' He gestured to the car park behind him, where a man in his early 40s was sat on a bonnet smoking a cigarette. I'd assumed he was a hotel bellhop.

I wandered over. 'Er, excuse me, are you the Interior Minister?'

'Yes, that is me,' said the man. 'I am Mohamed Said Kalombi.'

'Er, I'm from the *Sunday Telegraph* in London. I was wondering if I could interview you about pirates?'

'Why ever not?'

I pulled out a notebook and started grilling him – the first time, to my recollection, that I'd ever conducted an interview with a minister of state in a car park, while being glowered at by a suspicious ostrich.

Kalombi was a worried man, and not just because of the piracy. The whole of Puntland was suffering from deteriorating security, he said. There'd been a spate of kidnaps of foreigners in the past year, including a French journalist and two aid workers, and a growing threat from the Islamic extremists who now controlled much of southern Somalia. Bossaso had been hit twice by car bombs in recent weeks, attacks blamed on the Shabab, a group linked to Al Qaeda. Foreign aid agencies and businesses were pulling out, leaving people with even less prospects than before. As in the rest of Somalia, Puntland had vast numbers of jobless young males, all looking for ways to make men of themselves. Down south, it was militant Islam that offered them that chance. Up north in Puntland, it was piracy.

'Young people get drawn into the piracy because there is almost 100 per cent unemployment here,' said Kalombi. 'Now they see the chance to make millions of dollars through crime. It has become a 'flu, an epidemic. With their money, the pirates are buying more weapons, and even bribing the justice institutions. A whole young generation is becoming criminalised.'

There was little Kalombi could do about it. The Puntland government did not permit pirates to operate openly in Bossaso itself, although according to many people, the number of luxury villas springing up amid the shanty towns suggested it was awash with pirate cash. But the authorities' writ did not extend to the remoter stretches of the vast coastline, which now had numerous settlements where the pirate Jolly Roger fluttered unchallenged. The flow of ransom cash was so great that in some places, tiny, run-down fishing villages had undergone Torremolinos-style transformations into pirate boom towns. One village called Eyl was said to have become the modern Hispaniola, the island where the original pirates of the Caribbean lived in the 1700s. Residents were rumoured to have set up special 'restaurants' to cater for the diets of foreign hostages, while local mechanics were doing a kind of 'Pirate pimp-my-ride' service, equipping clapped-out wooden skiffs with souped-up engines. News reports about Eyl's new cottage industry had first surfaced several months ago, but no journalists had actually been there to write a first-hand account. I was hoping we might be the first.

As stories of the fortunes to be made in piracy had spread, more and more gangs had formed, with local warlords scrambling to get in on the act. The pirates of Puntland were thought to have netted at least $30 million in the past year alone, and even when the ransom was divvied up among a gang a dozen or two strong, it was still life-changing sums for people used to so little. For lower-ranking pirates there might be a new car or wife, and a lavish wedding with hundreds of guests. For their commanders, it might go on a flash new house in Bossaso, or a private bank account in Dubai – and also new hijacking ventures.

Ship owners were accused of paying up ransoms too easily, but argued they had little choice. A hijacked vessel could run up bills of $50,000 a day just in running costs and penalties for late delivery of goods. For the ship owners, it was cheaper to simply hand over a million dollars or two and get their ship and crew back quickly, rather than get involved in a stand-off that might run for several months. The *Sirius Star*, the oil tanker which had just been hijacked, was a case in point. It was a prize beyond the pirates' wildest dreams, the modern-day equivalent of a Spanish galleon packed with gold. The boat itself was less than a year old and had cost $150 million. And on board were two million barrels of oil – roughly a quarter of Saudi Arabia's daily output – worth a further $100 million. The pirates wanted $25 million, their biggest ransom demand yet, and a fortune by Somali standards. Yet to the owners and insurers, that was still only a fraction of what the whole package was worth, before you even took into account the lives of the 25 crew on board.

*****

We checked in and headed for the restaurant, only to bump into yet another minister. Dr Abdirahman Bangah, Puntland's acting head of fisheries, was taking afternoon tea, sheltering from the fierce sun under a wooden gazebo. He too was much exercised about the piracy problem – in particular, the failure of the outside world to stop it. In recent months, a multi-national naval force had been sending warships to patrol the Gulf of Aden, but so far their efforts had been hamstrung by legal red tape. Bangah had been particularly upset when a Danish warship had arrested 10 pirates, only to dump them back on a beach after deciding they lacked jurisdiction to prosecute. 'Where is the deterrent for people to join the pirates, if they think they might not even get arrested?' he demanded. 'They need to be much tougher.'

As it happened, just days before hijack of the *Sirius Star*, Royal Marine commandos from *HMS Cumberland* had shot dead a couple of pirates as they'd tried to attack a ship. Dr Bangah had apparently not heard about this, and, while he would no doubt have approved, I didn't bring it up. The first time a British warship had killed any pirates in centuries, and it happened in the very week that I, a British journalist, was in town trying to interview one: it was hardly going to make me popular in certain local circles, so the less the news was spread around, the better.

José and I ate a fried fish dinner in the restaurant, and then turned in. It had been a surprisingly productive first day. We hadn't even ventured out of the hotel yet, and we'd already met half the government of Puntland. Before going to bed, I wandered through the lounge to find my Somali-Belgian neighbour and a friend sprawled on the floor watching TV, surrounded by a vast pile of qhat leaves. My neighbour's companion, cigarette in one hand, qhat twig in the other, introduced himself.

'Hi,' he said languidly. 'I am the Minister of Health'.

2: Never let your daughter marry a pirate

ABDIWELI ALI TAAR'S business card hinted at just how lawless Puntland's coastline was. A printed logo introduced him as the head of the Somali Coastguard Service, under which a series of subheadings portrayed him as a busy man: 'Drugs. Counter-terrorism. People trafficking. Toxic waste dumping. Illegal fishing. Piracy.'

Rather less impressive than his business card was his ramshackle 'fleet' of Coastguard vessels, moored at Bossaso's rundown docks. We'd gone there on our second day, this time with our full complement of eight armed guards. They were crammed into the pick-up behind us, leaning out in all directions like the Anthill Mob from the Wacky Races. At the docks, a smell of rotting fish blew on the warm air, and a sign on the gate reminded a wayward populace to refrain from bringing in rifles, pistols, coshes, grenades, daggers or CS gas.

The fear of piracy had reduced the number of visiting ships to a few old barges from India and China, whose owners either figured their crews weren't valuable enough to kidnap, or simply didn't care. Tied up alongside them on the grey concrete quayside was Taar's entire armada – two decrepit launches, and a 40-foot motorboat with a sea-rusted anti-aircraft gun grafted onto the deck. This last was a marine version of a 'technical', Somalia's infamous contribution to improvised guerrilla warfare, in which an artillery piece was welded onto a pick-up truck. Compared to the frigates of the international anti-piracy force, the Coastguard's flagship looked like a fishing trawler with attitude. Taar, a cheerful, bespectacled chap with a goatee, was no admiral either. Prior to hunting pirates, he'd been living as an émigré in Canada, working as a cabbie.

His coastguard, however, did have one weapon in its armoury that the international force lacked – fear. The pirates weren't actually that scared of the foreign gunboats, knowing that because of their rules of engagement, they would only open fire as a last resort. With Taar's crew, they couldn't be quite so sure.

'When they see other Somalis coming, they get scared,' Taar told us with a grin. He was talking to us in his villa near the docks, a smart, modern place with proper air conditioning, something that marked him out as a man of status round here. 'If they see that you are serious about killing them if necessary, they will not kill their hostages. They want to make money, but they don't want to die.'

Taar took us down the road from his villa to the Coastguard's barracks, a walled compound that housed about 50 troops. Dressed in the same tatty paramilitary fatigues as our bodyguards, most were either grizzled old men or adolescents with wispy moustaches, giving them something of a *Dad's Army* look. Yet they'd learned their trade from people who'd been hunting pirates longer than anyone else – the Royal Navy. A London-based security firm called the Hart Group, staffed partly by former RN personnel, had mentored them between 1999 and 2002, after which the Puntland government had run out of money to pay them.

In the last two months, the Coastguard had conducted three successful operations against pirates. In one, they'd freed a group of Syrian sailors on a hijacked cement ship after a prolonged stand-off, during which one Coastguard man had been killed. Taar was confident that with a few extra gunmen, he could cleanse out a major pirate nest like Eyl, yet right now he didn't even have money for fuel. The week before, he'd gone cap-in-hand to meeting of UN donors in Nairobi, and played them a promotional CD showing footage of the bust on the Syrian cement ship. But the assembled company had refused to give him a penny. One official even warned him that if his clapped-out gunboat was seen by a foreign naval vessel, it might be mistaken for a pirate ship and fired at.

'I thought the video would impress them in Nairobi, but they haven't done anything,' he said. 'They are just not taking their responsibilities seriously on this matter, even though it is their ships that are being caught.'

I was sympathetic, but not particularly surprised. There were a few things that Taar's promo CD didn't mention, starting with the rather unorthodox tendering process for the coastguard contract. I'd read that Taar and his brother Hiff had won it largely because they'd backed the winning side in the civil war that briefly flared in Puntland in 2001. Then, when the government had run out of money to pay the Coastguard's $20-a-day wages, some of them had apparently turned to piracy themselves. In 2005, three Coastguard men who were supposed to be escorting a Thai vessel took the entire crew hostage, demanding $800,000 in ransom. They were later arrested by a US warship and were now doing ten years each in a Thai jail. Some of their shipmates, meanwhile, were said to be advising current pirate crews, their British-taught expertise earning them far more as poachers than it had as gamekeepers.

The Coastguard, though, was not the only part of Puntland's justice system to drift onto the wrong side of the law. One segment of Taar's promotional CD showed the pirates captured from the Syrian cement ship being loaded into a waiting police van at Bossaso docks. Several were sniggering, and one even waved to the onlooking crowds. They look like swaggering gangsta-rappers, not like men about to face harsh justice. While Samatar, the security minister, had pledged that pirates could expect either execution or long sentences in Bossaso's squalid jail, the gossip around town was that eight convicted pirates had recently bought their freedom by slipping $20,000 each to the Puntland government. For gangs earning millions in ransoms, that counted as a minor overhead. I asked Taar whether there might be any truth in such rumours.

He looked around for a moment, as if someone might be listening, and then spoke quietly.

'Of course,' he said. 'If the government really wanted to stop the piracy, do you think the Coastguard would lack the money to buy fuel?'

*****

Friendly as he was, Taar was not who we'd come to Bossaso to meet. The main prize was still to interview a pirate. In theory, this should not have been as hard as it might sound. The pirates were apparently keen to tell their tale to the world, claiming it was simply pay-back for all the years in which foreign trawlers had poached fish off the Somali coast. And besides, a good fixer could get you an audience with Satan and bring you back out alive. But the not-so-good ones will tell you that yes, Satan has agreed to be interviewed, but has postponed till tomorrow, then the day after, *inshallah*, and so on, until it becomes clear it will never happen, and I was beginning to get the feeling that Ahmed and Mustapha fell into the second category. First they'd claimed it would be no problem to go to Eyl and meet the pirate clans. Then they'd told us that it was several days' drive away, and that we'd almost certainly be kidnapped. As a compromise, Ahmed then offered to bring a local pirate he knew of to the hotel for us to meet. It sounded tempting until he mentioned, as if by way of recommendation, that this same pirate had been involved in the kidnapping of a French journalist last year. We decided against that too.

Eventually, it became clear that our only realistic hope lay behind the walls of Bossaso Central Prison, where a number of pirates, those whose friends had not yet bought them out of jail, still languished. It should have been simple to get access to them, as the Puntland authorities were supposedly keen to show that they were taking the piracy problem seriously. Instead, it became like the mythical hunt for buried pirate treasure. Every time Ahmed announced that everything was arranged, some last-minute obstacle would spring up. First, the security minister Samatar objected. Then the chief of police had to be consulted. Then the jail's governor wanted to be in the loop. Then, Samatar objected again, this time on different grounds, and the whole process started again. After three days of constant haggling, endless phone calls and several stand-up rows with Ahmed and Mustapha, we finally got in there on Saturday afternoon, just hours before the *Sunday Telegraph* went to press.

The jail was on the outskirts of town, down a long straight track that led to a sun-baked stockade squatting in the desert. It was like a Wild West fortress, a stone outer perimeter wall guarding an inner square that housed the inmates' blocks. We got into the outer courtyard, only to encounter yet more static from the chief warden, a rotund, languid character in sunglasses, who ran his fiefdom while ensconced on a sunlounger.

Three further hours of Kafkaesque discussions followed. First the warden wanted money. Then the pirates said they didn't want to talk. Then they said they would, but only if we brought them some qhat. Then the warden said qhat was banned in the jail. Eventually, he agreed to allow us in, but only for photographs. The guards let us through into an inner square, surrounded by big communal cages. Looking around, I realised why the authorities had given us so much grief about letting us in. The scene inside could have adorned any Amnesty International campaign leaflet on prison reform. Hundreds of arms waved at us through rusting blue bars, while in the unlit gloom beyond, grins of broken teeth and pairs of cataract-clouded eyes hovered in the darkness. Even from a distance, the smell of unwashed bodies was strong. The sight of two white visitors sparked uproar, possibly because it was the first entertainment anybody had had in months.

José snapped away, and we headed back to the hotel in time for him to send the pictures to go with the piece I'd filed that morning. I'd stayed up writing it right through until 5am, fuelled by chewing sachets of dried Nescafe in the absence of 24-hour room service. It's an old foreign correspondent's trick, handy for meeting deadlines when exhausted or jetlagged. The taste alone is disgusting enough to jolt you alert, and unlike the qhat that my neighbour was munching nextdoor, it allows you to keep a reasonably clear head. I needed it. The 'Despatch from the pirate coast' had not proved easy to bring to life, not least because the key characters – the pirates – hadn't made themselves available. Fortunately, the day before, we'd found another larger-than-life character to tell the story through – a fire-and-brimstone imam, who'd been giving sermons vowing God's displeasure on anyone who took the pirate coin.

'Do not take gifts from any pirate, and do not eat in their homes,' he'd warned. 'And do not let your daughter marry them – it is worse than sleeping with her yourself!'

The imam was an invalid, his legs withered by polio. He couldn't afford a wheelchair, so his friends ferried him around in a wheelbarrow instead. It was, I realised, every bit as bizarre a spectacle as seeing Long John Silver and his parrot walking along Bossaso docks. With the imam's help, I managed to knock out a 'colour piece' without racking up too many penalty points on my journalistic licence.

That night, José and I set about doing what most reporters do when deadlines have passed: getting drunk. As a Muslim state, Puntland was officially dry, but the hotel bellhops offered a discreet service in bottles of smuggled Ethiopian gin. We poured some into a mineral water bottle to disguise it, and retired to the open air restaurant. It had still been one of the hardest working weeks I could remember. From the moment we'd set foot here, we'd had to argue our case, be it with the immigration people, the prison wardens, Ahmed and Mustapha, and even our own armed guards, who seemed to think the best way to keep us safe was simply to keep us in the hotel all the time. They'd never turned up less than hour late, refused to work beyond about 3pm, and during the brief times we'd managed to go somewhere, tried to dictate what we did. Every day had felt like we had a coach party of whinging but heavily-armed schoolchildren in tow.

As the gin bottle rapidly emptied, we moved onto the only other intoxicant still available in Bossaso late at night, the infamous qhat. I'd tried it on my trip to Mogadishu two years before and had a fine time. Unlike cocaine, speed and other 'uppers', a group of people chewing qhat together do not necessarily degenerate into a series of competing monologues. Instead, your fellow motormouths actually seem like they have something interesting to say, which makes it great for after-dinner conversation. The problem is that to get the effect, you have to chew not just a few small leaves, but the equivalent of a medium-sized garden shrub. Sweet, sugary tea is served to dull the bitter taste, and rather than swallowing you spit it out, like chewing tobacco. But the effect only kicks in after at least an hour of mastication, which is long enough to leave your cheeks raw and your jaws aching the next day. And for all the conviviality it brings, there's no guarantee that the conversation will be particularly enlightened.

Around 10pm, we were joined by Ahmed, who'd been chewing since we got back from the jail. Rather than debating the finer points of Somali clan politics, we ended up discussing the British film director Guy Ritchie's divorce from Madonna. Details of the celebrity couple's failed marriage had emerged during the summer, and for some reason, Ahmed had been following it avidly on a celebrity news website. It was the first time I'd heard him speak on a subject with any real authority.

'U-understand one th-thing. Mad D-Donna should have more r-respect for Mr R...Ritchie, and sh-should not have left the family home like that,' he stuttered, his faltering English more staccato than ever from the amphetamine in the qhat. 'And what is she d-d-dancing around in public with only a small amount of c-clothes on? Wh-what husband would like his wife doing that?'

We all laughed, the tensions that built up over the last few days dissolving in the qhat juice sluicing in our mouths. I told Ahmed that if I ever bumped into Mr Ritchie back in London, I'd let him know that the people of Bossaso were scandalised by his wife's behaviour. Then I handed him a $10 note and sent him off into town to get more qhat. It was beyond midnight now and the streets were silent, save for the sound of crickets. But it wouldn't be hard to locate a few other chewers on an all-nighter. Ahmed was soon back with more bundles. We finally retired at 5am, the quarrelling of the working week forgotten thanks to a few hours' conversation at 78 rpm. We hadn't met a pirate, but at least we'd set Guy Ritchie and Madonna's marriage problems to rights.

I lay in bed, wired from the qhat and quite unable to sleep. The last time I'd chewed qhat, it had torn up the insides of my mouth so badly I'd been unable to eat properly for a week. It was around the time I'd started seeing my girlfriend, Jane, who I'd met via an online dating agency. It was about the only way someone with my peripatetic and unpredictable job could find a partner, as it allowed me to flirt online from anywhere in the world. When I'd got back from Mogadishu, we'd gone out for a dinner at a posh restaurant, where her date – who'd described himself online as 'pretty normal' – had cut up all his food into small pieces first, rabbiting on about getting stoned on some strange plant she'd never heard of.

To Jane's credit, she hadn't been put off by it, or by anything else about me, which was surprising given how different we were. Dating agency websites let you tailor your preferences on everything from politics, film and food through to whether you're looking for marriage or just a one night stand. Yet somehow, Jane and I had chosen polar opposites in each other. She had spent her life working for environmental groups and human rights NGOs, seeking not just to save the planet but to make it a better place. I'd spent my working life in newsrooms, bastions of professional cynicism. By rights, we shouldn't even have been on the same dating agency. It was one run by the *Guardian*, which, in theory, no self-respecting hack from the right-wing *Telegraph* should have been seen dead on. Unfortunately, I'd browsed the *Telegraph's* own equivalent, and found it seemed to cater mainly for ladies in their 50s looking for someone to share their passion for antique restoring. If that sounds like a stereotype of *Telegraph* readers, Jane was arguably a stereotype of the *Guardian* species. Like many green types, she wouldn't fly anywhere for holidays because it damaged the ozone layer. By contrast, I racked up about 100,000 airmiles a year. One friend laughingly called Jane my 'carbon offset'.

For two years, the partnership of Treehugging Lefty Woman and Vile Tory Boy, as our respective friends knew each other, had somehow survived. But the prospect of long-term commitment scared me witless. It was one thing to gamble my life in a warzone, quite another to gamble it on a woman, especially one who disagreed with nearly everything I said. And, besides, could I really continue spending half my time abroad if we had children? Getting up to change nappies every night would leave very little energy for rushing off to Heathrow at short notice, unless I began chewing qhat on a regular basis.

And so it was that the week before my assignment in Pakistan, we'd split up. We'd gone our separate ways one cold Monday morning, her face trembling a little as I'd walked out the door of her flat. It wasn't the first time we'd broken up, but on previous occasions, the option of reconciliation had never been kicked out of touch. This time, she'd emailed me saying that in order to properly move on, she didn't want to speak again for six months. Our relationship was ending the way it had begun, via the internet.

'You can contact me to tell me you've seen the light,' she'd written. 'Other than that, I don't want you to contact me at all. I'm sorry.'

Having not so much stared into the abyss as chucked myself right off it, I realised that I'd made a mistake. I'd thought about it for a few days, then emailed her from Pakistan to say I wanted to get back with her. This time I signed up for everything. Commitment, kids, in good times and bad, the lot. At the time, part of me had wondered whether I really meant it, or whether I was just panicking. But now, lying on the sweat-soaked mattress, staring at the ceiling fan, I felt I'd done the right thing.

Outside, the sky was lightening. There was the crow of cockerels, the purr of car engines and the murmur of voices, the sounds of Bossaso getting up to start another tough day. I would be facing a tough day myself. I'd always treated my body more as a nightclub than a temple, but even so, half a litre of Ethiopian moonshine and several kilos of qhat was likely to prove a punishing combination. As well as a brutal hangover from the cheap spirits, my jaws would ache and the torn-up insides of my mouth would feel like I had a dozen ulcers. As the old Somali saying went: 'Qhat makes you believe the whole world belongs to you, but in the morning you feel like they took away the keys.'

*****

The next day brought more than just a bad qhat come-down to deal with. Sometime in mid-afternoon, I staggered out of bed and headed to hotel reception to inquire when the next available flight back to Djibouti was.

The answer was, not for another three days.

I cursed. I was tired, hungover, and anxious to get home and see Jane. Besides, the longer I stayed in Puntland, the less relaxed I felt. With every passing day, it had become clearer to us just what a volatile place it was. All the local power brokers were on edge right now, spooked by the sudden international attention on the piracy problem, and the prospect of a power reshuffle in January's elections. The Kalashnikov-wielding Belgian in the hotel room next to mine was not the only one sensing trouble. Early on Sunday evening, as I was lying hungover in my room, there was a knock at my door. It was the Coastguard head, Abdiweli Ali Taar.

'I want to tell you about what is going to happen here,' he said in a low voice. 'There will be elections here in January, and then there will probably be some kind of war.'

'Really?

'Yes. Different groups trying to get power. Whoever loses the elections will not accept this. Puntland is a very dangerous place right now. When are you going back to London?'

'Oh, I'm not quite sure yet. Some time this coming week.'

I was lying. I knew exactly when we were leaving – Wednesday at 1pm. My ticket, purchased that afternoon by one of the hotel staff, was in a drawer. But one thing you never did in places like this was tell anyone your future movements.

'When you have made up your mind, let me know. I can give you an armed escort to the airport.'

I said I'd bear his offer in mind. In a way, I felt a lot more comfortable with Taar than I did with Ahmed and Mustapha. He had nothing obvious to gain by being friendly, unless he thought that as a reporter, I might be useful to him one day. Like seemingly everyone round here, it turned out he was planning on running in the presidential elections. But it would cause no end of trouble now to use Taar's guards rather than our own.

We killed the days before the flight by researching a feature about the local qhat market, a big row of wooden stalls in the centre of town where everyone came to buy their daily fix. Vendors sold qhat of various tastes and strength, covering their wares with sheets so that the leaves stayed moist and tender. The qhat cargoes were flown every morning from Kenya and brought to the market in pick-up trucks. Such was the appetite that each pick-up truck had guards armed with sticks to keep over-enthusiastic customers at bay. Demand for qhat was apparently at an all-time high thanks to the pirates, who found it a useful way to keep going during prolonged hijack negotiations. Many in the market saw them as local heroes, robbing the rich to give to the poor. 'Viva the pirates,' one lady qhat vendor told us approvingly. 'They are keeping us in business.'

That was one theory, anyway. The other explanation for the soaring qhat sales was that Ahmed was eating it all. He claimed he only chewed once a week, but since Saturday afternoon he'd been on the stuff non-stop. He seemed nervous about something, although neither José nor I could work out what. It was, as with so much of this trip, just another of the strange sub-plots that was pointless to try to comprehend.

*****

From: Colin Freeman
To: Telegraph foreign desk
Re: Departure from Somalia
Sent: 10.05pm, Tuesday November 25, 2008

'Planning to leave Somalia tomorrow (Weds). Taking the 1pm flight from Bossaso to Djibouti, flying Daallo Airlines Flight D3774, arriving 3pm Djibouti. Will call in and confirm all is okay when we arrive, fear slight risk of bureaucratic hassles on way out as our fixer here is bloody useless. If we don't get on the flight, I may be stuck here for yet more days.'

We finally left for the airport just before 11am, sending what is known as a 'last known whereabouts' email the night before. This is standard procedure for all transits in riskier destinations, containing information that the office can pass to the authorities if you vanish between A and B. Ahmed and Mustapha had for once turned up on time, as had a new set of bodyguards. We'd swapped them for the previous lot in the hope that they would be more punctual, although they looked no different from Gold Tooth and his pals, frankly, just another bunch of budget gunslingers in military fatigues.

José and I clambered inside the back seat of the 4x4, with Ahmed sat alongside us and Mustapha up front next to the driver. We headed out the gates, the bodyguards behind us in a single pick-up truck. As we jolted through the side streets, I could feel the stress that had built up over the last three days begin to peel away. Two of the last hurdles were already over: we'd paid Ahmed and Mustapha off without any great rows, and the guards had turned up on time. Now all we needed to do was to get the airport, negotiate any official hassle, and then wait for Air Leopardskin and the Russian pilot. Right now, I wouldn't care if he announced mid-air that we'd be diverting to the Congo for a spot of gunrunning, as long as he got us out of this cursed land of lotus eaters. I'd spent the last three days dreaming about this flight. José and I would toast each other farewell, first with a celebratory cup of water on the plane, then a beer in the Djibouti airport bar. After that we'd go our separate ways: he to Ethiopia, me to London, and reconciliation with Jane. Then, as one of the bodyguards turned to look at us, came the realisation that my qhat-chewing hotel neighbour had been right to be paranoid all along.

3: Kidnapped

I WILL NEVER FORGET the bodyguard's expression. He was one of the younger ones, a teenager with a hard, chiselled face like that of a seasoned lightweight boxer. Until now I hadn't even noticed him, he'd just been another figure in the smother of camouflage uniforms clinging to the back of the pick-up. Now, as we headed across a patch of open scrub, the pick-up had suddenly sped alongside us, and I could see his face pulled into a snarl, his eyes bulging, his teeth bared. For a fleeting moment I thought he might just be arguing with the driver over what route to take, expressing himself with the brusqueness that men with guns routinely do in Somalia. Then, as he and his companions leapt out of the pickup and ran to either side of our car, I realised we were being surrounded.

Our driver ground to a halt. To the left and right, the passenger doors opened. Outside the car, people were shouting and arguing in Somali. I glanced around, hoping there might be some innocent explanation. But to borrow Ahmed's expression, I understood one thing. We were being kidnapped.

'Shit,' said José, in a low, flat voice.

A guard reached into the car and tugged at my shirt, urging me to get out. I slid meekly along the seat, and jumped onto the hard gravelly ground. The guard, a tall, skinny fellow who looked about 21, had his Kalashnikov pointing at my stomach. We were no more than 20 yards from the nearest houses, but I didn't even think about trying to make a break for it. Being held at gunpoint has a mesmerising effect on the uninitiated. The overriding instinct is to do exactly what you are told. The guards gestured at us to get in their pick-up, and we did so without a hint of protest. To anyone watching at that moment, we probably looked like we were just changing cars because of a puncture.

Two guards leapt in the back seat either side of us and slammed the doors shut, wedging me in so tight it was impossible to move my arms. The pick-up roared off, wheels skidding in the gravel. I looked behind to see the other bodyguards in the back of the pick-up, guns at the ready in case anyone chased us. Their uniforms flapped in the wind as we gathered speed.

Then, darkness. Scrawny hands either side of us draped a scruffy green jacket over our heads, so we could neither see nor be seen. The musky body odour of the jacket's previous wearer mingled with my breath, now coming sharp and shallow. I could sense we were heading out of town, away from what little law and order Bossaso had. As we hurtled onto a rough back track, a narrow gap opened in the folds of the jacket. Through it I could see the desert that led towards the mountains, speeding past like a film on fast-forward. The driver was plunging through the rocky dunes with the speed and skill of a rally driver. Behind us, the rest of gang yelled at each other over the engine's mounting roar. There were laughs and whoops, the sounds of people who knew they'd got away with it. Where were Ahmed and Mustapha? No idea. Not that they were likely to be much help. The very men they'd hired to keep us from getting kidnapped were now kidnapping us themselves. Were *they* in on this, I wondered? Suddenly it felt as if forces unknown had been plotting this ever since we set foot in Puntland. As if all those conversations in Somali around us had been leading up to this very moment.

'Is there anything we can do, José?' I said weakly.

He made no reply. The bodyguard next to me, the tall fellow who'd dragged me out of the car, rapped me over the head with his gun butt for talking. But I had to ask. If we were going to try to escape, now was the time to do it rather than in the middle of nowhere. For a brief, mad moment I considered trying to lean forward and jerk the steering wheel, rolling the pick-up over. Then I realised it was a stunt I'd only ever seen work on TV shows like *The A-Team.* Colonel Hannibal's plans always came together, but mine, I suspected would not. Crammed in together like this, we'd all end up with broken backs.

I thought of trying to dial the *Sunday Telegraph* foreign desk in London via my mobile phone in my trouser pocket. Even if I couldn't speak to them direct, perhaps whoever picked up the phone would hear the gang's shouts in the background and sense something was wrong. But when I wormed my hand into my pocket, the guard to my right spotted the movement and grabbed the phone himself. As he did so, the jacket slipped from my head. He didn't bother putting it back. We were now right out in the desert, and he was obviously beginning to feel more relaxed.

And me? How did I feel? I'd spent much of my life reporting on other peoples' wars, tragedies and traumas, asking them to put into words how it felt when disaster struck. Now I realised why so many of them shrugged or began their response with the phrase: 'It's impossible to describe...'

It is indeed hard to do justice in words to what moments of extreme fear are really like. Most of us experience them so seldom that we lack the necessary emotional vocabulary. Nor, indeed do we really need it. At such times, our brains are designed to go into fight-and-flight mode, not sit around self-analysing. I was aware, though, of a feeling of detachment, a disbelief that it could actually be me, *yes, me*, that this was happening to, that of all the world's six billion people, I had scooped one of the jackpots in that day's global lottery of bad luck. The fear was there, but it felt strangely numbed, as if my brain had self-prescribed some strong natural Valium. Somewhere inside me though, a muffled voice was repeating the same emergency announcement, over and over again.

Oh my God. We have been kidnapped. This is bad. This is very, very bad.

The guards in the back of the pick-up were jabbering away, shouting instructions to the driver above the roar of the engine. In the conversation, only one word sounded vaguely familiar. It sounded like 'Kismayo', the name of a city in southern Somalia. Kismayo was not a place we wanted to go to. It was a stronghold of the Shabab militia, who'd imposed a kind of Taliban rule. The month before, they'd stoned a 13-year-old girl to death on trumped up charges of adultery and the Americans had launched missile strikes against the Shabab's leaders earlier in the year, claiming they were harbouring Al Qaeda fugitives. I'd no idea who'd snared us, but if they were taking us to be guests of the Shabab, we'd get a very hostile reception. At best, they'd probably use us as human shields in case the Americans carried any more airstrikes; at worst, it was a televised beheading. I tried to remind myself that no foreign hostage had yet been killed in Somalia – to my knowledge, anyway. But that muffled voice in my head couldn't help whispering: *'There's a first time for everything, you know.'*

The mountains drew nearer. Soon we were in the foothills, coursing along a dried-up river. The pick-up's tyres spun their way over beds of smooth, water-washed pebbles. Finally, when the trail got too steep, we ground to a halt in front of a thicket of trees. As the guards spilled out, I counted them. Seven, not the eight that we'd paid for. Fucking Ahmed and Mustapha. They'd even ripped us off on the number of kidnappers we should've had.

The guards ordered us out, and pointed to where the riverbed continued, up a sparsely wooded canyon.

'Imshi!' yelled one of them.

He was another teenager, with a face so thin and craggy that shadows cast across it even in the midday sun. White desert dust from the journey still covered his cheeks and forehead, transforming him into a grinning skull with black eye sockets, a Somali Jolly Roger. *'Imshi'*, I knew, meant 'walk' in Arabic. Just in case I didn't understand, he pointed to his gun and mimed a bullet going in my forehead. José and I marched off with our hands above our heads.

'Maa fi mushkilleh', I said.

It was Arabic for 'no problem', a phrase that I'd learned in Iraq. Mainly for use when there was in fact a very big problem indeed. We scrambled up the canyon, shoulders wincing in expectation of a bullet. The kidnappers fanned out, a couple ahead of us, the rest behind, guns drawn. José pulled alongside.

'Are you okay?' I asked him.

'Me, I am okay, yes. But I am concerned for my parents. They will be very worried. My father has a heart condition.'

I imagined some elderly Spanish man keeling over in front of the TV news, and tried not to think about my own father doing the same.

'Listen, man, we'll get through this okay,' I said, not really believing it. 'We'll just have to be strong, and...'

'IMSHI!'

Another guard, a bald, wizened guy in his 40s or 50s, interrupted us, pointing a finger to his lips.

Ten minutes further up, we came to a clearing and stopped. They gathered around us, guns drawn. A new fear hit me. What if they were just going to kill us? Just as I was thinking what a discreet, soundproofed spot this would be to shoot us and hide our bodies, one of them delved into a rucksack and handed us a bottle of mineral water. They obviously planned to keep us alive. For now, anyway.

'Imshi!'

The canyon steepened, bearing round to the right into a wide valley where we could see the start of the mountains proper. God only knew where we were. It was the emptiest, most barren landscape I'd ever seen. Trees and plants were almost non-existent. The valley slopes were strewn with sharp, twisted shards of black and brown volcanic rock, which clinked like metal as they dislodged under our feet. There was no path, forcing us to pick our way carefully like mountain goats. While José was wearing hiking boots, I had on only a pair of Next slip-on shoes. They'd been my default choice of work footgear ever since Baghdad, where my Iraqi translators had advised me against the standard war-reporters' get-up of combat trousers and hiking boots. It was too close to how US government officials dressed, they said, and therefore the equivalent of painting a target on one's back. Now, with every step, I was regretting ever listening to them, as sharp rock edges dug into the soles of my feet. If we carried on like this, I'd end up not just with ferocious blisters, but a broken ankle. Somehow, I doubted I'd be excused and sent home. I looked at my watch. 1pm. We should have been on the plane by now. Daallo Airlines Flight D377, with its leopardskin seats and complimentary water, now seemed like the gateway to a beautiful, parallel life, stretching away like a missed turning.

After an hour of yomping that would have tested applicants to the Parachute Regiment, we stopped on a pass half-way up the valley. Sweat was pouring off my forehead, stinging my eyes. As I searched for a rock comfortable enough to sit on, I saw the skull-faced kidnapper squatting down to take a crap, dropping his trousers with a practised ease that meant I didn't look away in time. Another kidnapper, the tall, wiry guy who'd been wedged next to me in the pick-up, rummaged in a small blue rucksack. Like a Scout leader, he produced a handful of Mars bars and handed them round. It struck a surreal note. *Mars bars*? I didn't even know they sold them in Somalia. The gang tucked in, chewing noisily and with their mouths open.

'Me, I prefer Snickers,' said José, with a grin.

I smiled back weakly. At least he was keeping his sense of humour. I'd feared he might be angry. After all, it was me who'd asked him to come to Somalia in the first place. We'd worked well as a team, we'd had fun drinking gin and chewing qhat on Saturday, but we were both still essentially strangers, thrown into this mess together. There was no telling what he'd be like to be held hostage with, or what he might vent on me if things started getting really rough. Weren't there stories about hostages who'd had to be kept in separate confinement to stop them attacking each other? He seemed okay now, but what about after a couple of weeks? Or months? Or years? He was probably thinking the same about me.

However long we ended up together, I knew all too well the horrors that we might be in for. Getting taken hostage was something I'd dreaded ever since becoming a foreign correspondent, the one great occupational hazard of a great occupation. During my time in Iraq, Baghdad had turned into the kidnap capital of the world, insurgent groups actively hunting Westerners and parading them in amateur movies released on the web. In the run-down hotel I stayed at, a former brothel called the Al Dulaimi, no less than six colleagues had been abducted, prompting rumours that the hotel was cursed. All had eventually been released, but some had been held for months on end, their terrified, haunted faces staring out from terrorist video nasties. They were still among the lucky ones. Other kidnap victims had been beheaded or otherwise killed, their last moments filmed for

Al Qaeda propaganda broadcasts. The fear of kidnap had been the defining experience of reporting in Iraq, squatting malevolently in one's mind during every waking minute, and sometimes intruding into one's dreams. It was what every correspondent dreaded most, the one ordeal that might arguably be called a fate worse than death. It had even given me the title of the book I'd written about my time out there, *The Curse of the Al Dulaimi Hotel*.

Come to think of it, if I live to tell the tale of this kidnap, sales might go up a bit. And if I don't, they'll probably go up even more.

Jesus, was this really the time to think about that? My mind was rewinding and fast-forwarding through every aspect of my entire life, re-assessing things in the light of what had just happened. Book sales aside, the changes were not generally for the better. Now, I'd no longer be remembered as Colin Freeman the intrepid foreign correspondent. Now I'd be forever remembered as Colin Freeman the kidnap victim, who fell for the glamour of foreign correspondence, but paid the price. Or Colin Freeman, the guy who went blundering around dangerous places to boost his ego, because he couldn't make a go of normal life. Whose family were now about to go through absolute hell worrying about him.

Guilt surged through me. All of a sudden, the last five years of my career – by far the happiest of my professional life – looked like one long exercise in reckless selfishness. I imagined the awful moment when my parents would get the call from the office saying that I was missing. They were both in their 60s. Even if I eventually got released, something like this could give one of them a heart attack. And all because their son thought it was fun to flirt with danger. Then there was Jane. Where did this leave us? She'd be going spare over a man who didn't even seem to know if he loved her or not.

'Imshi,' said the Scout Leader.

Mars Bar break over, we carried on up. The air was cooling with the altitude, but the sun was still fierce. Fearing sunburn and a headache, I asked for something to cover my head. I was handed the green jacket used to hood us during the getaway. Knotting its sleeves, I fashioned it into a headdress. The smell of its previous owner's stale body odour hit me again. I tried not to think what lice, fleas and other armpit-loving fauna might be lingering there. The gang thinned out, two on close guard, four in single file behind. A scout walked up ahead. Around us, mountains stretched on every side. Bossaso and the coastline were nowhere to be seen. I could see no huts, no path, no footprints, no litter, no sign that humankind had ever passed this way before. In terms of feeling far from civilisation, only being abducted by aliens would beat this.

I was reminded of a trip I'd done to Afghanistan in 2004, as a little light relief from Iraq. At the time, the US military was in yet another offensive to hunt down Osama bin Laden, who was still thought to be somewhere in its eastern mountains. I'd always found it surprising that they hadn't found him already, given all their manpower and technology, but once I got to Afghanistan I began to realise why. The place has a vastness and remoteness that simply no longer exists in the Western world. It first struck me on a trip to Bamyan, the village where the Taliban blew up some 1,500 year old statues of the Buddha. A few hours' drive out of Kabul, the driver had suddenly pulled onto a tiny, rocky sidetrack. I'd assumed he was about to take a piss. Instead, it was the start of the main road to Bamyan, another 12 hours' scramble up what wasn't much more than a cattletrack. Yet by Afghan standards, this was a good road. Other places, far further away, had none at all, just donkey tracks linking endless mountains and valleys. I ended up wondering not so much why the Americans hadn't caught Bin Laden yet, as why they'd ever thought it would be possible in the first place.

The mountains we were in now felt rather similar. Indeed, if the US really was 'closing in' on bin Laden in Afghanistan, this was probably the kind of place he'd flee to. Then, as we reached the crest of one mountain pass and marched down the other side, a lone figure appeared in the distance.

He was a boy, about 12 or 13, leading half a dozen donkeys towards us along a wide ridge of russet gravel. At first my heart leaped. Here, at least, was a witness, someone who might tell the outside world where we'd been seen. Then I realised it could lead to something horrible.

The kid approached, clocking our two white faces. I found myself thinking about a scene from the book *Bravo Two Zero* by Andy McNab, the former SAS man. During his unit's behind-the-lines mission in the Iraqi desert in Gulf War I, they'd come unstuck when a 15-year-old goatherd drove his flock into their hideout. Knowing he'd run off and raise the alarm, they'd contemplated shooting him, but let him go for the simple reason that none of them really wanted to kill a child. I wasn't so sure that the men who'd kidnapped us would have any such qualms.

Up ahead, two of the gang were now talking to the kid. The others watched closely. I could sense tension. The conversation didn't sound hostile. But I feared that any second, one of the kidnappers might smile, bid the kid good afternoon, and then put a bullet in his head.

Please God, don't them shoot him. For my sake, if not his. I don't want that on my conscience.

To my relief, the donkey caravan moved on. The herder gave us only a quick glance as he went past, as if it were entirely normal round these parts to see a couple of white men going out strolling with several local gunslingers. Maybe it was. Maybe other Western hostages had been dragged up here over the years. Perhaps whichever clan controlled this territory was in on the plot. That we were marching in broad daylight suggested the kidnappers weren't too worried about being seen.

As the herder went on his way, the gang motioned for us to rest again, perhaps to watch what direction he was taking. We squatted under a small, gnarled thorn tree, one of the few pieces of vegetation to dot the landscape. It looked every bit as hostile as the environment it had sprung up in, a weathered, grey trunk only shoulder high, its branches bristling with combs of inch-long thorns. Even the thorns had thorns, spiking out at right angles, making every twig look like the business end of a medieval mace. In Somalia, it seemed, even plant life knew that the best way to survive was to be armed to the teeth.

As we sat under what little cover it offered, the guards searched through our pockets again. They emptied my wallet, passing its contents for inspection by the old, bald fellow, who seemed to be in charge. He handed me back my credit cards, but for some reason viewed my Sainsbury's loyalty card with great suspicion, and confiscated it for further analysis. He also felt the outline of my money belt, tucked below my trousers, and gestured at me to remove it. There was about $4,000 in there in $100 bills, the remnants of the cash I'd withdrawn in Dubai. For the average Somali, it was the equivalent of about five years' earnings, like mugging someone in London and finding £100,000 in their pocket. For a fleeting moment I thought about chucking it into the breeze in the hope that they'd all run off to chase it, giving us a chance to escape. Then, meek as ever, I handed it over.

Still, at least they hadn't shot that kid. The only way to keep calm, I realised, was to remind myself that as bad as things were, they could easily get worse. True, when your sole consolation was that a child had not been murdered in cold blood right in front of you, it suggested you were having a rather bad day. But from now on, we'd have to look resolutely on the bright side. We weren't still in the car, hurtling down the road to be stoned to death in Kismayo. They hadn't executed us down in the clearing in the valley. We hadn't been split up. And José had been allowed to keep his cigarettes and lighter. As he lit one now, I watched enviously. I'd been a 20-a-day man back when I was a student, but had long since given up. Even in Iraq I'd kept off them, knowing that in stressful conditions it would be impossible to keep it to the odd one or two. This, though, was different. We weren't quite on Death Row, but were certainly in that territory where 'one last request' type indulgences could be looked on favourably. I gestured to José and he passed me the carton. *'Smoking is bad for you'*, read the health warning. These things are relative, I thought, inhaling for the first time since 1992.

It was now 5pm, and our shadows were growing tall on the rocks. By now, the office would be wondering why I hadn't called in yet. Word might even have got to them already of what had happened. I thought of the phone call that David, my boss, would have to make to both my parents and Jane, the one I'd always hoped he'd never have to do. Their numbers were listed in the foreign desk's 'next of kin' file, to be rung in the event that correspondents were killed, injured, arrested or suffered other misadventure. A couple of weeks ago, when Jane and I had looked like splitting up, I'd made a mental note to take her name off it.

'Where do you think we're actually going?' I whispered to José, as we got up to walk again.

'I don't know,' he said. 'I think they are taking us up to some cave in the mountains. That's what they did with that French guy.'

He was talking about Gwen Le Gouil, the French TV journalist kidnapped in Bossaso last December. José had told me about him over dinner one evening. Le Gouil had been doing a story about people trafficking, and had been abducted by one of the traffickers he'd gone to meet. They'd held him for about ten days. What state he'd been left in, José didn't know, although he did say he'd heard it was Le Gouil's first time in Somalia. That's what journalists always said of colleagues who came to grief. They were amateur, inexperienced, or reckless, new to the country, or whatever. There was always the search for some logical reason why it had happened, and the implicit reassurance that as long as one didn't make the same mistakes, all would be fine. The French journalists in our hotel and their Somali-Belgian fixer would probably be saying the same thing about us.

By 7pm it was getting dark. We'd been going flat out now for seven hours, although I didn't feel at all tired. Either I was fitter than I thought, or adrenalin was keeping me going. It was, though, becoming hard to see the ground in front of us. Every few minutes I was stumbling in my slip-ons. The guard up front was the only one who had a torch, the gang apparently worried that too many lights would draw attention. As we followed behind him, José and I noticed that the others were now lagging behind by maybe 25 yards.

Thoughts of escape crept into my mind. If the dark made it hard going for us, it would also make it hard for the gang. If we crept up on the guard ahead, thumped him over the head with a rock and grabbed his torch, could we buy enough time to dash off? By the time the others saw, we might be 50 yards away into the gloom. If we could keep up that lead on them, they might lose track of us. Also, down between the farthest mountains we could now see the glow of lights, some coastal town if my sense of direction was right. We had somewhere to head for. This was not some *A-Team* fantasy, but something that might just come off.

Under my breath, I discussed it with José. He'd had similar thoughts. The problem was what we'd do once we got away. We were on a plateau which stretched away into the night. What lay beyond it was anyone's guess. If it was a cliff, we'd be trapped. And even if it was a manageable slope, I'd never out-run the kidnappers in my slip-ons. We also had no water and no food, and only a vague idea of which direction to go in. Those lights could be a few hours' walk away, or a few days, it was impossible to tell. And once we reached lower ground, we'd lose our bearings completely in those winding valleys and canyons. Even if the kidnappers didn't find us, we could end up hopelessly lost, and dying of thirst. Every single stream and river bed I'd seen was completely dry. While Andy McNab might've managed it, I'd probably be found dead a few months later, my sun-bleached skeleton identifiable by my strange choice of footwear.

*****

As we debated our escape plan, I'd tried to remember what I'd learned about kidnappings on my 'hostile environment' course. Like nearly every other British journalist who travelled abroad these days, I'd been given training for the various hazards I might encounter, be it a car crash, a bullet wound, or a minefield. It was debatable just how much one could learn about such things in the classroom, but it was as much for the employer's benefit as the employee's. After all, the average middle-class journalist, armed with little more than a humanities degree, was ill-equipped to survive a pub brawl, never mind a warzone. If someone who'd never encountered anything more hostile than a hungover news editor lost a leg in a minefield, there was the potential for a big negligence lawsuit.

Filling this knowledge gap was a flourishing cottage industry in 'hostile environment' courses, run by ex-members of Britain's special forces. The very phrase 'hostile environment' was perhaps a clue as to why newspaper HR departments liked them. They expressed the chaos of somewhere like Somalia in the language of health and safety speak, as something with predictable, manageable risks, like the dangers of working with heavy machinery or hazardous chemicals. The courses usually lasted a week and taught a mixture of first aid and tips for how to handle yourself in warzones. If a colleague gets blown up in a minefield, for example, the golden rule is not to run to help them – you'll probably step on a mine yourself. If fleeing a gang of men armed with Kalashnikovs, keep in mind that their weapons are only accurate up to 25 metres. If someone's lung is punctured by a bullet, remember you can use a credit card to seal the hole.

Or was it a 50 pence piece? To be honest, I'd never bothered committing much of it to memory. Rather like the sailors of old who never learned to swim, my attitude towards trouble had been rather fatalistic. If you landed in deep water, your chances of being able to pull yourself out by your own means were very limited. It was one thing performing artificial resuscitation on a dummy in a classroom. It was quite another trying it on a real, live person, who might also have their organs spilling out, while also under fire. About the only thing I could remember from the first aid course was the recipe for making Temazepam from a mixture of high street painkillers. It sounded like a terrific hangover cure.

Then again, the idea of hostile environment training was not to qualify you for SAS membership, but to give your panicking, traumatised mind something to focus on when it all went wrong. Sure, you might not be much help to someone whose legs had been shredded by a roadside bomb, but trying ineffectually to stem their bleeding was better than just going into a blind panic. This was especially true for kidnaps, where the lack of immediate danger to life and limb allowed the mind plenty of leeway to run amok. The kidnap section of the course had been run by a wiry, moustachioed ex-SAS man known only as 'Mick'. His was the one class I'd paid proper attention in, as I was just about to head back for another stint in Iraq. And, if I remembered correctly, one of his main recommendations was that if you spotted an escape opportunity, you should seriously consider it. You might not get another, and, if there was a chance you might end up in the hands of Al Qaeda, it was worth the risk.

Could we really do it? We wouldn't actually have to clobber the guy up ahead of us, just push him over hard and then run. If my hostile environment training was right, we'd be quickly out of range of their weapons. Besides, they wanted us alive, not dead. Who knew, perhaps they'd just panic and give up. Just then, though, the guard up front stopped and turned, waiting for the rest to catch up. Our window of opportunity closed. I should have felt disappointment. Instead I felt relief. Deep down, I knew I lacked the guts to do it, mainly because of the beating I feared we'd get if they caught us. We squatted down for another rest stop. The wind was strong now, chilling our sweat-soaked clothes.

'Look, they are about to pray,' said José.

I looked over to see a row of kneeling silhouettes. They had their backs to us, staring out across the valley. If we got another chance to escape, at least we now knew which direction Mecca was. Not that that the gang's trust in God was complete. One kidnapper was skipping prayers so that he could continue to watch over us. A low murmur went up against the wind.

'Allah Akbar. Allah Akbar...'

It was the opening words of the Muslim call to prayer, the chant of 'God is Great', familiar to me from years in the Middle East. Yet as I watched, a chill swept over me that was nothing to do with the temperature. There was something sinister about seeing a bunch of kidnappers evoking the name of the Almighty. It felt like a perversion of the act of prayer, as if the huddled figures in front of me were addressing not the entity above, but the one down below.

As we rested, I grew colder. Given that we'd climbed non-stop all afternoon, I estimated that we must be at least 4,000 feet up, the height of Ben Nevis. I took off the jacket from round my head and put it on. José, though, was wearing only a tee-shirt.

'I am cold,' he said to the gang, only half-miming a shiver.

'Maa fi mushkilleh,' they replied, waving their hands dismissively. No problem.

'No, mushkilleh, my friends,' he insisted, standing up. 'I am cold. Give me jacket.'

'Maa fisch.' We don't have. They gestured at him to sit down.

'Come on. I am cold! COLD.'

A sweatshirt was produced. José was right to persist. Now was the time to try to set some ground rules, to get them used to the idea of providing us with some minimum care. It was one of the key 'conduct under capture' tips from Mick, the kidnap expert. As we sat shivering, I tried to remember some of the others. Try to stay calm, but don't worry about feeling scared or guilty – that was natural. Eat and drink where possible, there was no telling when your next meal might be. Expect visits from clerics or holy men, interrogations about your religion, or accusations of being a spy. Try to be the 'Grey Man', neither passive nor aggressive. Yet try also to build a rapport with your captors. Make a point of asking for cigarettes, drinks, food, toilet breaks and so on. That made you come across as a fellow human being, which would make it harder for them to kill you if ordered to. In practice, Mick said, they often just outsourced that task to someone else. But at least you'd die leaving a better-fed, slightly happier-looking corpse.

'Imshi.'

We staggered on for another couple of hours, getting lost, retracing our steps and clambering up to a plateau. It was now approaching midnight. From the gang's rucksacks came a bunch of cheap woven mattresses. A kidnapper chucked one down in front of us and folded his hands against his head, mimicking a pillow. This was where we'd be spending the night. We lay down side by side, wriggling uncomfortably on the rocks. I grabbed a large, flat stone, hoping it might work as a pillow. It was now extremely cold. Some other lesson in my hostile environment course had said that in situations like this, it was best to share bodily warmth. Frankly, I didn't particularly want to do 'spoons' with José, but if it was going to stop him getting hypothermia, I was obliged to offer.

'José, mate, don't take this the wrong way, but I think it might be a good idea if you lay right next to me. It will shelter you from the wind, and we can share our body warmth.'

'It's okay man. I will be fine.'

'Seriously, it's a good idea. Just lie with your back to me, and I'll, er, put my arms around you.'

I shifted forwards and lay against him, putting one arm around him in rather awkward fashion. Even in the circumstances, I felt like some adolescent trying it on with a reluctant teenage girl. It reminded me that we still didn't really know each other very well. I might as well have said to him: 'Listen, on my hostile environment course, they said the best way to fight off hypothermia was to have sex.'

Eventually I gave up and lay on my own, tucking my trousers into my socks to minimise the breezes chilling my clammy skin. Ten yards away was the silhouette of a lone guard, on sentry duty while others rested. If we stayed all night here, we'd be suffering from exposure by dawn. Just as I was debating whether we could build a wall of rocks around us to keep the breeze out, the gang began getting to their feet, apparently too cold to sleep here themselves. We stumbled back the way we'd come for half an hour, before turning off into a hollow where several huge boulders were piled together. In between them was a gap big enough for us all to shelter in. We lay down on what smelt like goat droppings. Compared to where we'd been before, it was passably warm. I drifted off to sleep, wondering what kind of nightmares I might dream, knowing that waking up would bring little relief.

4: The Somali Arsenal Supporters Club

ON THE PREVIOUS occasions that we'd decided to go our separate ways, Jane had always said the thing she dreaded most was waking up the next day. She'd roll over in bed and realise that I wasn't there, that I wasn't off on some foreign assignment, and that there was a whole day to get through before she could go back to sleep and switch off again. As I drifted off that first night, I feared I was in for the same thing. I'd wake up wondering why there were rocks digging into me, and why I was staring at a boulder, not a hotel ceiling. And then it would hit me.

Kidnapped.

The reality jolt, I feared, might catch me sufficiently unprepared to spark the all-out panic attack that I was sure would come sooner or later.

Fortunately, my brain seemed to have spent the night on some kind of standby setting. I woke up feeling like I'd never really gone to sleep. The kidnappers were already up, muttering in low voices. José and I staggered to our feet like new-born goats, limbs stiff and half-asleep. A kidnapper rolled up our mattress and we were off, the pre-dawn light casting a purple glow behind the mountains.

We trekked up one side of a valley to where it steepened into a cliff. At the foot of the rock face was an alcove about 15 feet wide and head high, thorn bushes guarding it from prying eyes. As we drew near, I could see some of the gang already lounging in one corner. Like some giant eagle's lair, it was lined with the detritus of previous occupants: scraps of litter, bits of blanket, and clumps of torn-up bush grass used as bedding. How many other poor bastards had been dragged up here before, I wondered.

A kidnapper spread out a mattress for us. In the opposite corner, the Somalis were making a campfire, using armfuls of sticks picked up in the valley. Dried and bleached by the sun, they formed a smokeless blaze within seconds of being lit. A large, battered pot was produced and filled with water, while out of a rucksack came plastic packets of spaghetti. Each packet was smashed several times against a rock to break the strands into smaller pieces.

Pasta, Somali-style. A reminder that this land had once been colonised by Italy, as part of Rome's belated bid to join the European scramble for Africa. In the first half of the 20th century, tens of thousands of Italians had colonised the eastern half of the Somali country, bringing their love of fine food, good coffee and elegant design to cities like Mogadishu. Compared to the mineral-rich Congo, or the prime farming lands of Kenya or Zimbabwe, Italian Somaliland, as it was known, offered relatively little of value. It was more a 'vanity colony' to boost Italy's international prestige, something that came to matter a lot during the Fascist era of Mussolini. The Italian presence went into decline post-war, and by the time the Somali government collapsed in 1991 nearly all of the Italian émigrés had returned home. Judging from what José and I were about to receive, they'd taken their knack for good pasta with them. A kidnapper fished out a single metal plate from a rucksack, piled a heap of spaghetti onto it, and placed it before us. It had been boiled for least 25 minutes, and was soft and clammy. The Italians had clearly never taught the Somalis the meaning of *al dente*.

We were also handed a can of Chinese-made baked beans in tomato sauce, which José poured onto the spaghetti. Pasta was one of my favourite dishes at home, but that was when it came with sun-dried tomatoes and fresh pesto from my posh neighbourhood deli. This, by comparison, looked like something that a greasy spoon with pretensions might have dreamed up in the 1970s.

There was also the question of how we were supposed to eat it.

'Do you have fork, spoon?' I asked the gang, prodding demonstratively at the steaming, intestinal mass before me.

'Maa fisch.'

Of all the meals to eat without cutlery, spaghetti was probably the least convenient. Now I realised why the cook had smashed it into small pieces first. I took a handful, raised it above my head and fed it into my mouth like a sword-swallower, fighting a strong urge to retch. As Mick would have pointed out, we didn't know when we'd be getting our next meal.

With neither cutlery nor appetite to speed things along, eating the spaghetti took about half an hour, by which time it was cold, congealed and even less appealing than before. Just getting a plate, though, counted as VIP treatment. The Somalis ate theirs straight out the pot, circled round it like a bunch of hyenas on a kill. Afterwards they produced a huge, soot-blackened kettle and made tea. A kidnapper poured out a cup for us, fashioned from the bottom half of a mineral water bottle. It was very sugary, but given that it had been boiled, was a source of clean water, something that we were otherwise running low on. There was a communal jerry can of drinking water, but I wasn't sure of its provenance. Trying out yet another of Mick's survival tips, I'd poured some water from the can into an empty mineral water bottle I'd found and put it out in the sun. Apparently if you left water in direct sunlight for four hours, the ultra-violet rays would kill off any bacteria. José hadn't looked convinced.

José and I passed the tea between us and had a smoke, feeling ourselves relaxing a little. At least we were getting a chance to rest and re-fuel. It was now 1pm, roughly 24 hours since we'd gone missing. The office would definitely know now that something was wrong. All manner of other explanations – missed flights, broken mobile phones, road accident, arrest – would have been ruled out. I wondered if anyone back home had had any sleep. Jane probably hadn't. Every time I thought about her, tears pricked my eyes.

'Tell me your life story, José,' I said.

I'd heard some of it during the qhat night in Bossaso, but now I wanted to hear it in proper detail – mostly because I wanted an excuse to tell him mine. Having got us into this dreadful situation, I wanted to explain what had led up to it, to make sense of things while there was still time.

We spent the next couple of hours swapping our respective tales, like two souls sitting in some waiting room to the afterlife. Our career paths turned out to have much in common. José had actually started out as a journalist rather than a photographer, and, like me, had somehow ended up on a mind-numbingly dull transport beat. Around the time I was writing about roadworks for the *London Evening Standard*, he'd been on a magazine devoted to the affairs of the Spanish municipal bus sector. Bored out his mind, and overdoing it on drink and drugs, he'd taken up photography instead, heading, as I'd done, to the nearest convenient warzone. First he'd gone to Colombia, spending time in the jungle with the FARC rebels. Then for the last two years he'd been freelancing in East Africa, covering wars in the Congo and Sudan, and a coup in the Comoros Islands. Transport journalism clearly had a lot to answer for in terms of giving people a moth-like fascination for danger. Perhaps Ernest Hemingway had started off on some magazine about trams or bus conductors.

The enthusiasm with which José spoke of his new life reminded me of my own days in Iraq. There was that heady joy of being your own boss, of being free to come and go as you pleased, of knowing that if it got boring, you could just relocate elsewhere. A hand-to-mouth existence, for sure, but not much different, really, from being a staff man, who could get sacked on an editor's whim anyway. It was, though, a lifestyle for a singleton, as I'd been back then, and as José was now. I told him about my ups and downs with Jane.

'I'm glad I emailed her about getting back together before this happened,' I said. 'Otherwise it would have been even worse. She'd have thought I didn't want to see her any more, yet she'd still probably be worrying about me.'

He nodded. I wondered if he could really relate to it. The life of the roving foreign freelance was, in a sense, a rejection of most things that passed for a normal existence – the proper job, the steady partner, kids, and so on. Because it was considered to be a gutsy thing to do, it was seen as a valid lifestyle choice, rather than just another way of dropping out. But what happened if things went wrong, as they had now?

'Do you think you'll ever come to somewhere like Somalia again?' I asked him.

'I think so. This is what you expect at some point in your career.

We just have to hope we get out okay. And you?

'I think this might be my last trip to somewhere like this, to be honest. I think it's a reminder not to push things too far.'

It probably wasn't what he wanted to hear. But I did feel like I'd had a timely warning about how sooner or later, this line of work was likely to end in tears. All the better then, maybe, to settle down and have children, as I'd pledged in that email to Jane just eight days ago. I wasn't normally a believer in God or Destiny, but right now, it did feel as if some guiding hand was nudging me in a certain direction. Right now, I'd quite happily go back home, give up my job and procreate, eking out the rest of my days as Jane's dutiful house husband if needs be. The past 24 hours had been sufficient adventure to last the rest of a lifetime. I didn't mention any of this to José. The last thing he needed was his fellow hostage banging on about Destiny. That could wait until we'd been chained to each other in a cave for five years.

Around 4pm we broke camp. The fire was stamped out and covered with rocks, the kettle and spaghetti pot packed into a rucksack. Guns were checked, magazines removed, inspected and refitted. Each inspection produced a familiar click-crunch sound from the weapon's innards that set my nerves on edge. Two guards headed off up the valley as scouts. We were on the move again.

'Wayn al-aan?' I asked, pointing with my finger down the valley. Where now?

'Sajarra,' came the reply. Sajarra? That meant car.

'Sajarra fi wayn?' Car to where?

'Sajarra fi Bossaso.'

A car to Bossaso? Christ, perhaps we were going to be released. It often happened like this in kidnap situations. Whoever had ordered the abduction would lose their nerve, especially if a big hue and cry had gone up, as it probably had in our case. Our kidnapping might already be on the news. Down in Bossaso, Samatar, the bumptious security minister, would surely be getting calls from the Foreign Office. Maybe Ahmed and Mustapha had gone to the cops. Or, if they'd been in on it, perhaps they'd been arrested. In which case, they were hopefully getting waterboarded by a couple of visiting MI6 officers.

Even if we weren't about to get released, I'd rather be held hostage in Bossaso than up here in the mountains. We might have a room with beds, a toilet, reading matter, perhaps even a TV. I wouldn't mind if we didn't have the BBC or CNN. Compared to the entertainment options available in a cave, I'd be quite happy with imported Egyptian soap operas. Then again, maybe they'd stick us in a darkened cellar and chain us to a radiator, like the Archbishop of Canterbury's special envoy, Terry Waite.

Either way, though, I felt something approaching optimism as we staggered off down the path again. We were now 24 hours into the kidnap, and my much-feared lapse into all-out shock and panic hadn't happened. Now, the only real threat to my sense of calm was when I thought about Jane or my family. I decided to stop thinking about them. I felt guilty, knowing they'd be unable to do the same about me, but they'd understand. The priority had to be looking after my own mental well-being, to minimise the sources of stress.

My mood was further improved by the fact that we were heading off the mountains and into a valley. The air became warmer and stiller. Insects droned in the background. It looked like we might be getting closer to inhabited territory, as the gang were proceeding more cautiously. Every now and then one of the scouts would scurry back and confer with the others. I was impressed by how well they worked together. While the older bald guy, whom the others called Miro, appeared to be vaguely in charge, everything seemed to be done by consensus, not command. No-one ever raised a voice. And they were clearly very fit, especially one guy that José dubbed the Sherpa. He had super-thin, bandy legs like a high-jump champion with rickets, yet he could scale the slopes without even breaking into sweat. There he was now, heading back up the valley to get a better view of the ground ahead. He'd vanish into a dip in the rocks, then reappear a minute later, far higher up than you'd expect him to be.

By early evening we were out of the mountains and into a plain of hillocks and dried-up river beds. It was flatter, but no easier. The ground was just as uneven as before, the rocks digging through my slip-ons and into the arches of my feet.

'Cam sa'a fi sajarra?' I asked. How many hours to the car?

'Sa'a-tayn'. Two hours.

Two hours later, I asked the same question again. And got the same answer. And two hours later again. As I realised we were being lied to, my upbeat mood wilted. José was flagging too, complaining of being thirsty. Just before we'd left the cave, I'd drunk the water that I'd left out in the sun, gambling on the sterilising properties of ultraviolet light. José had politely declined it, just as he'd turned down my offer of a body-warming man-cuddle the night before. Now, though, the gang had run out of water completely, and what little José had left inside him was being sweated out.

Twilight came. We picked our way over a moon-like landscape of bare rocky knolls and meandering hollows, where stunted thorn trees crouched like witches brewing a spell. Occasionally I would walk into a protruding thorn bush twig, suspended in the gloom like a trip wire to a booby trap. One nearly stabbed me in the eye. When the ground did briefly smooth out, it proved deceptive.

'At least the going has got a bit easier now,' I said to José as we hit one flat section. A second later I tumbled over, picking up a long, bleeding scrape down one shin.

By around ten o'clock, I was thirsting too. It hit all of a sudden. I'd been thinking about the hotel in Dubai where I'd stayed *en route* to Bossaso, and where I should have been staying again last night. Among its many comforts was a fully-stocked mini bar. While normally my mind's eye would dwell on the chilled beers inside, now it lit on the bottles of mineral water. Straightaway, my insides felt raw and dry, like a rash in need of some soothing balm.

Soon, all I could think about was getting to the car and finding some water. At one point, we saw a pair of distant car headlights, flashing on and off as a drug smuggler might signal to a ship. But like a mirage in the desert, the beams disappeared as we got near, and then our route veered off in another direction. By now I was beginning to lag behind. I gave myself a psychological pep-talk, like a football coach trying to inspire a losing team at half-time.

Remember, every step is ultimately a step in the right direction, even though we don't know where we're going. The longer you walk, the sooner it'll all be over. Yes, these may be trite, 'game-of-two-halves' sporting clichés, but it's all we've got...

Eventually the headlights reappeared again, this time with the distant sound of passing vehicles. We were now definitely near a road, and presumably, a car and water. Eventually it came into view, a highway running up a long, sloping embankment. Occasionally a convoy of three or four elderly trucks rumbled their way up, engines grinding with the effort.

We lurked in a culvert until the road was quiet, then half the gang swarmed up the scree slope of the embankment, disappearing over the other side. The Sherpa grabbed my arm, gesturing that we would follow suit and that we should stay low. I crept along as he bid me, half-bent over, not really caring that I was helping us to stay undetected, thinking only about the car and the water. We dashed across like a pair of rabbits, went down the other side, and carried on into the bush again.

'Sajarra?' I asked. *'Wayn sajarra?'*

'Sajarra ma fisch.'

Fuck! No fucking car after all! And no fucking water! Lying bastards! For the first time, I began to feel like I couldn't go on any longer. It was now around 1am. We'd been on the move for nine hours without a drink. My mouth felt as dry as the ground beneath my feet. The Sherpa and his pal, anticipating my reaction to their deception, put their arms around my shoulders, half-supporting, half-coercing. The sound of the road grew fainter, as did the voice in my head telling me to keep going. Now it was no longer a football coach, but a punch-drunk boxer's ringside buddy, slapping him in the chops and saying if he didn't pull himself together, he was finished forever.

How much longer could we go without drinking? Much more of this, and we'd be seriously dehydrated. Then again, if our captors were anything like as tough as Somalis were said to be, we could be going for a long time yet. It was a quality frequently noted by visitors, that the people here seemed extremely hardy – products, like the thorn trees around us, of a landscape indifferent to the needs of most forms of life. In a book I'd read by Gerard Hanley, a British Army officer stationed in Somalia during World War II, he'd told of a wounded Somali soldier who'd walked for 14 miles while holding his guts in hands. After a doctor had sewn him up, he'd gone back to soldiering again.

While that tale was from half a century ago, I suspected things hadn't changed much. It wasn't that unusual in the world's more untamed corners, where the sheer demands of everyday existence seemed to forge human constitutions of a different league. A journalist friend who'd spent time with US Army medics in Afghanistan had told me how they were constantly amazed at Afghans' capacity for survival. Afghan soldiers would be brought in from the battlefield sometimes, often with what the US military doctors assessed as clinically fatal injuries. Then, in defiance of all known medical precedent, they'd pull through. Captain Speke was struck by same thing among the brawl-loving Somali porters at the docks in Aden, who often sported knife wounds so deep that it was 'marvellous how they ever recovered from them'.

All of which meant there was every chance this lot were going to walk us until we passed out. And then probably kick us awake, force us back on our feet, and walk us some more. Horrible and exhausting as it would be, they could probably squeeze plenty more miles out of us yet.

We scrambled on like zombies, eventually taking a break on a rock plateau. When they gestured for us to move again just minutes later, José decided he'd had enough.

'Muy, muy,' he said, pointing to his throat. Water. Water.

I joined in. *'Muy. Muy.'*

'Maa fisch,' said Miro. *'Imshi.'*

'No fucking way, my friend' said José, raising his voice. 'I need some fucking muy. Muy. MUY!'

'Maa fisch!' barked Miro, looking round anxiously, as if someone might overhear. He pointed with his gun. *'IMSHI!'*

José swore in Spanish and then yelled right in his face.

'I am not going anywhere until you find some fucking muy, bastard! What are you going to do, fucking shoot me? Well go ahead. Then you will have wasted all your fucking time dragging me over your fucking mountains!'

He sat back down. The gang, seemingly taken aback by his defiance, conferred. The word 'fuck' came up several times, as if they knew it might be a rude word and were mildly shocked that he'd felt it necessary to use it. Eventually José's Ghandi-style protest tactics paid off. One of the kidnappers disappeared with the jerry can. He was a hillbillyish fellow with a high, bald forehead, and his mouth showed not just his long, yellow teeth but also his gums, as if his face was stretched too tight over his skull. He directed the way much of the time, leading me to guess that he must be a local, hired for his knowledge of the area. Sure enough, ten minutes later he was back, with the jerry can half-full. How he'd managed to find a well round here was a mystery, although my admiration for his water-divining prowess was undermined by my suspicion that if he'd been able to find it now, he could have found it hours ago when we'd first asked. José drank first, me eyeing the can like a junkie watching someone cooking a teaspoon of heroin. He passed it over. It was mossy-tasting but cool, and spoiled only by the fact that there wasn't quite enough to go round. British to the end, I felt obliged to offer it around among the kidnappers rather than finish it all myself. They shook their heads.

Half an hour later, I realised why. In a clearing, we came across a large red and white metal barrel, standing on its own. For reasons unknown, someone had put a full water urn here, just when a group of passing kidnappers might need it. They prised the rusting plug from the top with a rock, tilted it and began pouring water into the jerry cans. It tasted a lot cleaner than the water the Sherpa had located earlier. Until José choked suddenly, and spat a small, brown, slimy object onto the ground. Closer inspection revealed it to be a lizard. A dead one.

'Did that come from this barrel?' I asked, fighting the urge to retch every last drop.

'No, I think it was in the bottom of the can already. It must have been in the water that guy found us. I fucking nearly swallowed it.'

What kind of bacteria, I wondered, inhabited water that had a decomposing lizard in it? Not the kind, probably, that could be killed off by a few hours of ultra-violet light.

Marching resumed. Fatigue took over from thirst as our main source of torment. As dawn broke, we reached the edge of a plateau that looked down into a valley several miles wide, a Somali Grand Canyon. We climbed to the bottom, where the kidnappers laid out our mat in under a tree and bade us lie again. A bird in the branches above gave a soft, descending whistle, the only friendly sound I'd heard in days. As I lay there trying to sleep, it made me want to cry.

As the sun gradually nudged the shade away, another group approached. About eight of them. Judging by the shouts, they were accomplices. Was this a shift changeover? I hoped not. Since the existing bunch hadn't actually mistreated us so far, I had no interest in swapping them for some new bunch that might.

The newcomers had brought provisions. One handed José and me a withered carrier bag, containing two bottles of water, a couple of limes, and two packs of cigarettes called 'Business Royals'. Not a brand I'd ever heard of, but one that observed the unwritten rule I'd noticed in global tobacco marketing – namely, that the more run-down the country, the more aspirational its cigarette brands were. When someone lit up in the Third World, they were never just a smoker, they were a Sportsman, an Aristocrat, a Playboy or whatever. Still, puffing on a Business Royal did make me feel vaguely human again. Especially when José pointed over to the far side of the riverbed, to a gleam of a blue metal under a distant tree.

'*Sajarra?*' I asked, glancing to the nearest kidnapper.

'*Sajarra,*' came the reply.

*****

Several Business Royals later we headed over to the tree next to the car.

Another eight men were lying in its shade. As well as Kalashnikovs, they had a couple of belt-fed medium machine guns. Two of the men had bullet-belts wrapped Rambo-style around their shoulders, the ultimate in African militia bling. The presence of the belt-fed guns worried me. They were a step up from Kalashnikovs, a hint that these guys wouldn't give us up without a fight.

'Hello, and how are you?' beamed one of the men with bullet-belts. It was the first English anyone had spoken.

'We are okay, thank you,' I replied.

'Where are you from?' he asked.

'London.'

'Spain.'

'Ah, Londonspain,' said Bullet Belt. 'Very nice,' he added. 'Welcome.'

It was, to my recollection, the most effusive reception we'd had since setting foot in Puntland.

'What is happening here?' I asked. 'Where are we going? Why have you taken us?'

'Yes!'

Bullet Belt smiled again, nodded, and wandered off. Either I'd stretched his English beyond his conversational limits, or he was under instructions not to talk too much.

We smoked another cigarette each, fell asleep for an hour, and woke up to be escorted towards the car, a blue Hilux 4x4. I noted down the registration plate, 13-539, in the vague chance that I might one day meet a policeman who was interested to know. José and I clambered in, followed by at least a dozen others, sitting on the window ledges, standing on the sideplates and perched on the bumpers. We lurched briefly along the valley for a mile and then transferred to the back cabin of a large, non-articulated truck. Our spirits rose. There was no way it could have got here without a half-decent road. Perhaps we were getting near Bossaso after all, and freedom. As it ground into gear, we lit a cigarette each and began joking about who would play each other in the movie of our kidnap.

'Brad Pitt for you, José, maybe,' I said. 'And what about me?'

'Er, let me think... Danny DeVito, maybe?'

'Danny DeVito? But he's old. And small. And bald.'

'Exactly,' José said, sniggering.

'I'm 38, by the way, not 60. And I'm not bald, just receding. Nor am I a midget.'

'I'm sorry, I can't think of anyone else.'

'Thanks. Just what I need right now.'

By now the two of us were laughing away. It felt good. Bonding in captivity and all that. Slightly crazed, yes, but defiant. The curtain briefly drew back and a kidnapper peered in, clearly wondering what we found so funny.

The truck meandered through a maze of dried-up river channels, seeking spots where it could clamber from one to another. Sometimes it would get stuck and people would pile out to place stones under the tyres. It was dark again by the time we stopped. Around us on all sides were towering butterscotch cliffs and rock pillars, reminiscent of the Arizona backdrop of so many cowboy films. It wasn't Bossaso though.

Brad Pitt and Danny DeVito spilled out, no longer so cheerful now that the hope of a comfortable bed had gone. We slept by the lorry, then at first light headed into a nearby canyon. Just as I began to fear another marathon walk, we sidetracked through a pile of Stonehenge-size boulders and into a side crevice. At the end was an alcove, clearly our next cave hideout. It was even better hidden than the first one. As we approached, I half expected to see Osama bin Laden rising to his feet to greet us.

As we inspected our new surroundings, the hard-faced young kid whose snarl I remembered from the start of the kidnap wandered over. So far, none of the gang except Bullet Belt had said a word of English. But now he spoke in a broken pidgin.

'You. From where you?'

'Spain,' said José.

'Britain,' I added.

I wondered whether honesty was the best strategy. It generally was, but if these guys turned out to be Shabab sympathisers, saying you were from Britain, with its enthusiastic military presence in Iraq and Afghanistan, wouldn't be the best introduction. To my surprise, it turned out to be the perfect ice-breaker.

'Ah, Bree-tan,' he said, grinning. *'Man-kester United. Leeva-pool. David Beck-ham. Thierry Henry.'*

The international language of football. Spoken even here, among the kidnappers of Somalia. And a perfect opportunity for a bit of rapport-building. Alas, I am not much of a sports fan, save for a passing interest in snooker born of a misspent 1980s youth. If he had name-dropped Alex 'Hurricane' Higgins or Terry Griffiths, I'd have been fine, but with football I was struggling.

'Ah, yes!' I said. 'Thierry Henry. Arsenal!'

A frown swept over his face. Had I offended him?

'Thierry Henry, Barcelona,' he said.

José nodded by way of confirmation.

'Thierry Henry transferred to Barcelona last year.'

We both sniggered. I was being corrected on my knowledge of the Premier League transfer market by a Somali kidnapper. He got the joke too. He grinned, pointed to his chest and introduced himself.

'Faisal,' he said.

We began swapping the names of various English footballers, men who probably didn't even know where Somalia was, never mind that they had followings here among its kidnapping fraternity. Men like *My-kill Owen*. And *Paul-a Scoles*. And teams like *Jew-ventiss* and *Barce-nola*. No, you say Barce-*lona*. *Yes, Barce-nola. Barce-nola good.*

Through a combination of miming and pidgin English and Arabic, Faisal gave us some insights into what had led him to a kidnapping career. He claimed to have been left an orphan a few years ago after a government militia had killed both his parents, a point he made by running a dirty finger across his throat. With nobody to look after him, and no prospect of work in Bossaso, he'd taken his chances on a people-smuggling boat, only to be deported home after getting as far as Greece. His sister he claimed, had had better luck, and was now apparently in *Bree-tan*

'Really?' I asked. 'Where in Britain?'

'In Leeva-pool.' Faisal mimed someone reading a book. *'Her. Make.*

Study.'

Could his sister really be a student in Liverpool? It was possible, I supposed. I nodded and smiled, as if to confirm what a small world it was. Faisal beamed back. Perhaps he was wondering whether I knew her.

When the conversation petered out, he went off the camp fire, assembled another plate of spaghetti for us, and brought it over along with a tin. This time it was imported Chinese tuna. A fish once caught in great numbers here in Somalia, that had once been one of its few export industries. And the demise of which, in a roundabout way, explained why we'd ended up stuck here in the first place.

5: Tuna And Toxic Waste

'How did the pirates start? The warlords ran out of people to rob on the land, so they robbed from the sea instead.'
(Old Somali joke)

IF SOMALIA'S HARSH, ARID landscape seems less than inviting to the foreign visitor, so too does the sea that surrounds it. As Air Leopardskin touches down on the coastal airstrips at Bossaso or Mogadishu, the eye is caught by the huge, barrelling waves that charge in from the Indian Ocean. The entire coastline would be a surfer's paradise, were it not for the scavenging sharks attracted by the many rubbish slicks, some of whom will readily snack on a human leg. Seen from a window of an incoming plane, the sharks appear as a vast shoal of silver slivers in the water, big enough to remain visible from a very great height.

These forbidding waters do, however, offer an abundance of something frequently in short supply on land – food. While droughts devastate Somalia's crops every ten to 15 years, the sea hosts some of the world's richest fishing grounds, from squid and shrimp through to swordfish and lobster. Top of its marine delicacies is yellowfin tuna, a torpedo-shaped game fish with lean, tender meat, which gathers in shoals up to five miles long. Tuna fishing used to be one of Somalia's few thriving industries, putting both food and money on the table in dirt-poor coastal settlements like Eyl. But throughout the 1990s, local fishermen began facing tough competition from bigger, better-equipped trawlers from Asia and Europe, for whom Somalia's unpoliced waters were an under-fished, quota-free paradise. While the tin of tuna that José and I were putting on our spaghetti had 'Product of China' written on it, there was a good chance the meat inside had been netted somewhere off the Somali coast, shipped thousands of miles to a canning factory on the Chinese mainland, and exported back again.

The competition infuriated the Somali fishermen. It wasn't just that the poachers were stealing their fish, they were exporting it back to Somalia's own markets at prices that often undercut their own product. Their response to this threat to their livelihood, though, paved the way for another, much more lucrative industry, to take its place. Borrowing weapons from friends, the Somali fishermen formed their own vigilante patrols, waylaying the foreign poachers at gunpoint and exacting punitive on-the-spot 'fines'. At first they took just cash and equipment, but as time went on, they would seize the entire vessel, demanding ransoms from the owners. They gave themselves names like the 'National Volunteer Coastguard of Somalia', the 'Somali Marines' and even the 'Somali Navy', whose real-life counterpart hadn't put to sea since the early 1990s. Local warlords got in on the act, lending extra weapons and militiamen, and from there on it was just a short step to outright piracy. Soon Somali 'Coastguard' teams were targeting not just marauding foreign trawlers, but seafarers of all sorts: cargo ships, luxury yachts, even UN food shipments earmarked for the starving in their own country. Fellow Somalis seafarers were not spared either. When José and I had wandered among the wooden fishing skiffs at Bossaso docks, we'd come across many tales of fishermen being preyed on by pirates.

'We were out on the sea once and a group of pirates approached us,' said one fisherman, Mohammed Abdullahi, as he stood smoking on a dirty grey beach littered with rotting fish heads. 'At first they asked us for water, and when we said we had none to spare, they pulled weapons and forced us to give them most of what we had, as well as our fish catch. We were lucky to get back to shore without dying of thirst.'

Had Mohammed ever felt tempted to take the pirate coin himself, I asked? He shook his head. No, he'd heard the sermons from the imam in the wheelbarrow, and knew Allah did not approve. But he couldn't speak for the other fishing crews around us, most of them young men like him, with families to feed. On a good trip out to sea, Mohammed said, each crew member could earn the equivalent of between $5 and $10 a day. It was a pittance compared to what even the lowliest pirate deckhand would make on a share of a million dollar ransom. Fishing was a mug's game, especially if, like Mohammed, you also got robbed by the pirates yourself. It was no surprise, therefore, that many fishermen had concluded that catching boats would be far more profitable than catching tuna. According to a recent report in the *Los Angeles Times*, the port of Hobyo, another pirate boom town like Eyl, now had all but four of its 80 fishing vessels dedicated to piracy.

What made piracy even more tempting as a career option was the reluctance of the owners of foreign vessels to kick up much of a fuss. The hijack of the *Sirius Star*, which had brought José and me out here in the first place, had made international headlines, but only because it in showed that the pirates were now a threat to oil shipping, a strategically important trade. Before now, most acts of piracy hadn't even been reported to the authorities. Foreign trawler owners had generally preferred to cough up ransoms in private than complain in public, knowing they'd get little sympathy if they'd been fishing illegally in the first place. Payments flowed into Somali-owned bank accounts in Dubai and Djibouti, where opaque banking rules meant a few million more dirty dollars did not attract unwanted attention.

*****

The Somalis' sense of grievance came not just from what foreign vessels were taking out of Somalia's waters, but what they were putting in. Ever since the late 1990s, there'd been talk that the Somali coast was being used as a dumping ground for toxic waste. The culprits were said to be Mafia-run firms from Somalia's old colonial partner, Italy, for whom illegal waste disposal was a lucrative sideline to their standard businesses of drugs and extortion. Suspicions of this washed up in the aftermath of the Indian Ocean tsunami of 2004, in which Somalia, luckless as ever, was the only African nation to be badly hit. While the world's attention focused mainly on the devastated tourist beaches of Thailand and Indonesia, the monstrous waves also hurtled 3,000 miles west across the Indian Ocean, hitting Somalia harder than anywhere else in East Africa. Puntland suffered worst of all, with at least 300 people killed and about 50,000 made homeless. As locals salvaged the debris of their demolished villages, they found dozens of rusting steel barrels, leaking what appeared to be hazardous chemicals and hospital waste. After receiving reports of people in towns such as Hobyo suffering unusual skin infections, ulcers and breathing problems, the UN despatched experts to investigate. However, in the tsunami's chaotic aftermath, the area was even more lawless than normal, and the team had to pull out before they could conduct a detailed probe. Proven or not though, it gave local pirates yet another charge on which to arrest passing ships. Not long after, hijacked seamen found themselves being waylaid by men calling themselves 'The Somali Toxic Waste Militia'.

Such profitable vigilantism had parallels with earlier ages of piracy, much of which was committed by so-called 'privateers' – private gunships given government commissions to hunt down ships of enemy states during war. Many privateers carried on their plundering in peacetime, to the point where line between privateer and pirate was so blurred as to be meaningless. The Somali pirate armada sailed under a similarly threadbare flag of political convenience. Whether they were righteous defenders of their seas, or simply opportunist brigands, depended on who you asked. Somali politicians were keen to portray it as a response to the marauding foreign vessels, as were many Left-wing commentators in the West. Yet like that much older scandal of Africa's coastline, the slave trade, the haste to blame foreigners meant the role of local middlemen was often overlooked. The foreign trawlers and toxic waste dumpers did not always sail into Somali waters uninvited. Instead, they often paid huge amounts for dubious 'licences' issued by ministers in the various self-declared Somali authorities that had sprung up since the collapse of central government in 1991.

As with the 'minister of health' who I'd seen chewing qhat in our hotel in Bossaso, these people were often ministers in name only. Indeed, some were not ministers at all. Take, for example, another 'minister of health', Nur Elmy Osman, who struck a waste dumping deal worth $20 million with an Italian firm back in 1991. The 'Somali government' which he claimed to represent was in fact just another faction clinging to a patch of turf in Mogadishu. Yet that did not stop him signing a deal to allow the dumping of 10 million tonnes of toxic waste in Somalia over 20 years. That particular agreement, brokered in a hotel room in Rome, was rumbled by the Italian government before any waste was dumped. But other shady transactions were thought to have gone ahead and, as with most business connected to Italian organised crime, people poked their nose in at their peril.

In 1995, a tribal chief called Abdullahi Musse had complained that 'Western companies, probably Italian', were dumping chemicals off the Puntland coast. He wanted the outside world to act, and gave an interview to Ilaria Alpi, a gutsy Italian female reporter who travelled to Bossaso to meet him. But before her investigation was complete, Alpi was shot dead in the street in Mogadishu. Some reckoned she was just the victim of just another random Mogadishu street killing. In Somalia, they pointed out, not even foreigners were guaranteed the dignity of a meaningful death. But others, including her parents, were convinced she had been silenced to stop her exposing the Mafia's Somali rackets. Her murder had never been solved.

Equally murky deals were hatched over fishing rights. Fishing in Somali waters was a rough game at the best of times, with ships routinely carrying arms for protection, and sometimes robbing each other rather than catching fish themselves. One trawler fleet owner did so by mounting a Soviet-made anti-aircraft gun on one of his ships; a quick burst fired over the bow of another vessel a few miles away was all that was normally needed to persuade them to stop and meekly hand over their catches. According to a marine conservation charity, Oceana, Spanish trawlers wishing to fish illegally in Somali waters had routinely paid local 'officials' thousands of dollars for 'licences', effectively a combination of bribery and protection money. Having some dodgy paperwork, though, was no guarantee that a ship could go about its business safely. According to reports in the *Indian Ocean Newsletter*, a publication with a keen nose for the scandals of the East African seafaring community, there were frequent hijacks when such deals went sour.

Since as far back as early 1990s, Italian fishing firms had been striking agreements with the Majerteen, a major Puntland clan, allowing them to fish in 'Majerteen territorial waters' for an annual fee of $200,000. However, one Italian trawler was then boarded by the clan's 'maritime inspectors' and forced at gunpoint to sail to Bossaso, where the inspectors levied a $270,000 'fine' for using fishing nets with too fine a mesh. This was less a fisheries conservation measure, and more a simple ransom demand. The trawler was freed after the money was paid into a Djibouti bank account, one of several 'fines' said to have put around $1.5 million into clan coffers.

Yet history suggested that today's Somali pirates were simply following in a long tradition of preying on passing ships. In 1986, an American historian, Wayne Durrill, had done a study into life in northern Somalia in the mid-1800s, drawing on records from the British colonial office at Aden. He discovered that Puntland clans like the Majerteen had made a handsome living from looting British and Dutch vessels bringing silk and spices from India. Armed with just spears, knives and a few elderly flintlock rifles, the Somali clans could not attack such vessels directly. But they didn't need to. Instead, they just waited for shipwrecks on their coastline, something that happened all too frequently thanks to the treacherous currents that swept along the coast.

Once again, coastal geography played in the Somalis' favour. Just south of the very north-east tip of Puntland is Ras Hafun, a sandy peninsula that sticks 25 miles into the ocean, with an abandoned lighthouse that marks the easternmost point on the African continent. As the currents running up the East African coast surged around Ras Hafun's flanks, they created a whirlpool effect that could fling unsuspecting East Indiamen onto the jagged coastline of the Majerteen heartlands. Two or three boats a year would come to grief in this fashion, and if the sailors didn't drown in the shipwreck, they often wished they had once they made it onto land. Waiting for them would be tribal looting parties, who would often slaughter the survivors before stealing whatever was left of the boat's cargo. The pickings were so lucrative that the

Majerteen even had a Muslim holyman stationed in the mountains inland, whose job was 'to pray day and night that God will drive Christian vessels ashore.'

*****

Judging by the accounts from those who lived to tell the tale, being shipwrecked in northern Somalia in the 1800s would have made the ordeal that José and I were facing seem fairly tame. The nearest friendly port was several hundred miles down the coast, while the interior was known as a place where even hardened explorers like Captain Speke came to grief. Even by the standards of what was then still very much the Dark Continent, it would have counted as *Here Be Dragons* territory.

Henderick Portenger, a soldier on board a British East India supply ship called the *SS Weisshelm*, wrote an account of life as a castaway in a book called the *Narrative of the Sufferings and Adventures of Henderick Portenger*. The title does little justice to the horrors described within, and although it begins with a testimony from his commanding officer that Portenger was 'not addicted to exaggeration' one cannot help wondering if it might have been embellished. But if even a fraction of what he claims was true, it made the *Adventures of Robinson Crusoe* look like a package holiday.

On the evening of June 7, 1801, Henderick and 20 other soldiers were travelling on the *Weisshelm* from Calcutta to Egypt, when currents began sucking it towards the northern Somali coast. Clearly the prayers of the holyman in the mountains were answered that night. The *Weisshelm's* nightwatchman fell asleep, and by the time the alarm was raised it was too late to stop the ship being impaled on jagged rocks offshore. After a night of being pounded by waves that 'appalled the stoutest hearts', those on board swam to the mainland, using planks, hen coops and rum kegs as flotation devices. Six of Portenger's detachment of 20 soldiers drowned, along with many of the crew. If I had wondered whether José might blame me for our current predicament, it was nothing compared to the guilt consuming the sleepy watchman. As the survivors lay recovering on the beach, he drank a long draft of rum and hurled himself off a cliff.

Before the day was out, Portenger would be thinking the watchman had done the sensible thing. That afternoon came 'a group of the savage inhabitants of this miserable coast', brandishing flintlocks, swords and spears. First the natives stripped them of their clothes and possessions. Then they began shooting at everyone in sight, at which point Portenger and his comrades fled for the nearby mountains.

For the next two months, the castaways wandered the coast in search of help, sleeping in caves, living hand-to-mouth, and gradually dropping dead from thirst and starvation. Food was leaves and roots, crabs washed up on the beach and the occasional wildcat. Water was from brackish, stagnant pools shared with monkeys, although when really desperate, Portenger also drank seawater, and even his own urine. It was a hint of what José and I might face if we ever tried to escape.

Reduced to 'skeletons of skin and bone', he and a companion stumbled into a village where locals gave them shelter in return for doing odd jobs. They were eventually picked up by a passing British warship that had got becalmed offshore, having spent 197 days as castaways. Some 40 years and numerous shipwrecks later, British officials in Aden struck a deal with the Majerteen under which they would be paid to look after castaways rather than harm them. By then, though, the profits from the looting had already made the Majerteen the most powerful clan in northern Somalia.

Meanwhile, the *Narrative of the Sufferings and Adventures of Colin Freeman and José Cendon* continued. True, we had tinned tuna rather than raw crab meat, and while the supplies of water had been limited at times, we hadn't yet been reduced to drinking our own urine. But cushy as it was compared to Portenger's sufferings, I wasn't sure if I could handle 197 days here. I ate what I could of Faisal's spaghetti and lit a Business Royal, wondering what would happen next.

6: Proof Of Life

From: Joe Jenkins, deputy foreign editor, Daily Telegraph
To: David Wastell, foreign editor, Sunday Telegraph
Sent: Nov 26, 2008, 1.55pm

'Have you seen this?'

Agence France Presse - News Alert
Bossaso, Somalia: A British and French journalist were reported kidnapped in a northern Somali city, officials said Wednesday

YOU DON'T GET much more safe and suburban than my parents' house in Kent. They live in the commuter town of Sevenoaks, on a quiet, tree-lined street that might have been the setting for a 1970s sitcom like *The Good Life* or *The Fall and Rise of Reginald Perrin*. Mock Tudor frontage is still in vogue, lawns are neatly mowed, and between 7 and 8 o'clock every morning, front doors disgorge a stream of smartly-dressed commuters on the stroll to the nearby station (just 30 minutes to Charing Cross, as the estate agents like to boast). When my parents first moved down there from Scotland, it felt like moving into a different world. Neighbours spoke like BBC newsreaders, there was a residents' association run by a retired Wing Commander, and crime was almost non-existent. Kent Police used to train rookie coppers in Sevenoaks, before moving them onto tougher beats like nearby Tunbridge Wells. It is not, in short, a place where people normally fret much about kidnapping.

The peace of my parents' Home Counties idyll was disturbed in the early afternoon on November 26th, just as they were sitting down to lunch. The phone in the hallway rang, and my Dad picked it up to hear the voice of the *Sunday Telegraph's* foreign editor, David Wastell.

'I am afraid we are rather worried about Colin,' he said. 'He was due to leave Somalia this morning, but he didn't make the flight he was supposed to be on. I hate to say this, but we think he may have been kidnapped. We can't quite be certain at this stage, but we felt we had to tell you. We didn't want you hearing it on the news first.'

My parents hadn't even known I was in Somalia. I go away so often I don't always get round to telling them. If it's somewhere dicey, my Mum often prefers not to be told anyway. They'd known I was in Pakistan the week before, but hadn't heard about the sudden re-route in search of pirates. Dad listened to David, thinking: '*Something that only happens to other families has just happened to us.*'

Then he went through to the kitchen to tell Mum. Lunch no longer seemed appealing. The kettle was put on instead. They rang my older sister, Linda, who is a hospital doctor, and my brother Richard, who sells greetings cards and gifts for living. He got a tearful phone call from my Mum as he drove along the M25 from a meeting. He went straight to the house, to find her crying at the kitchen table. 'At least I have one son safe,' she said, barely looking up.

Like most brothers, Richard and I have given our mother ample cause for worry in the past. Sevenoaks, despite its charms, can be a dangerous place – especially if you get drunk and try to slide down the handrail of the stairs at the railway station, as Richard did ten years ago. He slipped off, fell straight down about 20 feet, and spent the next three weeks in intensive care, narrowly avoiding brain damage. Horrible as it was, that at least fell into the realm of ordinary domestic crises. Friends and neighbours rallied round, and my doctor sister was there to act as an in-house expert. This was very different. None of my family knew anything about kidnapping. It wasn't something that happened to ordinary people. My brother's extensive range of greetings cards, with their 'get-well-soon' and 'deepest sympathies' messages, did not include one saying: 'Hope your son gets freed soon'. Nobody had the slightest idea what they were supposed to do now. Come to think of it, they weren't even sure exactly where Somalia was.

My Dad, Richard and brother-in-law, James, gathered round the light-up globe on my parents' sideboard, one of several ornaments that have been there since about 1972, along with pictures of their offspring sporting various unfashionable haircuts. There, glowing on a map of Africa that still showed Zimbabwe as Rhodesia, was the land where I was being held, a jagged yellow triangle jutting into the blue of the Indian Ocean. Puntland wasn't even marked because it hadn't officially existed at the time. On the internet, they got a more up-to-date picture, not that it brought much reassurance. Of all the grim places they knew I'd been to over the last five years, this looked by far the worst. No government. No foreign embassies. Wars, piracy, famine, Islamists.

'Bossaso is a port rife with armed gangs smuggling everything from arms to migrants across the Gulf of Aden,' one web page pointed out helpfully.

'Best not show any of this stuff to your mother,' muttered Dad.

*****

The following afternoon, with still no word of what had happened to us, my parents were invited to the *Telegraph* offices in London. Firms that send staff to dangerous places, be they journalists or otherwise, are taught that rule number one if an employee is kidnapped is to try to keep the next of kin on side. Explain what is going on, demonstrate that heaven and earth is being moved to sort things out, and they will hopefully show some faith in you. Look like you're disorganised or attempting to dodge responsibility, and they will quickly conclude that this is probably why such-and-such ended up a hostage in the first place and start raising hell. Legal threats will be made, complaints made to the press, or in the *Telegraph*'s case, other media, and the whole thing will become a great deal more complicated than it already is.

No charm offensive, though, could stop my family feeling like they'd stumbled into some bizarre thriller movie as they arrived at the *Telegraph* offices in Victoria. They were ushered discreetly down a corridor away from the main newsroom and into a special 'incident room' that the paper had set up, already complete with maps of Somalia on the wall. Sat opposite them were assorted executives and a lean ex-military man in his mid-30s who introduced himself as 'Mark', a specialist in kidnap situations. Mark worked for a corporate security firm that the *Telegraph*'s insurers retained for emergencies of this sort. Most big companies have them on hand for problems in countries where Scotland Yard and the Foreign Office may not be able to do much, or may even be unwelcome. Knowing little of such things, my family simply referred to Mark thereafter as 'that James Bond type'.

Eyeing each other up over the coffee and biscuits, neither hosts nor guests quite knew what to make of each other. My family had never met any of my colleagues before, and what they'd heard about them from me probably wasn't terribly reassuring. Newsrooms can be stressful, combative places, and sometimes the only way to relieve 'creative tension' after a lousy week at work is a good, long whinge about your bosses. Like all good parents, my Mum and Dad had listened sympathetically to my rants over the years without actually paying the slightest attention. So they had no way of knowing whether the people they were now putting their faith in might be that 'useless-idiot so-and-so' or that 'pillock such-and-such'.

My bosses weren't relishing the meeting either. Journalists are used to dealing with grief-stricken, stressed families, but normally only for as long as it takes to conduct a 'speaking-from-the-family-home' interview piece. Here, they had such a family right in their office, who might, for all they knew, start kicking off in very aggressive fashion.

Also sat at the table, feeling equally awkward, was Jane, who was still down as my girlfriend on the next-of-kin form. At the time, my family still didn't know her that well, and the last thing they'd heard was that we'd split up. Jane now found herself having to explain that we'd agreed to get back together again the night before I'd gone to Somalia, which didn't really sound very plausible. She likewise didn't really know anyone from my work. Like José and I up in the cave, the kidnap was throwing lots of relative strangers together, facing an ordeal of a kind that none of them had any experience of.

Mark gave a briefing. Scotland Yard and the Foreign Office had been informed, as had the Spanish authorities. The paper had formed its own special crisis team to deal with the situation, restricting the information flow to a few key staff. The foreign desk had been doing their best to piece together what had happened, liaising with Agence France Presse, the wire agency that José nominally worked for, which had good contacts in Somalia. Print-outs from AFP reporters' conversations with various Puntland officials were piled on the table. The responses so far didn't shed much light.

'No one so far has claimed this kidnapping,' Abdulkebir Musa, an assistant minister for seaports, was quoted as saying. 'We haven't had any sign from the driver or the car.'

'A police operation is under way,' said Bile Mohamoud Qabowsade, an advisor to the president. 'All the exits of Bossaso have been closed and an investigation been launched in an attempt to collect witness accounts on who might have kidnapped them.'

How reliable the accounts from the Puntland authorities were, nobody could be sure. It remained unclear who had taken us, or why. Mark said it could be days or even weeks before any kidnapper got in touch, and that they might issue a ransom demand. To my mum's horror, he warned that they might try to ring the family home. Dreadful thoughts danced in her head of picking up the phone in the hallway and hearing my voice at the other end, screaming for her and Dad to sell the house so the gang wouldn't cut off another of my fingers. Mark told Mum and Dad that if the kidnappers did get in touch, they were not to speak to them, but to give them a number for the crisis team. They would have someone on hand round the clock.

The paper had also managed to get a voluntary news-black out on the kidnapping. Within hours of it breaking on the news wires, the *Sunday Telegraph*'s editor, Ian MacGregor, had contacted other newspapers and TV channels asking them to refrain on reporting it for the time being. This was a common tactic in hostage situations. The idea being that the less fuss there was in the media, the less the hostage-takers would think they had grabbed anyone important enough to be worth holding. To that end, my family and Jane were asked not to tell anyone else about the kidnapping either, other than close friends.

My family and Jane took Mark at his word. Pretending life was going on as normal might be better, in a way, than simply sitting around and going to pieces. Jane went back to work, telling colleagues she had unspecified 'family difficulties'. My parents, who are both retired, concentrated on housekeeping, gardening and preparing for Christmas, not that it promised to be much of an occasion. Whenever the phone rang, my mum feared the worst. She was terrified that if the kidnappers called, she'd forget the phone number for the crisis team, so she had it written down on pieces of paper next to every phone in the house, along with back-up copies in her handbag. The *Telegraph* crisis team agreed to ring every afternoon at 5pm, but each call brought little more news, nor did those from a family liaison worker provided by the Foreign Office.

By Saturday, four days after I had gone missing, nobody was any the wiser. There was a wealth of conflicting accounts emerging from Puntland. There were claims that we'd entered the country illegally, and that we'd refused to use bodyguards. There were reports that Ahmed and Mustapha were either complicit in the kidnap, or had been abducted along with us. Then, on the Saturday morning, officials in Bossaso announced that they'd found the spot where we were being held and had surrounded it with 60 armed police. 'The policemen are around their hideout. After two, three hours, they'll have the hostages with them,' a Puntland official told AFP breezily.

London did not share his confidence. Mark feared it would lead to a bloodbath in which both José and I would be killed. The crisis team spent the day frantically ringing officials in the Puntland government, pleading with them to call the operation off. By the end of the day, however, it became clear the government claims were completely untrue. There were no police within miles of us, never mind some crack team. But it also meant there was still no real word on whether we were alive.

In the meantime, Jane and my family tried to go about their daily business pretending nothing had happened at all. It was not easy. Kidnapping exerts a particularly cruel emotional toll on the victim's next-of-kin. The threat of death looms large, but at no fixed time or date, so there is no prospect of 'closure'. And unlike the car crash victim or cancer patient clinging to a life support machine, it is harder to attribute to the will of God or the disinterested hand of fate.

Instead, there are malign human actors involved, whose intention all along is to drive a bargain by fear and terror. It is no surprise that hostage negotiators often say the real target of a kidnap is not the victim, but their loved ones.

On Sunday afternoon, unable to bear another miserable day at home, Mum and Dad decided to face the outside world. They walked down the road to a party hosted by their friend Dick, one of the few other people they'd confided in. In case anything important happened while they were out, they gave the crisis team Dick's home number to ring. Neither really felt in the mood for socialising, nor were they quite sure what to say if anyone asked where their globe-trotting journalist son was at the moment. But after several glasses of wine, both found themselves relaxing a little for the first time since Wednesday afternoon. Then Dick wandered through the crowd and whispered discreetly to them. 'Phone call for you. Take it upstairs.'

Dad took the call. It was the *Telegraph*, saying that they'd had finally had a call from me. Dad told Mum. She went back downstairs, trying not to cry.

*****

'I don't like the look of that guy,' whispered José, as we sat on our mat in the corner of our new cave sometime on the morning of Day 5. We'd begun to count the days numerically, like contestants in some Stone Age version of *Big Brother.*

'Which guy?' I glanced at the armed men sitting on the far side of the cave. Frankly, I didn't like the look of any of them.

'The one with the turban on. See? Next to the camp fire. Standing up now.'

José directed my gaze while keeping his own to the ground. We were instinctively wary of ever pointing at any particular kidnapper, or even making them aware we were talking about them.

'You see him now?' he said. 'The one who came with the second bunch of kidnappers. He looks like he is some kind of religious guy. And he's been reading the Koran to the rest of them.'

My eyes lit upon a tall, thin youth, clad in a dirty white robe and sandals. He wore a loosely wound turban of faded pink cloth, and unlike the rest of the gang, carried a pistol rather than a Kalashnikov. That wasn't the only thing that marked him out. His appearance was more Arab than Somali. His face was long and slender, with high cheekbones jutting out from coffee-coloured skin. On his chin he had a small goatee. He was about 20, and, to the mind of a paranoid, kidnapped Westerner, a dead ringer for a young Osama bin Laden. In the evenings, he'd been reading out aloud from a thick, yellow-covered Koran, the gang gathered round like children having a bedtime story.

True, there was no shortage of bin Laden lookalikes in Somalia. While the Al Qaeda leader was raised in Saudi Arabia, his ancestral village is in Yemen, from where many people resettled in Somalia several centuries ago. The question was what exactly this particular lookalike was doing here with us. He might just be here as some sort of chaplain, giving the gang spiritual guidance for the kidnap mission. Or he might be the point man for some kind of Islamist group, perhaps whoever'd ordered the kidnapping in the first place. His evening lectures might be all about the evils of the infidels on the other side of the cave. True, assuming that someone was from Al Qaeda because they read the Koran was a little like assuming your local vicar was a fundamentalist Christian because he read the Bible. But I couldn't help sharing José's unease. The hostage experience is not one that nurtures a generous outlook to one's fellow men. Besides, most vicars I'd met didn't officiate as reverends-at-large for armed kidnapping gangs.

Later that day, after a meal of rice and tuna, we got a chance to put José's fears to the test. The Teacher, as we'd nicknamed him, wandered over to talk, accompanied by the football-loving Faisal. Like Faisal, he turned out to have a tiny smattering of English. We strung out another conversation about football teams as long as possible, only coming to a halt when I mentioned Hibernian FC, the team from my home town of Edinburgh. News of the feats of 'the men of Easter Road', it seemed, had not yet reached the cavesfolk of northern

Somalia, and there were blank looks all round. Then, seeking a new topic of discussion, the Teacher brought up religion.

'I, Muslimeen,' he said, pointing at himself and Faisal. *'You. From which, you? Christiyan?'*

'Christian,' I said.

I wasn't really. Other than a few youthful stints at Sunday School, my attendance record at church was the same as my attendance record at Easter Road, which was to say, nil. And right now, for all the predicament we were in, I hadn't felt desperate enough to pray. But in his 'conduct under capture' lesson, Mick had said it was better to lie and say you were a Christian than admit to being an unbeliever. For all their talk about Christian oppressors, militant Muslims had even less time for Godless atheists. Nor did they really do agnostics, or woolly Anglican 'God-is-whatever-you-deem-it-to-be' stuff. You either followed God United FC or you didn't. If you appeared to doubt the existence of the Almighty in any way, they'd lose far less sleep about slitting your heathen throat, should circumstance require. Just to be on the safe side, I pointed to José too.

'He is also Christian,' I said, baptising him before he could say otherwise.

The Teacher nodded approvingly. Sensing he might have sway with the gang, we pressed for some concessions that might make life more comfortable.

'My friend, we need to wash,' said José, miming the act of taking a shower. 'You have soap? Water?'

'Maa fisch.'

'And we need to shit,' José added, gesturing vaguely to his rear. He picked out a scrap of tissue from his jeans pocket. 'You have some of this?'

The Teacher shook his head and picked up a rock. *'This. You. This.'*

'No... no. We must have this... tissue,' said José.

'Yes, tissue,' I chimed in.

God only knew what infections you'd pick up wiping your arse with a rock. To our delight, Faisal went off, rummaged in a rucksack, and came back with a handy-pack of tissues for each of us.

Anxious to seem grateful, we kept the conversation going. We tried politics. As with religion, the discussion was done on very black and white terms. Different world leaders got either the Thumbs Up or the Thumbs Down, although our new friends seemed to know less about politicians than they did about football. Barack Obama got a thumbs-up, but so too, confusingly, did George W Bush and Tony Blair.

'What about the Shabab?' I asked nervously. We might as well find out sooner rather than later. The Teacher put three cocked fingers to his head, and twisted them back and forth. It was an Arab gesture for one who is not of sound mind.

'Shabab. This crazy. Al Qaeda. No good.'

Thank *God* for that. We hadn't the faintest idea whether he was telling the truth, of course. But it was still a comfort. A cheery thumbs up for the Shabab would have killed the conversation even quicker than mentioning Hibs FC.

*****

That afternoon the Teacher wandered over again. *'You,'* he said. *'You call you country, you. England. Spain.'*

He raised an imaginary telephone to his ear, and gestured that we were to follow him. Together with Faisal and two other guards, we headed out the cave and picked our way up a steep slope, strewn with dagger-shaped rocks. After not standing up for two days, it was hard to keep steady.

'This. Is. A. Difficult. Position,' cautioned The Teacher, mustering his longest sentence yet.

After twenty minutes of scrambling, we saw some of the gang sat next to a thorn tree near a ridgetop. We flopped down alongside them, a fresh layer of perspiration on our clothes, now stiff as cardboard from the sweat of the past few days. Sat fiddling with a mobile phone was a big, heavily-set fellow who'd driven the truck that had delivered us here a couple of days ago. He was built like a middleweight boxer, with a grin that made his lower teeth jut out like a crocodile's. He had a calm, steady expression that looked as if he might enjoy trouble. As he tried to get a reception on the phone, I tried to make a note of any distinctive features that marked our location. Opposite us was a cliff several hundred feet high, and a soaring rock pillar that flared into a huge fist of stone fingers. The mountains were shaped into long, narrow, tableaus of wind-blasted rock, like upturned ships' keels. It was a harsh, savage landscape, but also starkly beautiful.

The big guy's mobile phone rang, a chirpy tinkle that sounded odd on such a man in such a place. He spoke into it for several minutes, then handed it to me. I heard the static of a poor line, and then a voice in deep, heavily-accented English.

'My name is Ali, I am an English teacher from Bossaso. I am acting as interpreter for this gang. Can you hear me?'

'Yes, I can hear you.'

'I am not on their side, I am acting in a humanitarian capacity. I am just trying to help you. Do you understand?'

'Yes, Ali, I understand.'

Somehow, I doubted he was acting purely out of altruism. Ali was probably a 'chewer', as they called them in Iraq, someone who presents themselves as a go-between in hostage situations, but who is actually an affiliate of the kidnap gang. Still, right now he was our only chance of getting a message to the outside world. It sounded like he was calling from his family home. I could hear children's voices in the background. What a charmer, running a hostage operation in front of his kids.

'Is there anybody you want me to call for you?' he said.

'Yes, I want you to call the number of my office in London,' I said.

I didn't want to ring Jane or my family. It would be too much of a shock for them, and I wouldn't have trusted myself to keep my composure. In any case, the office was more likely to have someone waiting for me to ring.

I gave Ali the number for the main *Telegraph* newsdesk. He dialled it on a separate mobile phone, and then created a crude connection by putting the two handsets on loudspeaker and holding them together. The arrangement allowed Ali to earwig on the conversation, and presumably also prevented anyone tracking down where the kidnappers' mobile phone signal was coming from. But it also made the line full of crackle and feedback, and it kept on cutting out. It was only on the third attempt that I finally heard the newsdesk phone ringing.

Eventually a woman's voice answered. 'Hello, *Telegraph* newsdesk.'

'Hello, my name is Ali, I am calling from Somalia. I would like to speak to someone from the *Sunday Telegraph*.'

I listened anxiously. He had chosen the worst possible time to call. Sunday mornings were notorious for elderly *Telegraph* readers calling in to complain that their paper had the TV listings wrong, or was missing a supplement. Either that, or it was some nutter claiming to have slept with Prince Charles, or to have proof that Tony Blair was part of a Masonic conspiracy to rule the world. Or, indeed, claiming to represent a kidnap gang from Somalia. Because there was only a skeleton staff on Sundays, such calls would often get short shrift from the newsdesk, who'd just pretend to listen while someone burbled away at the end of the phone. Or that was what I often did, anyway. I half expected the woman's voice to tell Ali: 'Really, that's very interesting. Can I suggest you ring back on Monday morning? I'm sure someone will be happy to discuss this with you then.'

I cut in. 'Hi, this is Colin Freeman here from the *Sunday Telegraph*. Who is that?'

'I'm sorry, the line's very faint. Can you repeat that?'

'It's Colin Freeman here. I'm ringing from Somalia. I've been kidnapped...'

'Pardon? Who did you say you were? The line's very faint.'

Jesus, any second now she'd put the phone down. Luckily, the woman showed more patience than I normally did. I blurted out a message, not waiting for her to ask questions.

'If you can hear me, this is Colin Freeman from the *Sunday Telegraph*. I am in Somalia with a photographer called José Cendon. We have been kidnapped. We are being held in some mountains near Bossaso, but physically and mentally we are both fine. Did you hear that okay?'

'One moment, please,' said the woman. 'I am just going to pass you on to our home news editor.'

A man's voice introduced himself, I couldn't make out who. I went through the spiel again.

'Did you get that?' I asked

'Er, yes,' he said.

'Are there any questions you have for me?' I asked.

'Er, yes, when exactly were you kidnapped?'

'Last Wednesday.'

'And where?

'In Bossaso.'

'And you were leaving the hotel as it happened, yes?'

'Yes.'

'And you're in Somalia, right?'

'Er... yes.'

Christ, was the paper not even aware of what had happened? Or had this guy just not been told? Poor bastard, he'd probably come in expecting a quiet Sunday shift, hungover from the night before.

The phone went dead again, and we rang back. This time, though, the newsdesk had got their act together. I was given another mobile number to call and to ask for 'Nick.'

I was half expecting 'Nick' to be some Foreign Office type. Instead, it was Nick Meo, my colleague on the foreign desk. Why they'd picked him to do it, I didn't know, but he was a good choice. He was a cheerful, unflappable character who'd been through some scrapes himself over the years. Only last month, he'd been travelling in a US army vehicle in Afghanistan that had been hit by a landmine, killing its top gunner. While he'd never been kidnapped, he'd have an idea of I was going through, and was therefore the kind of person I wanted at the end of the phone.

Nick explained that he had been appointed as the intermediary for any calls between the kidnap gang and London. Then he asked some 'proof of life' questions given by our families, things only we would know the answer to. For me it was the name of my first primary school teacher, the name of the house in the Lake District that we used to go on family holidays to, and the name of my favourite surfing destination in the Canary Islands.

'Do you know what the people holding you want?' asked Nick.

'No, they haven't told us anything yet. They don't speak English. But we are being treated well, and we have water and food.' I said. 'And cigarettes,' I added. Suddenly that seemed very important.

'Are you under any duress to say that you are okay?' Nick asked. He was gambling, I guessed, that Ali's English wouldn't run to the word 'duress'.

'No honestly, we are fine,' I said. 'I just want to say to Jane and to my family that I am sorry for all the worry I am causing them.'

'I'll tell them you're okay,' Nick said. 'They'll be very happy to hear that.'

I tried to think of something that would convince them I was coping.

'The mountains we're in are actually very beautiful,' I said. 'If it wasn't for the circumstances, it would be like an amazing backpacking experience.'

It was true, in a way. Somali Kidnap Tours Inc had every ingredient of the average adventure travellers' fantasy. Mountains that no tourist had ever visited, sleeping rough in caves, and being guided by 'genuine' locals, who didn't ruin their authenticity by boasting about some Finnish gap-year student they'd slept with.

'Also Nick, please tell everyone that I am really sorry about causing the office all this trouble.'

I meant that bit too. As a foreign correspondent, you were paid to go to dangerous places and come back out alive again, not end up being a hostage. I had a sneaking suspicion that when I got back, the office might quietly find an excuse to get rid of me.

'Don't worry, mate, no-one is blaming you here,' Nick said. 'It's just a job that went bit wrong.'

That was something of an understatement.

The line went dead again. Ali asked if we needed to speak any more. I said no. Nick now knew everything we had to say, and Ali could now call him direct to relay whatever it was this gang wanted.

José and I wandered back down the hill, only to be re-directed to a new hideout. This time it was just a gap in between two large segments of rock, open to the sky. We smoked a celebratory Business Royal each, relieved at having got proof of life back. At least our families would know we weren't dead. Five days might have seemed like a long time, but it was fairly businesslike by the standards of some kidnaps. José said that when he'd worked in Colombia, he'd heard of hostages being held for six months before they got any word out to their families at all.

As night fell, we lay on our mat and looked out over the stars, discussing our prospects and chuckling at what Ali had said after Nick had rung off. He hadn't approved of me comparing our experience to a backpacking holiday.

'The gang holding you won't like it if you sound too happy,' he'd said. 'This isn't a holiday, you know. You need to sound more scared.'

Hearing us sniggering away, one of the kidnappers wandered over to see what was going on. 'Shshh,' he said. He gestured at us to sleep, as if admonishing a pair of naughty schoolboys.

7: Stone Age men

NOTWITHSTANDING THE FACT that he was giving spiritual sanction to our illegal abduction, the Teacher took a shine to José and me. Keen to improve our level of communication, he would come to our corner of the cave each morning and hold a short language class, asking for basic words in English and giving us their Somali counterparts. Given that we taught each other largely by pointing to whatever was around, the lessons departed somewhat from the standard language school fare. Rather than 'Shopping at the market' or 'Meeting the family', we learned odd words like *hubud* (bullet), *massas* (cave) and *rashasha* (belt-fed machine gun). But it passed the time, and besides, the other pupil in the classes was Yusuf, the man who seemed to be the gang's main leader. He was about my own age, with a boyish face and a quiet, self-assured manner that suggested he was in charge for his brains rather than his brawn. Not that he seemed like someone to be trifled with. Inside a laptop case that he carried at all times was a pair of wood-handled stick grenades, along with a copy of the Koran. Giving him English lessons kept us in his good books. After lesson one, a tin of pineapple chunks was produced. After lesson two, we each got a fork and spoon.

Thanks to the educational policies of Somalia's late dictator, the Maoist-influenced Siad Barre, learning Somali was easier than it might have been. In 1972, in a typical act of despotism-in-the-name of progress, he'd scrapped the old Arabic alphabet in favour of a Latin one. The changeover had rendered half the nation's printing presses obsolete overnight, but it did mean that the Teacher could write down each Somali word for us. It was still complicated though. Like a rewired typewriter, the 'x' in Somali script swaps places with the 'h', while 'c' sounds like 'a', and there is no 'p' or 'v'. Most words we found hard to pronounce intelligibly. Being British, the first one I asked to learn was *waxadmasantaxay* (thank you), which, in my mouth, sounded more Geordie than Somali. Try as I might, I could never convey my gratitude properly as the kidnappers handed over our daily dollops of rice or cigarette rations. The Teacher and Yusuf did rather better, mastering both 'How are you?' and 'I am fine, thank you'. I resisted the temptation to teach them to say 'I am a kidnapping bastard, thank you'.

English was not Yusuf's only subject of study. Along with his Koran, his laptop case also contained a thick history book in a shiny yellow jacket, which he spent many hours poring over. Occasionally, he would read out aloud to the younger members of the gang, who would sit attentively, as if worried that he might hand out worksheets later on. Watching him vaguely reminded me of Stringer Bell, the gang leader in the TV cop show *The Wire*, who runs a team of teenage drug dealers while studying for a college degree. What history Yusuf was reading exactly I had no idea, although one day he wandered over and pointed to a line on a page. Two words stood out amid the dense Somali jumble of x's, h's and c's. They formed a name: 'Richard Corfield'.

'*This. This British,*' Yusuf said, pointing at the text and then at me.

Full marks to Yusuf. Like Speke and Burton before him, Corfield was another dedicated emissary of empire who had visited Somalia in the early days, although unlike them, he did not return back alive to tell the tale. Instead, he became the most famous scalp of the so-called 'Mad Mullah,' Mohammed Abdullah Hassan, the man who led Somalia's first modern war against foreign occupiers.

A tall, fearless fighter who was farmed for both his fiery anti-Western oratory and his ability to avoid capture, the Mullah was in many ways the Osama bin Laden of his time. His jihad against the foreign 'infidels' proved one of the fiercest anti-colonial insurrections of the period, while his habit of keeping a running commentary to his enemies presaged bin Laden's videotaped messages to the West.

'I like war, but you do not,' he would snarl in open letters addressed to the British public. 'Our men who have fallen in battle have won Paradise.'

Born in 1856, the Mullah grew up in the northern territory known as British Somaliland, part of the three-way colonial carve-up that created Italian Somaliland to the east, and French Somaliland – now Djibouti – to the west. With little of value in the desert interior, the British colonial footprint was actually relatively light: HMG's presence was confined largely to a few hundred officials in the coastal towns, which sent livestock across the Gulf to the more valued British port at Aden.

However, to the Mullah, who had fallen under the influence of hardline Saudi clerics during a youthful pilgrimage to Mecca, the mere notion of Christians ruling Muslims on their own soil was abhorrent. His guerrilla campaign from 1899 to 1920 mobilised some 20,000 fighters at its height, and, in classic insurgent fashion, targeted not just the occupying presence but any Somali tribes who co-operated with it.

Tasked with suppressing the rebellion was Corfield, a Boer War veteran who led the Camel Constabulary, a mounted unit that used the one animal properly adapted to Somalia's desert conditions. Such was the Mullah's effectiveness as a guerrilla fighter that Corfield was under orders not to confront his forces directly, but as the bloodshed between the tribes grew ever greater, Corfield refused to sit on the sidelines. One sultry August afternoon in 1913, his 110-man force fought a pitched battle with nearly 3,000 well-armed supporters of the Mullah, killing an estimated 450 of the enemy, but losing 36 constables in the process, including Corfield himself.

Knowing British vengeance would be severe, the Mullah vanished back into the bush, and despite a British bombing campaign – one of the first uses of airpower against an insurgency – remained at large for another seven years, eventually dying of influenza. A century on, though, he was still remembered in Somalia as a classic Muslim resistance fighter, not least because of an extraordinary poem he dedicated to his vanquished enemy, titled simply 'The Death of Richard Corfield.'

Reminiscent of Bin Laden's crowing, mocking addresses, the poem advised the dead Corfield's spirit on what he should say to Heaven-bound souls, as he was dragged the other way towards Hell.

'You have died, Corfield, and are no longer part of this world. When, Hell-destined, you set out for the Other World, those who have gone to Heaven will question you...

'Say to them: 'With fervour and faith they attacked us.' Report how savagely their swords tore you.

'Say: 'As I looked fearfully from side to side, my heart was plucked from its sheath.'

Say: 'My eyes stiffened as I watched with horror, the mercy I implored was not granted.'

Such was the Mullah's way with both the sword and the pen that he was said to remain an inspiration to jihadists of the modern creed. During the US occupation of Mogadishu in 1993, resistance leaflets had reportedly quoted verses from his ode to Corfield, while today, the Shabab were also rumoured to hold him in high regard.

But what was Yusuf's take on him, I wondered? Was it merely intellectual curiosity? Or was he too, a follower of some kind of anti-Western cause, for whom the Mullah might be a hero? It was now a week into our captivity, and I still could not really tell who our captors were or what their purpose was. For all that the Teacher had suggested that they weren't affiliated to the Shabab, they didn't exactly come across as common criminals either. Common criminals, I imagined, wouldn't pray together five times a day, as this lot did, nor would they spend their spare time reading history books or the Koran. They'd most likely also be chewing qhat, of which I had not seen a single leaf in the cave so far. Could they be some kind of political militia? If so, what did they want from us?

On Day 8, we finally found out. We'd been taken up to the nearby mountaintop again for a phone call, and as Yusuf sat talking to Ali on the phone, the Teacher stood in front of us.

'*Okay. Phone London you,*' he said, pointing at me. '*Your family. Three meel-yon dollar.*'

'And you...' He pointed at José. *'Your family, three meel-yon dollar.'*

He gestured with his AK47. *'No dollar? This, you. After two days.'*

José and I looked at each other queasily. At least we were worth the same amount. From the way the Teacher had priced us out separately, I thought he'd been about to offer a discount on José, as if, as a mere Spaniard, he commanded less in the international hostage market than a citizen of an aggressive imperial power like Britain. It might also have meant he got freed before me.

Yusuf handed me the phone. It was Ali, who called Nick again. I told him of our new status as the Six Million Dollar Men.

'They say that if we don't pay them $3 million for each of us in 48 hours, they'll kill us both,' I said.

'That's going to be a bit difficult,' said Nick.

'How do you mean?'

'Well, obviously your family don't have that kind of money. And neither the British government nor the *Telegraph* pay ransoms. They should also realise that you were in Puntland just doing your job, reporting on the problems of the Somali people. We really think that they should just let you go, without any conditions. I want to remind them that *they are responsible for your welfare*. If anything happens to you, *it is their fault*.'

There was little left to say. Back at the cave, José and I spent the rest of the day trying to work out what would happen next. We didn't think the gang were really serious about killing us. Not yet anyway. If they really were after a ransom, it was also likely that $6 million was a kind of starter for ten, and that they would negotiate. It felt strange to be given a price tag, though. I thought of the various things you could buy with $3 million. A two-bedroom townhouse in Mayfair. A dozen Rolls Royces. Ten kilos of uncut cocaine. Or, if you were a Somali, a brand new SUV for everyone in your clan, with change left over for the mother of all qhat parties. It seemed rather a lot for a grubby hack like me. I could imagine a senior diplomat commanding that kind of figure, or some famous face from CNN. But me? Then again, how did anybody decide how much people were worth in the first place? Was there some kind of committee that circulated informal price guidelines? Still, at least our guys were thinking big. It would be embarrassing to die for want of say, $50,000.

Yet even if my family or the *Telegraph* were willing to pay a ransom, I didn't think the British government would let them. Other countries like France and Italy were said to have coughed up for hostages in Iraq recently, but Britain was supposed to have a policy of never negotiating. It was a hangover from the days of empire, a strategy to deter upstart foreign powers from detaining HMG's colonial footsoldiers around the world. The hitch, though, was that it was forged in a time when there were other ways of bringing polite pressure to bear on local officials, like bringing in the Royal Navy to shoot up their port. These days, I wouldn't want to lay on odds on the Foreign Secretary diverting *HMS Cumberland* from its anti-piracy patrol to shell Bossaso.

Still, we couldn't even be sure it was money they were really after. I knew from covering kidnaps in Iraq and Afghanistan that they were always murky affairs, partly because abduction was often seen as a dishonourable tactic in the first place. Hence kidnappers often disguised not only their identities, but their motives. Sometimes they cited political reasons when it was actually financial. Other times they cited financial reasons when it was actually political, or a mixture of both. In Somalia, it was not unknown for factions to kidnap or kill foreigners simply to undermine the authority of whichever rival faction was in power. The media hullabaloo over a missing or murdered Westerner made it look like they couldn't control their own turf. Our own abduction might be nothing to do with money and just the product of the myriad clan feuds that raged here all the time. Back in Bossaso, I'd sensed tension between the coastguard head, Abdiweli Ali Taar, and the government, whom he'd accused of being in cahoots with the pirates. I'd painted him out as a bit of a hero in the piece I'd written. Had someone perhaps had us kidnapped just to undermine him and his presidential campaign? Or could he even have done it undermine someone else? Round here, anything was possible.

We'd just have to hope that whoever was trying to free us back in London knew what they were doing. One liked to think there was some Foreign Office or M16 desk officer with contacts in this region, who knew which clan chiefs might be bribed, or if necessary leant on, to help. Then again, there might not be. One of the problems of having a secret service was that you never really knew whether they were all-powerful, as they liked to hint they were, or utterly useless. If the Foreign Office's only contact in Bossaso was, say, the qhat-chewing minister of health, we'd have plenty more time for Somali lessons.

*****

One of the reasons I'd fled to Iraq from the *London Evening Standard* – and ultimately wound up in this cave – was to avoid any more 'doorsteps'. Alongside the 'death knock' – where your task is to visit the home of a bereaved family and secure an interview with them – the doorstep ranks as one of the most unenviable tasks in any newsroom. While the death knock requires the tact of an undertaker, the doorstep requires the skills of a sentry. Step one is to park up with a photographer outside the house of some celebrity, politician or other person 'in the news'. Step two is to ring the doorbell, fire a few questions, and wait for them to say either 'no comment' or 'piss off'. Step three is to wait a while, and then repeat step two again. And again. And again. The idea being that eventually, they will tell you something just to get rid of you. It is roughly the same principle applied by malodorous beggars in parks and shopping centres, and carries some of the same risks. The police may be called, or if you pick someone in a bad mood, you may get punched.

Over the years I spent hours, days and sometimes entire weeks on doorsteps. I besieged philandering politicians in Westminster townhouses. I waylaid murder suspects on south London council estates. And I hounded enough celebrities to fill a copy of *Heat* magazine: the Gallagher brothers from Oasis, most of the Spice Girls, Les Dennis, Amanda Holden and plenty of other C-listers whose names no longer mean anything. All the name-dropping in the world, however, cannot disguise the fact that doorstepping is like being on a stake-out in a very dull cop movie.

You did, however, get to know your photographer very well, hanging around with them from dawn to dusk. This can be a mixed blessing. Like many professions who work together, photographers and reporters treat each other with friendly rivalry. We reporters – who, of course, are never known to stereotype – see photographers as the rough trade of the news industry, doing a job which involves little more than sticking a digital camera in someone's face. The nickname among reporters for a photographer is a 'monkey', a name coined by none other than Prince Philip, who once likened a press pack that followed him round the Rock of Gibraltar to its resident colony of Barbary Apes. 'Monkeys', it will be no surprise to learn, regard reporters as stuck-up arses, and nickname us 'caption writers'.

To be fair – and in case, God forbid, I ever end up doorstepping again – I should stress that most photographers I have worked with are charming, erudite people who have made a wet day outside Ann Widdecombe's house far more fun than it might have been. Indeed, it was a photographer who originally suggested I quit the *Standard* for Iraq, while doorstepping the late Cheryl Barrymore in 2002. All the same, if I'd known that becoming a foreign correspondent would lead one day to me being stuck in a cave with a photographer I'd never met before, I might have thought twice.

Happily, José was shaping up to be a very companionable fellow hostage. Frankly, the conditions we were in could have put any human relationship to the test. We spent 24 hours a day on the same mat together, eating from the same plate, sleeping under the same blanket, and waking each other up at night with our snoring. Yet as Day One became Day Five, and Day Five became Day Ten, I found myself liking him all the more.

Partly it was because his basic conduct-under-capture persona was similar to mine. He was easy-going, didn't panic or complain, and was neither confrontational nor timid when dealing with the gang. But he was also good company. I'd feared that it might be difficult being stuck with a non-Brit, even one who spoke good English as he did, simply because we'd have a limited amount in common. As a hostage, there is only so much time that can be spent musing profoundly on the nature of life and death: it is helpful to be able to while some of the hours away talking light-hearted twaddle. Had I been with a photographer from the office, we would probably have passed a great deal of time on subjects like 'Worst New Romantic bands of the 1980s', favourite children's telly from the 1970s, and that great moral dilemma game: 'If your life depended on it, who would you rather have sex with? (choose two equally unappealing celebrities).' But while José had never watched *Grange Hill* or *The Magic Roundabout*, and lacked an opinion on whether Valerie Singleton would be better in bed than Thora Hird, he was extremely well versed in the books and films of my own language.

He'd read Dickens and Hemingway, Orwell and Steinbeck, had picked his way through the Elizabethan English of Shakespeare and the broad Scots of Irvine Welsh. He knew what a psychological Western was, and could discuss the finer points of the works of Sam Peckinpah, Lars Von Trier, Wong Kar Wai, and numerous other directors I probably should have heard of, but hadn't. If anything, it was me who came across as the cultural ignoramus, frequently looking blank when he mentioned some prominent artistic figure from my own country. Yet we found many mutual tastes, some of them endearingly obscure. I was delighted to learn, for example, that I had been taken hostage alongside a fellow fan of the 1973 film *Pat Garret and Billy the Kid*, with its cameo appearance by Bob Dylan.

We also swapped anecdotes about the places we'd worked and the stories we'd covered. We discovered mutual friends in the journalist hubs of Nairobi and Jerusalem, and, in what often made for much more entertaining conversation, people we both disliked. Frontline journalism is great fun, but it does attract a number of people who take themselves rather too seriously, simply because they write about conflict rather than celebrities. Indeed, one of our best early 'bonding moments' was a bitching session about a well-respected and award-winning photojournalist, whom we took great glee in slagging off for his well-meaning, but slightly pompous remarks about 'bearing witness'. True, neither of us had ever actually met him, nor did we know whether he was the self-important twit we made him out to be. But such was the boost to cave morale that we let that small point pass.

Gradually, in between the whistle of the soot-blackened camp kettle that started the morning, and the final call to prayer that signalled darkness, we learned a lot about each other, forging a friendship in days that might normally have taken years. Soon I could have answered 100 different 'proof of life' questions about José, including some his family probably didn't know the answers to. He was from Santiago di Compostela, a small town in Galicia that is one end of a famous pilgrim route across northern Spain. His favourite drink was rum and coke. His favourite bar was the Medusa, a little place tucked away in Santiago's old town, where they also did good tapas. His favourite bands were Iggy Pop, the Smiths and Pink Floyd. He preferred the Rolling Stones to the Beatles, but like me, didn't reckon they'd done anything good since *Exile on Main Street*. He'd been one of the 'cool kids' in his school (I was more one of the 'square' ones). He'd once spent a dismal summer working in London, stacking video tapes in a warehouse, and sharing a flat with a crack-smoking Turkish landlord. And he'd also slept with a great deal more women than I ever had. True, 'monkeys' were notorious for exaggerating things like that. But even so, it sounded like his time sharing a bed with me was probably his most celibate period for a while.

*****

All the same, no amount of buddy movie-style bonding could stop Stone Age life being generally very boring. Each day, the routine was identical. We'd wake up to the low hum of our kidnappers' dawn prayers, followed by the crackle of firewood being lit and the murmured exchanges with those coming off night guard duty. Around 8am we'd have tea and smoke the first of our daily cigarette ration, sometimes Business Royals, sometimes Rothmans. And then the rest of the day would start. If you could call it that. There was, frankly, nothing to do. We had no books or newspapers to read, and the Teacher, despite our pleadings, would not give us a pen and paper so that we could keep a journal. He even objected when we scratched out the markings for a chessboard on a flat piece of rock, claiming it was a map on which we would formulate an escape plan.

'He may be a teacher, but he is a thick bastard, just a villager,' grumbled José.

Eventually, having appealed to Yusuf, the gang leader, clearance for the chess set was given. The pieces were fashioned from small pebbles wrapped in cigarette foil that we twisted into different shapes. A single spire made a bishop, a bent spire made a knight, a pair of spires made a queen, and so on. Under the Teacher's watchful gaze, we began what would become a long-running tournament.

'Get your spies away from my pieces,' muttered José, as an ant crawled from my end of the board to his.

It worked surprisingly well, although occasionally we'd get confused as to which piece was which, or a game would be scuppered when the entire set blew away in a gust of wind: normally when I was winning, or claimed to be. Spain soon established a convincing lead over Britain.

From a cigarette packet torn into 52 tiny squares, we also made a set of playing cards, using a piece of charcoal from the fire to daub crude symbols on them. Crosses, circles, dots and triangles took the place of diamonds, hearts, clubs and spades. It was a fiddly procedure, but was vaguely satisfying, in a Bird Man of Alcatraz sort of way. The ingenuity of the human spirit, and all that. Unfortunately, having spent an entire morning making the cards, neither of us could remember any decent card games. We tried poker, but it was hard to get excited when all you had was pebbles as chips (we only got about five cigarettes a day each, so they were too valuable to gamble).

A makeshift version of Scrabble, with a vast pile of charcoaled vowels and consonants, was little better. I even tried our own version of *Countdown*, the Channel Four game show, much to José's bemusement.

'We each take nine letters from the pile, then we have 30 seconds to make the longest word we can,' I explained.

'Come on, man, I am Spanish, you have to give me more time than that. English is not my first language.'

'Okay, we'll do a minute. In fact, two minutes. That'll make it more exciting.'

I dished the letters out. AEGTRPUYT.

Two minutes later, we showed our respective hands. I had GREAT. José had TARGET.

'Well done, you beat me!'

'Okay, so what happens now?'

'Er... we do the same again.

'Is that it?'

*****

Otherwise, the sole distraction was a battery-powered radio that the kidnappers occasionally allowed us to listen to, on which we could sometimes pick up a very faint signal from the BBC World Service. Of our own abduction, we heard nothing, although we did hear reports about the ongoing piracy crisis. There was talk of the multi-national naval force sponsoring some kind of land invasion against the pirates in Eyl, a prospect that alarmed us. I could see us being sold on to some pirate gang to use as human shields. Also worrying was the ongoing reports of the mounting casualties of the global recession. I didn't fancy hearing Nick on the phone telling me the *Telegraph* had gone bust.

Much of our time we spent simply watching the kidnappers as they went about their daily business around the camp. Gradually, what had previously been an anonymous gallery of suspicious, distrustful faces evolved into distinctive characters and personalities.

Yusuf was the clear leader, while his co-commander was the big fellow who'd driven the truck, who was also our main source of smokes. His name, we later found out, was Mousa, but José dubbed him the Guy of the Cigarettes. The rest of the gang seemed careful to avoid ever using their names in front of us, but we made up nicknames for them anyway. There was Skullface, the skinny kid who'd threatened to put a bullet in my head as we'd fled Bossaso (that apart, he proved quite friendly). Then there was Skullface 2, who looked like his emaciated older brother; The Mirror Man, who was always checking his hair in a hand-held mirror; The Trekker, who'd found the water when we'd both been pining with thirst; The Smoker, a tall fellow in his mid-20s who rolled his own cigarettes, and The Hobbit, a near-dwarf with a curled, tapered beard and high-pitched voice. Some, like the Sherpa, were reserved. Others, like the Mirror Man, showed a naive friendliness. At one point he offered to give us his email address so we could correspond with him if we ever got back home.

While José and I were bone idle, the rest of the camp hummed with activity. There were round the clock rotas of cooking, cleaning, tea-making, weapons maintenance, and guard duty. Every so often, a small party would disappear off to get more supplies, returning a day or two later with bulging hessian sacks. They sweetened the tea so heavily that the sugar sack was as big as the rice one.

The gang brought a certain ingenuity to life in the cave, with a range of tricks that would have been useful on Mick's hostile environment course. They powered up Yusuf's mobile phone by cutting the wall plug off a charger, paring the bare flex down to its bare wires and attaching them to several HP2 batteries taped together. It took most of the day to charge a phone on, but it worked.

Flavour for the cooking pot came from crystals of rock salt that the Trekker sourced from the nearby mountain slopes, the sort of stuff people paid a fortune in my neighbourhood deli back home. Bread they would make by running up a dough of flour and water, fashioning it into large, flat pancakes, and then sticking it in the embers of a fire made from very light brushwood. Somehow, the fine ash did not stick to the dough, and half an hour later it would be pulled out, dusted off and served up like nan-bread from a curry house. It was quite palatable – unlike the cloudy beverage they concocted from the fat that rose to the top of the boiled goat stew, which they relished as some kind of health drink, but which made me want to retch whenever I looked at it.

They also taught us how to brush our teeth with a stick torn from a tree. You chewed the end into strands, moistened them with your tongue, and then applied it like a wet paintbrush across your teeth. Provision for personal hygiene was otherwise rather thin. With barely enough water even for drinking with, we washed just once a week, using half a bottle of water and a handful of Omo washing powder. It refused to lather at all, and left you with grit grinding in your armpits.

But while our Stone Age lifestyle afforded us the odd jeer when we heard items about 'Green living' on the World Service, I worried what its long-term health impact would be. When José had first mentioned that we might end up in a cave, I'd imagined somewhere with at least a few camp beds maybe, or a generator to provide electricity. I hadn't thought it would be literally just a cave. I had no idea what the seasons were in Somalia, but it would be rough going if it got wet or cold. So far the weather had been one of our few allies – warm and sunny every day, without being too hot – but a few tropical storms could change all that, especially up in these mountains. And God only knew what other creatures we were sharing the cave with. We knew there were mosquitos and ants, we feared there was probably lice, rats, ticks, and possibly all manner of poisonous insects and spiders.

Somalia, like much of sub-Saharan Africa, was also home to numerous diseases that could undo a soft Westerner like me. Malaria, Dengue Fever, typhoid, sleeping sickness, rabies, giardiasis, Yellow Fever – the list in the *Lonely Planet Guidebook to Africa*, I remembered, ran over several pages. We might also get scurvy because of the lack of fruit and vegetables, plus whatever ailments might be lurking in the water we were now drinking. At first we'd been given bottled stuff when they'd resupplied, but soon that stopped, forcing us to drink from the big communal can, which had started life as a diesel container. Not only did it have a slightly oily bouquet, we had no idea what kind of well it was drawn from. Gerard Hanley, the British Army officer stationed in Somalia during World War II, had written how the water in many wells contained minute shards of crystallised gypsum – invisible to the eye when you drank, but painful as hell when you tried to piss. The crystals acted like tiny hooks in the tissue of your urinary tract, and had left many a squaddie wondering how he'd caught the clap when there was no brothel within 100 miles.

Malaria was the thing that scared me the most. Something like one in fifty mosquitos carried the malarial parasite, I recalled, dishing it out in various grades of severity. Type 1 malaria was like bad flu. Type 4 you were lucky to survive. And even with the milder forms, the symptoms – blinding headaches, raging fevers, terrible chills – would be hard to cope with in a cave. One of my best friends at university, Richard, had had two bouts of malaria while working as an English teacher in Malawi, and it had left him bed-ridden for several years. We might also pick up any amount of bugs from the desperadoes sharing the cave with us: tuberculosis, HIV, Hepatitis A, B, C and beyond. Not that it would necessarily take some exotic ailment to lay us low. With no access to medical help, a bad bout of diarrhoea could finish us off.

Yet in those first couple of weeks of captivity, we found ourselves coping better than expected. If anything, the despair that had clouded the first three days lifted a little as we rose to the challenge. At the same time, our world shrank rapidly, as did our expectations of it. It soon felt surprisingly natural to wake up each morning on the stone floor, nod good morning to José, and contemplate another long, empty day. As long as tea was on its way, and a cigarette close at hand, I was reasonably content.

Even the gang seemed relaxed. On Day 12 they held a party to celebrate the Muslim festival of Eid Al-Ahda, marking the end of the annual pilgrimage to Mecca. A goat was sacrificed and cooked up, guard duty kept to a minimum, and extra prayers said all around. Then, during the afternoon, the gang had a kind of 'Puntland's Got Talent' contest, featuring Koranic recitals, a jumping-over-a-stick game, and a press-up contest. Noticing that they were all fairly useless at press-ups – even the super-fit Sherpa – I entered myself and won with 25 in a row. It wasn't quite Paul Newman winning the egg-eating marathon in the prison movie *Cool Hand Luke*, but it drew a generous round of applause anyway.

'*Waxadmasantaxay,*' I shouted in my best pidgin Somali, wondering vaguely what the Somali was for 'champion'. I settled for just shouting 'Arsenal!'

8: Soldiers of God

'So how many times did you go to Somalia before, José?'
'Four times. Mainly to Mogadishu.'
'How was it?'
'Bad, mostly. Always fighting. And you? Did you ever go there?'
'Just the once. When the Islamists were in power.'
'How was it?'
'Pretty good actually. Peaceful and safe. Not like bloody Puntland.'
'Really? Tell me about it, my friend. We have all day...'

MOGADISHU, OCTOBER 2006: As 50 pairs of flip-flopped feet marched past in unsteady, slapping goosesteps, Colonel Abukar Sheikh Mohamed cracked an approving grin from under his sunglasses. The ragged column of soldiers on the red, sandy soil in front of him did not look much to be proud of – none had a uniform, and several were minus a full set of eyes, hands and ears. But given the unpromising material he'd started with, he was prepared to overlook the lack of spit-and-polish. Here at the Hilwayne Camp, a disused army barracks just outside Mogadishu, the phrase ''orrible little men' was not a drill sergeant's term of endearment, more a simple statement of fact. The recruits on the parade ground were all former members of Mogadishu's warlord militias, the drug-crazed gangs of killers, robbers and rapists who'd run amok for the past 15 years. Now, the Islamic Courts Union, a new religious movement that had seized control of the city a couple of months before, was 'rehabilitating' them into its ranks.

'Some of these men were alcoholics, others chewed or smoked drugs all day,' said Colonel Mohamed, gesturing with a long, thin twig that he used as a swagger stick.

'But now we have taught them the Islamic religion, they cry about their past sins and obey only the word of God. They do not even smoke cigarettes. Discipline is the first priority.'

The column reached the far end of the drill ground, next to a derelict barracks where some rusting technicals were parked.

Brows dripping in the midday sun, they executed a messy about-turn and headed back. Many of the eyes swivelling front had the bloodshot, rolling glaze of years stoned on qhat, marijuana and Ethiopian gin. They were dressed like most really poor Africans, in a wardrobe of throwaways from better-off countries. One trooper wore a sweatshirt advertising a car garage in Michigan, another had shellsuit bottoms in the colours of the Brazilian national football team. A third wore a teeshirt identifying him as a member of a college athletics team in Ohio. Their commanders didn't look much better. The Colonel's deputy had recently had his nose shot off, and sported a white strip bandage across his face that made him look like the pop star Adam Ant. But on their final march past over the parade ground, the soldiers put the hands to their sides, raised their heads, and gave the chant that was ringing alarm bells not just among Somalia's neighbours, but across the globe to Washington.

'Allah Akbar!,' went the cry. God is Great!

Some 13 years on from *Black Hawk Down*, and Somalia was once again the stuff of American nightmares. This time, though, the problem was not the warlords of Black Hawk Down infamy, but a movement that had proved to be their very nemesis. Fed up with the way the warlords had carved the city into a series of warring fiefdoms, a coalition of sheikhs and clerics called the Islamic Courts had banded against them, realising that religion might bring unity where clan politics had brought only discord. Over recent months they'd driven the warlords out, imposing law and order via Sharia courts, and giving captured militia fighters the chance to save their souls in the religious boot camp at Hilwayne.

Amazingly, it seemed to be working. Peace had returned to the city's streets for the first time since 1991. Shops and businesses were reopening, as had the port and airport. People were no longer raped and carjacked at random. Émigrés were returning home. In the coastal towns outside Mogadishu, where the Courts were now extending their writ, even the piracy was being stamped out.

The Courts argued that turning Somalia into an Islamic state was the only way of disciplining such an unruly nation. But peace also had its price. In return for banishing the warlords and their drunken, drugged thugs, the Courts expected people to submit to an austere interpretation of the Koran. Music, films and dancing were frowned upon, and women encouraged to wear the veil. There was talk of making it compulsory to pray five times a day, and of even banning men from chewing qhat. Yet on Mogadishu's wrecked streets, many long-suffering residents seemed willing to give the rule of God a try. The rule of mankind, after all, had so far failed them utterly, be it the warlords, the US-backed peacekeepers, or the dictator Siad Barre, whose 20-year reign of terror had ended in 1991.

The prospect of Somalia falling under the yolk of some African Taliban was not welcomed elsewhere. The West, having largely ignored Somalia for the previous decade, was now watching anxiously again. Of particular concern were training camps like the one we were now stood in, where the Courts were using short, sharp, Sharia shock treatments to create their new Islamic army.

As the men before us ended their drill, I wandered over to speak to them. Faces crowded all around me, apparently keen to be interviewed. But just as I looked round for Duguf, the interpreter, I felt his hand on my shoulder, dragging me away.

'Stay away from them, they are dangerous,' he said.

'But I need to interview them,' I protested.

'You see how they were gathering around you then? You were about to get robbed, just like the Spanish journalist I brought up here a while back. They stole his cameras.'

'Can't you get one of the commanders to keep watch?'

'Even they can hardly control them. Take it from me, I know these kind of guys. See how they cannot stand still? See how they are always look from side to side, and over their shoulder? That is the sign of people who have killed many times, maybe a dozen or more. So now they live in fear. Always checking that nobody is coming to take revenge.'

The soldiers headed off to prayer class, Colonel Mohamed shouting words of encouragement in their ears. As the senior drill officer for Somalia's new Islamic army, he clearly took a certain pride in recruiting such unholy warriors to his cause. Yet no amount of rehabilitation was ever going to give this lot a clean bill of health in Washington's eyes. The outside world hadn't really cared about them when they were robbing, looting and raping. But once they started praying, that was a different matter altogether. Unholy warriors were Somalia's problem. Holy warriors could end up as everybody else's.

*****

It's a complaint frequently voiced in the world's more restive cities that the foreign correspondents who shape their image to the wider world only ever visit when there's trouble. Check into the Commodore in Beirut or the Europa in Belgrade, and sooner or later, the receptionist, cleaner or barman will inquire wearily why you never come when things are quiet.

They have a point, to a point. As the old newsroom adage goes, 'if it bleeds, it leads'. Mogadishu, however, is an exception to this rule. Having been at war for nearly 20 years – far longer than most other places manage without a break – Somalia's capital is news when it is at peace.

I'd had a call about the 'Mogadishu-in-tranquillity-shocker' story from a freelance photographer friend, a Frenchman called Corentin Fleury. Peace wasn't exactly Corentin's normal gig either. Unlike me, he was a combat zone specialist, a seasoned gambler rather than an occasional flutterer, who was prepared to take genuine rather than calculated risks. He hadn't been in the game any longer than me, but already his track record of conflicts rather tore a strip off my own war reporting credentials. I'd first worked with him during an attempted military coup in Chad in the summer of 2006. When I'd met him in the hotel bar, I'd expected some grizzled veteran twice my age. Instead, he was only 24, although by the sounds of things, he'd done well just to reach that age. During the US siege of Fallujah in Iraq two years before, he'd been the only Western journalist unembedded inside the city, a mission that ran equal risks of being either killed by the Americans or beheaded by Al Qaeda. At first I hadn't believed him, but when I'd got home I'd seen his pictures in *Newsweek*. When he'd finally left Fallujah, he'd been arrested and questioned for a week by the Americans. They couldn't understand how any Westerner – even a Frenchman – could be crazy enough to go there in the first place, never mind come out alive.

Now, though, he was suggesting a trip that for once, wouldn't involve the prospect of bloodshed, be it his, mine, or anyone else's.

'Do you want to go to Mogadishu?' he'd said. 'There is this group called the Islamic Courts Union that has taken over the city. They have been fighting with the warlords, who the CIA was supporting.'

'The CIA?' I asked doubtfully. Call me a sceptic, or indeed a complacent fool, but in my limited experience, most stories that involved the CIA were the same as those involving UFOs, Mossad, or the death of Lady Diana. They were fascinating, compelling, and generally utter rubbish. Especially if you worked for the *Telegraph*, which was not known as a prominent mouthpiece for anti-American conspiracy theories.

'Why would the CIA fund the warlords?' I asked. 'I mean, they're the bad ones, aren't they? The ones who've been going around killing everyone all the time?'

'Yes,' said Corentin. 'But the Americans think the Courts are linked to Al Qaeda. They don't like the warlords much, but they like Islamic extremists even less. So they've been paying the warlords to fight them. It's all part of the war on terror. I was there in a few months ago when the Courts first started fighting the warlords. Now they have completely defeated them and got control of the whole city.'

CIA involvement or otherwise, the prospect of Islam taming the world's most lawless city, and succeeding where the outside world had so spectacularly failed, was a story in itself. Plus I'd never been to

Somalia before, and rather fancied the idea of racing around with a team of armed bodyguards, as Corentin said we'd have to do. Especially if it was, in fact, relatively safe.

*****

A few weeks later I was aboard my first ever Air Leopardskin flight to Mogadishu from Djibouti. I was amazed that a place like Mogadishu even had scheduled flights, although getting tickets did involve a rather bizarre ring around of Somali grocers in west London, who sidelined as airline agents in the back of their shops.

Our Antonov touched down on a runway that ran right along the seashore, narrowly missing a few members of the public who seemed to be wandering freely around. We pulled to a halt near a large, open air shack that passed for an international arrivals terminal. It was, by all accounts, a sign of the city's startling progress. Until the month before, the airport had been shut because of fighting, and the only place to land was an airstrip two hours' drive outside town.

Waiting for us was a fixer called Duguf, a freelance cameraman for Agence France Presse. He'd worked with Corentin during his last visit. He spoke English in short, very quick bursts that made him sound rather like a garage rapper and weren't that easy to understand, but he'd been in the news business in Mogadishu for more than a decade, which spoke fairly well of his survival skills. Unlike Ahmed and Mustapha, he'd done his homework in advance of our arrival. He brandished a paper from a Courts official approving us as 'fit and proper people', handed an airport official $30, and loaded us into a four wheel drive. Behind it was an elderly Hyoshi pick up with eight armed guards. The make-up of our personal security detail was a lesson in the diplomatic balancing acts that fixers in Mogadishu had to play. Four of the gunmen were from Duguf's own clan, the other four were hirelings from the Courts militia. As long as the balance of power in town was a little fragile, it was worth paying everyone to be on your side.

We drove off out the main airport gate and into town, bouncing over potholed roads. Duguf and Corentin reminisced about their last stint together back in May, when the Courts had driven out the remaining warlords. It sounded rather more in Corentin's usual line of work. At one point, their car had been hit by a shot from an anti-aircraft gun mounted on a technical. By some miracle, the shell capable of taking out Cold War jets from several miles away had done nothing more than cripple the front wheel.

Elsewhere, however, the various artillery manned by Mogadishu's warring factions over the years had been more effective. There was barely a single building that didn't look like it had served as the frontline in some last stand for control of the city. Unlike Baghdad, where only a few neighbourhoods bore heavy battle scars, here every block seemed to have hosted its own local Stalingrad, with combatants who'd fought with more enthusiasm than skill. The bigger buildings resembled chunks of gorgonzola cheese, yellowing whitewash veined with green mould, corners and sides gnawed away by bullet marks of all calibres.

Until a few months ago, driving through any one of these mini-ground zeros would have been perilous. Like gangland Los Angeles, every single neighbourhood was controlled by a different warlord, who would demand money or favours for the dubious privilege of passing through his turf. Going from one side of town to the other was a constant obstacle course of checkpoints, manned by militiamen who were drunk, high and aggressive. If you were wealthy or influential, you'd negotiate passage with a few small bribes, or by name-dropping a few heavy clan connections. If you weren't, you might find your vehicle confiscated with a demand for $500 'car tax'. Failing to pay would see it sent to the local 'car slaughterhouse', a yard where it would be cannibalised for spare parts. No-one was exempt. Even buses serving the few schools still running in Mogadishu were forced to cough up daily tithes. Argue the point, or try to appeal to the militiamen's sense of fairness, and there was every chance you'd be killed on the spot.

Now it was different. As we sped towards our hotel, the only gunmen I saw were our own hirelings in the wing mirror. Around us were signs of a city getting on with life as normal. There were donkeys pulling carts full of firewood, children playing, and the usual armies of street hawkers that make every African downtown a drive-through shopping experience. Occasionally, Corentin would remark that we had just passed through some neighbourhood completely off-limits on his previous visit. Now we could pull over wherever we wanted. At a general purpose store where Corentin stopped to buy extra batteries for his cameras, the proprietor, Abdullah Noor, spoke warmly of the city's new masters.

'In the last month a new sense of life has come to the business,' he said, stood behind a counter full of cheap Chinese watches and calculators. 'We even feel safe enough to open at night. There may be Islamists who are extremists, yes, but the majority are okay. One hand controlling things is better than many.'

All the same, as we drove off again, I noticed Duguf looking edgy as another SUV blocked the road. It looked like it was just trying to do a three-point turn, but rather than wait to find out, Duguf ordered our driver to take another route down a side alley. Clearly, Mogadishu wasn't yet that safe, something Duguf confirmed as we drove past a patch of wasteland a few minutes later.

'Do you know of Martin Adler?' he said. 'This is where he was killed three months ago.'

I remembered the name. A freelance cameraman from Sweden, he'd been covering a political rally when a lone gunman had wandered up to him, shot him in the chest, and then vanished into the crowd. The Courts claimed it was the work of some warlord faction, trying to undermine their claims to be running a safe city, although as with most Mogadishu murders, nobody really knew.

I'd bumped into Martin in Baghdad the year before. We had had a pleasant lunch in a hotel together, but like so many fleeting encounters, I hadn't caught his surname. It was only some weeks after his death, when I'd discovered his business card during a routine rummage through the pile in my office desk, that I realised that 'Martin from Baghdad' was actually Martin Adler, murdered in Mogadishu. It wasn't the first time I'd discovered a dead man's business card in my contacts drawer: he was in there along with an aid worker and a contractor friend who'd both been killed in Iraq. They were a reminder of the risks of spending too much time in places like this, as if Death shuffled the pack every so often and said: 'Pick a card. Any card.'

The hotel was a nondescript two-storey building that squatted unadvertised behind a barbed-wire topped wall. Lunch was in a dimly-lit dining hall upstairs, where the only other guests were some engineers from China, one of the few countries still sending people to work here. I didn't envy them. They came in for six straight months at a time, with nothing to do except work during the day and sit in the hotel at night. Entertainment was restricted to a ping-pong table and a TV in the dining room that seemed to be stuck on a cookery channel.

That afternoon Duguf took us on a tour what was left of the city's historic landmarks. In the old diplomatic quarter were a few reminders of the days when Somalia had still been a functioning state. There was the old parliament building with its Cleopatra-style spike, the office of Somali Airlines, the Italian Club, the Russian embassy, and the Italian-built cinema. Now they were just tangles of collapsed facades and broken pillars, thorns and cactus flourishing where once there'd been windows and doors. Somali looters had stripped away much of their brick and metal innards, the painstaking stonework of some Italian mason ending its days propping up some tin roof in a shanty town.

The Italian-built Catholic Cathedral was the worst hit of all, devoid of most of its roof and walls, one 70-foot high buttress still reaching defiantly towards the heavens. It had been gutted back in 1991, first by fire and then by looters, who'd even dug up a bishop's coffin. We wandered up its grand old staircase and into what was left of its interior. Today, according to Duguf, the only communions the cathedral hosted were gangs of drug addicts seeking sanctuary from the Courts' pious gaze. High up on the wall, above the evil-smelling remains of someone's cooked goat supper, was a carved bust of Jesus, his carefully-chiselled features chipped by gunshot. He stared down on the desecrated soil below, despairing, perhaps, at the futility of the divine mission on earth.

'It is all very sad,' said Duguf, as Corentin walked round taking moody frames. 'In the old days Mogadishu was so beautiful, with lots of Italians living here,'.

'Do you think it will ever be peaceful again?' I asked.

'Maybe. But it will take 20 years maybe. Perhaps even 40 years.'

*****

Jesus wasn't the only saviour to have retired defeated from Mogadishu. On the first floor of the derelict Europa Hotel, in a room overlooking an empty swimming pool, was a graffitied drawing of a hawk's head floating beneath a parachute. Underneath was a caption in Italian: '*2 lug 93, I falchi c'erano.*' 'The Hawks were here, 2 May 1993.'

It was the scrawl of some Italian army paratroopers' unit, part of the multi-national peacekeeping mission that lasted just two years here in the early 1990s. Composed of some 30,000 well-armed and well-intentioned soldiers, the mission should have been one of the UN's finest moments. All they had to do was rein in the feuding clan mafias that had seized control of the city since Siad Barre's fall, and stop them stealing the food aid that was supposed to be easing the country's famine. World opinion was behind them, galvanised by TV pictures of starving Somali kids robbed of their daily bread by larcenous militiamen. Children would be saved, the weak protected from the bad by the strong, courtesy of a new world order unencumbered by Cold War ideology. Yet a mission that should have been as popular as Live Aid soon became mired in bloodshed and controversy. The new world order ran into conflict with that other, much older world order, the clan system, which was what had pulled Somalia apart in the first place. For all that different clans might resent each other, they resented outsiders interfering in their affairs even more.

Like the former Yugoslavia, which was engaged in similar self-destruction at the time, Somalia's turbulent social dynamics had long been kept in check by its resident dictator. Mohammed Siad Barre.

'Comrade Siad', as he preferred to be known, was a chain-smoking ex-army officer who came to power in a coup in 1969. He never quite gained the notoriety of other African tyrants like Idi Amin or Mobutu Sese Seko, but his career still bore all the hallmarks of the classic Cold War despot. He flirted militarily with both East and West, led Somalia into a disastrous Cold War scrap with neighbouring Ethiopia, and set up his own East German-trained spy network that killed, tortured and terrorised his people. In the manner of Chairman Mao, he also produced a little blue book outlining his thoughts for Somalia's future, including such original insights as 'less talk and more work'.

Like Tito in Yugoslavia, however, Barre recognised that his country's warring clans were a threat not just to his own power, but the whole idea of a functioning nation state. As long as people owed allegiance to their clan rather than their country, it would be impossible to field a proper army, establish law and order, or run a government properly. That would make Somalia vulnerable not just to chaos from within, but to divide and rule from enemies outside, in particular its Christian neighbour and long-time adversary, Ethiopia. In Barre's little blue book, he even recruited Marx to his cause, likening the struggle of clan interests in Somalia to the battle of class interests in developed nations.

'Tribalism was the only way in which foreigners got their chance of dividing our people,' he remarked.

Unlike the rest of his Marxist doggerel, the idea of 'anti-clanism' went down well at first, appealing to the sense of nationalism that swept many African states in the post-colonial 1960s. In the words of a Somali song from those more optimistic times, it was not 'who do you know?' that was important, but 'what do you know?'. 'Cousin' was out as a greeting, 'comrade' was in. But like most dictators' attempts at social engineering, anti-clan policies were implemented crudely. Somalis were banned on pain of jail from asking each other what clan they belonged to. When, instead, they started asking 'What clan did you *previously* belong to?', that was outlawed too. In the countryside, the Barre regime introduced Soviet-style collectivisation of pasturelands, in a bid to undermine the clans' rural power base. Nomads were told to abandon the camel herds they'd tended for thousands of years and start new lives as farmers and fishermen. Clan rebellions against this assault on their authority were put down brutally. Menfolk were killed, women raped, and water wells smashed, leaving herds and owners to die of thirst.

Inevitably, tensions began rising, and as Barre himself should have predicted, foreign powers saw the chance to meddle. By the mid-1980s, his government was fighting several insurgencies against clan militias armed by Ethiopia. Fearing rebellion within his security forces, he put ever more of his own Darod clansmen in key positions, accelerating the very dynamic he'd pledged to eradicate. In January 1991, Mogadishu was invaded by forces loyal to the warlord Mohamed Farrah Aideed, a senior figure in the Habr Gidr, a rival clan to the Darod. Barre was duly ousted from his marble floored villa with its private zoo, sparking the events that would set the scene for nearly two decades of anarchy.

Having fled the capital, Barre's armies headed south towards the border with Kenya, into the lush, river-fed farming valleys that were Somalia's breadbasket. To slow down the rebel forces that were chasing them, they embarked on an 'eat, slash and burn' strategy to ensure their pursuers would march on empty stomachs. Grain stores were looted and destroyed, fields set ablaze. The result of this Pyrrhic exit strategy was a widespread famine, which international aid efforts were ill-equipped to deal with. Relief shipments arriving in Somali ports were routinely hijacked by clan militias, who either sold it to their own people or exchanged it for weapons. Up to 300,000 people died from malnutrition, and as TV broadcasts began showing footage of starving, pot-bellied Somali children, the outside world finally decided it was time for some tough love. 'Operation Restore Hope', launched in December 1992, saw detachments of heavily-armed US Marines land on Mogadishu's beaches, authorised by the UN to use 'all necessary means' to sort things out.

Rather like the American mission in Iraq a decade later, things went well at first. Swarming up the beaches in the dead of night, the only hazard the Marines met was a blizzard of flashbulbs from the worlds' press. The Marines quickly restored supply routes throughout the country, easing the famine, while UN officials set about bringing the various warring factions to peace talks. Yet the anxiety for quick results meant officials neglected to do their history homework. If they had done, they might have paid more attention to the cables they got about Somalia from Smith Hempstone, America's ambassador in neighbouring Kenya. 'Somalis, as the Italians and British discovered to their discomfiture, are natural-born guerrillas,' he'd warned.

*****

Had America heeded Hempstone's advice, Hawa Elmi might have been a much poorer lady than she already was. We went to her house on the morning of our second day in town; it was an overgrown shack somewhere in a maze of narrow backstreets, but a location well-known to every foreign press fixer in Mogadishu. Hawa, a loud, gap-toothed and slightly dotty widower, was nicknamed 'The *Black Hawk Down* Lady', in honour of the chunk of crumpled metal that lay in her back yard. It was a fragment of fuselage from one of the US helicopters shot down over her home in 1993. For a fee negotiable on the door, she allowed visiting journalists into her back garden to photograph it and hear her story of how it landed.

Frankly, it wasn't the greatest war tourism experience in the world. The five foot long, twisted fragment could have a piece of scrap from Mogadishu's 'car slaughterhouse', for all I could tell. Yet if you could pick just one exhibit to sum up the failure of Operation Restore Hope, this wouldn't be a bad choice. It was a burnt, shapeless symbol of how the formidable US military machine had, in the end, been brought crashing to earth by the backstreet gunmen of Somalia.

The helicopter that plunged into Hawa's back garden one hot October afternoon had originally been trying to sniff out Mohamed Farrah Aideed, the warlord who'd ousted Siad Barre. Aideed had started out on cordial terms with the foreign forces, assuming that as Barre's nemesis, he would be the natural candidate for them to install as the country's new ruler. But as the peace talks had progressed, it had dawned on him that the UN's blueprint for a political settlement did not see him as its leader. Instead, they wanted a set up in which all clans would be first among equals, something of a departure from the traditional winner-takes-all approach of previous clan power struggles. Deprived of what he saw as the due rewards of victory, Aideed withdrew the hand of friendship from the international force and took up arms instead.

The 'Eisenhower of Somalia', as Aideed liked to call himself, launched his first major strike against the peacekeepers in June 1993, when his forces ambushed a UN contingent of Pakistani troops. 24 Pakistanis were killed, with some of their bodies later found skinned and disembowelled. The UN put up 'Wanted' posters of Aideed around Mogadishu, declaring a price of a $25,000 on his bald head. But efforts to catch him backfired repeatedly as ordinary Somalis got caught in the crossfire. A month into the hunt, the US missiled a house in Mogadishu where Aideed was wrongly believed to be hiding. Instead they killed 73 of his clan elders, who, ironically, had been meeting to discuss ways of ending his rebellion. The botched bombing prompted a U-turn in attitudes to the foreign presence, as the city's international press pack learned to their cost later that day. Upon arriving at the scene of the airstrike, four foreign newsmen were beaten to death by an angry mob.

The US kept up the hunt. Letting Aideed go, they reasoned, would make a mockery of the whole law and order project. In early October, word reached them that two of his senior henchmen were at a house in one of his strongholds in Mogadishu. This time, rather than risk another missile strike, the Americans despatched a special forces snatch squad in a convoy of Black Hawk helicopters. Almost straightaway, things went wrong. One of the soldiers in the Black Hawks fell during the rope descent, plunging some 70 feet and injuring himself badly. Minutes later, another Black Hawk was downed by a rocket propelled grenade, killing both pilots. Then another two helicopters were hit, one managing to struggle back to base, the other crash-landing a mile from the ambush site. As reports of the battle came in over the military radio, US commanders listened in bewilderment. Black Hawks were supposed to be too fast to be at risk from RPGs, especially those aimed by qhat-crazed Somali militiamen

Meanwhile, the hue and cry had gone up around the city. Within a few hours, some 90 US soldiers, including a back-up ground convoy, were under siege from a mob of thousands of Somali gunmen. An urban answer to Rourke's Drift ensued, the Somalis repeatedly attempting to over-run the American positions. By the time an armoured rescue convoy finally reached them the next morning, 18 US soldiers were dead and another 83 injured. Between 500 and 1,000 Somalis died as well – proof, depending on one's point of view, of how the Americans had abandoned all rules of engagement and shot at everything in sight, or of how their opponents, in true Somali warrior style, simply kept coming no matter what. Either way, it was the biggest gun battle US troops had been in since Vietnam.

Yet for America, the real horror lay not in the US body count, but in what their Somali foes did with some of the dead servicemen's bodies afterwards. Footage shot by a Somali cameraman showed white corpses being dragged through Mogadishu's dirt alleyways, as a mob cheered and celebrated. Americans went into shock when they turned on their TVs. This was supposed to be a humanitarian mission, wasn't it? And anyway, what kind of savages did this, even in war? Just as TV pictures had led America into Somalia, now they hauled it out. Switchboards at Congress were jammed with callers wanting to know why decent US citizens were dying needlessly for a bunch of ungrateful Africans, and when the hell America was leaving. Six months later, they got their wish. In March 2004, the US military withdrew, followed by the rest of the multi-national force a few months later. Operation Restore Hope was quickly dubbed Operation Abandon All Hope, with Somalia's future left in the hands of its warlords once again.

Yet the ramifications of *Black Hawk Down* went well beyond Somalia. Just like Vietnam 20 years before, it raised a collective doubt in America about the wisdom of getting involved in other people's wars. For much of the next decade, Washington lost its appetite for military do-gooding abroad, ignoring other equally urgent cries for help. US troops were kept well away from the 1994 Rwandan genocide, despite the death toll climbing into hundreds of thousands. In the Balkans, it was not until 1999 that America was persuaded to bomb Milosevic's Serb forces, by which time most of the ethnic cleansing had been done. Only 9/11 forced a rethink. In one hot afternoon on the streets of Mogadishu, the hopes that the post-Cold War world would be an easier, simpler place to police had been dashed forever.

*****

As a graveyard for foreign troops and a no-go zone for aid workers, Mogadishu had spent the next decade written off as an ungovernable basket case. Yet had a free market economist been sat alongside Corentin and I as we cruised around in our armed convoy, he might have noted much to his satisfaction. In the absence of any government, the city had become one of the world's purest bastions of free market capitalism. The average citizen might well get gunned down in his prime, but he didn't want for cheap international phone calls, schools for his kids, or even electricity and water – as long as he was prepared to pay for them.

Just as our $20-a-day gunmen filled the role of police, a few dollars a week could hire you people to take your garbage away, deliver barrels of fresh drinking water, or even connect your house to a satellite internet service. After the stifling socialism of the Barre regime, the state had been rolled back completely, and when Adam Smith's invisible hand wasn't blasting away with a Kalashnikov, it often ran things better than in other African capitals. International phone calls, for example, were among the cheapest in the world. A *New York Times* reporter had once counted no less than 45 private clinics, five rival airlines and 55 competing electricity firms, whose generators spawned the tangle of cables that festooned every street

There was freedom of speech too in Mogadishu. Or free, at least, to those who could hire enough muscle to fend off anyone they offended. While radio stations and newspapers did not have to worry about censors or licence fees, certain other precautions were necessary in a place where upsetting someone might result in more than angry letter to the Editor. Horn Afrik Radio, whose breezeblock studio we visited on our second day in town, had been set up by three Somali émigrés who'd quit a comfortable life in Canada to give Mogadishu its own answer to the BBC. Where other radio stations might splash out on a traffic helicopter, here they'd spent part of their start-up cash on two technicals and a squad of bodyguards. But after six years on the airwaves, their phone-in shows had become such a hit that their best defence was their listeners. When one local warlord took umbrage at their reporting and despatched his toughs to shoot the studio up, there'd been a public outcry and he'd backed off.

The editorial director of Horn Afrik was one Ahmed Abdisalam Adan, a bespectacled, urbane figure who met us in his offices on the outskirts of town. He prided himself on his station's journalistic objectivity. He had a policy of hiring staff from across the clan spectrum, and would sometimes invite different warlords to argue their case on air, in Mogadishu's own version of the BBC's *Question Time*. But no amount of BBC-style impartiality stopped it being the most dangerous job in local radio on the planet. Adan himself had been shot at on occasion, while several colleagues had been murdered. It was, he said with mild resignation, all part of the job. He spoke in the way a local newspaper boss back home might talk about publishing an embarrassing correction.

Because of his station's hard-won neutrality, Adan was a good man to come to for an opinion about the Courts. The city's new rulers had been a topic of hot debate on Horn Afrik's phone-in shows, and like most of the callers, Adan could see both good and bad in them. Over tea, he explained how things had got so bad in the first place. Since the collapse of the government, Somali clans had reverted to settling their feuds using the system of blood money, the tribal equivalent of modern-day compensation culture. In the old nomadic times, it had worked tolerably well: there was a generally agreed scale of payments, with compensation for a murder being anything up to a hundred camels, worth the equivalent of $40,000. But that was in the times before the country had been flooded with Kalashnikovs, which brought an industrialised efficiency to the business of score settling. So many people got killed when feuds erupted these days that the blood money market had experienced its own version of a stock market crash, bottoming out at as little as $200 for a life. Blood money became known contemptuously as 'rubbish bag money', because the cash was often handed over in several bricks of Somali shillings wrapped in a bin liner. Life had become quite literally almost worthless.

'Two hundred dollars was not much in anybody's money,' said Adan. 'So instead of looking for compensation, the clans would revenge any killing by going to whichever clan did it and killing one of their most prominent men. That was usually a businessman. Eventually the businessmen said to themselves, 'How do we stop our people doing this?"

The answer, he said, was the Courts. The way he described them, they sounded like a kind of militarised Rotary Club. Local entrepreneurs raised money together to hire gunmen and technicals, and then installed a few clan elders in a local mosque to act as judges. They dished out their judgments according to the Koran and Sharia law, which had the advantage of being widely understood. True, many of old timers sitting in judgment were not exactly experts in Sharia law. Rather than consulting the latest works in modern Islamic jurisprudence, they used texts that were often hundreds of years old. But it didn't really matter. The average punter in the street was happy to see justice of some sort, any sort, being meted out.

'The Courts started out just within each clan, and the idea was to rein in the bad apples within their own communities,' Adan added. 'When that proved quite effective in creating law and order, they started to co-ordinate their activity across the city.'

By 2004, the Courts had extended their jurisdiction to large parts of Mogadishu, well aware that there was little chance of any proper government in the foreseeable future. The UN had been trying to create one for years, picking various clan heads to set up a 275-member Transitional Federal Government (TFG). The result, however, had been little more than a fighting, squabbling talking shop. Some were minor leaders who had no real influence, some were exiles who spent most of their lives outside Somalia, and others were warlords with blood on their hands. Such was their lack of support that they didn't even meet in Mogadishu, which was considered too dangerous. Instead, their headquarters was in Baidoa, a more tranquil city 160 miles north west of the capital.

As the TFG floundered from a distance, it was the Courts who gradually won credibility on the ground. Yet in early 2005, Adan's radio station found itself reporting on a string of killings of senior Courts leaders. Suspicion fell on Mogadishu's remaining warlords, who saw the Courts as less an Islamic peace-and-love jamboree, and more a Trojan Horse for an African Taliban and an end to their own freewheeling ways. To some extent their suspicions were justified. While the Courts' financiers were mainly businessmen interested only in peaceful trading conditions, their spiritual leaders were mainly Islamists, some linked to militant causes abroad. Then, in early 2006, the warlords launched the 'Anti-terror coalition', an alliance of militia leaders dedicated to kicking the Courts out for good.

Yet as the city echoed yet again to the sound of gunfire, Adan and other well-connected people in Mogadishu noticed something odd. It wasn't just the way in which the warlords suddenly claimed to be banding together in a fit of altruism. The city's main weapons souk at Bakara Market, where you could buy everything from $800-a-pop RPGs through to $50,000-a-time bespoke technicals, was suddenly awash with cash.

'In 2005 loads of dollars flooded into the weapons market, thousands of new dollar bills all in sequence,' said Adan. 'It was coming from the warlords, who were buying as many guns as they could to attack the Islamic Courts Union. But someone was giving them the money to do so, and there wasn't much doubt who it was.'

'Who?' I asked. 'The CIA?'

Adan smiled. 'We never saw any signature on any piece of paper, of course. But you know how anxious America is about terrorists at the moment. Anyone who presents themselves as the terrorists' enemies can become America's friend.'

There was, of course, no hard proof of what he was saying. Nobody had actually filmed or photographed CIA planes landing on airstrips in the dead of night and handing over suitcases full of crisp US dollars, despite lots of claims that this had happened. But Washington had never denied it outright, and in many ways it made sense. After all, with the war on terror at its height, and America increasingly bogged down in Iraq, the CIA was as worried as the warlords about Somalia falling to an Islamist government.

If so, unfortunately they'd backed the losing side. Whatever reservations Somalis had about the Courts, they were far more popular than the warlords, who, prior to their 'anti-terror coalition', had been the chief sponsors of terror in Mogadishu. With public opinion on their side, the Courts soon gained the upper hand in the struggle with the warlords. Some fled, others switched sides, leaving the Courts in control of the entire city. It was the stuff of nightmares for Washington's foreign policy makers – an Islamist regime taking over a failed state, backed not just by guns, but by popular mandate. To many in Mogadishu, Islam was now seen as the harbinger of peace, while America was seen as the backer of the scumbag warlords, whose raping, murder and pillage had mattered not a jot to the West.

*****

To see what ordinary Somalis thought of their new Islamic masters, Duguf took us to a neighbourhood on the south of the city once notorious even by Mogadishu standards. 'Bermuda Triangle' was a slum that had once been the haunt of groups of unaligned freelance gunmen, so crazy that even the warlords didn't want them. The area got its nickname because people who went in often didn't come out again. Even now, Duguf wouldn't let us stop for more than about 15 minutes. But that was enough to confirm that things had changed.

'When the warlords were here every kind of bad thing happened – rapes, murders and stealing,' said Omar Ali, 30, sitting on a red, sandy boulevard where large lizards lurked in the palm trees. 'If I bought food for my children, they would take it off me sometimes.

But since the Islamic Courts Union kicked out the militias, we can walk around at midnight without worrying. Even you, a foreigner can come here.'

A similar story was told by the casualty records at Mogadishu's main Medina hospital. According to its director, Sheikhdon Elmi, gunshot admissions were down to less than 30 a month. That was still a lot for a city of just one million people, but less than a fifth of what it had been before the Courts took power.

The basic act of allowing people to go about their daily business unmolested was probably all the Islamic Courts needed to do to remain popular. In that respect, they were not unlike the Taliban, who'd also got their foothold in power through providing basic security. In the civil war that had followed the Soviet pull-out of Afghanistan, the various mujahedeen groups had behaved just like the warlords in Mogadishu. It had become impossible to travel anywhere without risking one's life or livelihood at the hands of checkpoint thugs. So when a then-little-known cleric called Mullah Omar had led a stand against them, he'd won immediate support.

The big question now, though, was just how much the Courts would follow the Taliban in strictures on lifestyle. Many of the calls to Horn Afrik's phone-in show were complaining that the Courts militias were stopping shops from selling music CDs, and shutting down the little booths that showed films and Premier League football matches. And while most people didn't mind the odd public flogging of a thief, they didn't care for endless radio sermons on the importance of Islamically pure behaviour. Somalis, after all, had traditionally followed Sufi Islam, a school that generally preached tolerance and moderation. Ultra-orthodox Islam, the kind that chided its followers during their every waking moment, didn't really suit the national character.

Mindful of this, the Courts had so far been at pains to present themselves as a force of moderation. They'd set up a 'Supreme Judicial Committee' to hear appeals before executing or flogging anyone in public. And they'd so far steered clear of any ban on qhat, fearing it could be the single biggest thing that could spark a backlash. Yet as in every political movement, there were moderates and hardliners. The courts' chief of security for Mogadishu, Abu Utayba, was on record as saying that people who failed to pray five times a day should be shot. He'd also featured in a jihadist promo video that praised bin Laden and introduced Somalia as 'the new Afghanistan'. The Courts' PR department claimed it had been fabricated by their enemies, or at least wasn't officially endorsed. Washington was also claiming that the Courts' main spiritual leader, Sheikh Hassan Dahir Aweys, had links to Al Qaeda. As luck would have it, Aweys walked right into our hotel one evening for a meeting.

A septuagenarian with a red henna-dyed goatee, skull cap and thick glasses, the man sitting in the hotel lounge not look like much of an international terrorist. Yet according to his various US, Interpol and UN rapsheets, that was exactly what he was. The US had him on its post 9-11 'linked to terrorism' list, while the UN Security Council had him down for an asset freeze, travel ban and arms embargo under its schedule of 'individuals associated with Al Qaeda'.

Aweys had picked up these credentials largely as a result of his involvement with Al-Itihaad Al-Islaami (The Union of Islam), a now-defunct Islamist group that had sprung up in the wake of collapse of the Barre government. Composed of some 1,000 men, its main beef had been a territorial scrap with Ethiopia over the disputed Ogaden border region, which it lost badly. But some Itihaad members stood accused of cooperating with the Al Qaeda cell that carried out the 1998 US embassy bombings in Nairobi and Dar es Salaam, in which 224 people were killed. Others were suspected of kidnapping and killing aid workers in Somalia in the 1990s. The US believed that Aweys' was harbouring suspects from the embassy bombings, and would doubtless shelter other Al Qaeda fugitives if given the chance.

If Aweys was a bin Laden protégé, however, he was rather better at PR than the average Al Qaeda operative. When I rather nervously put it to him that he was considered a terrorist by many, he responded not with an anti-Western rant, but a mildly-offended shrug.

'We are not the Taliban,' he said. 'We don't want labels, we want help to rebuild a society that has been destroyed. If the world doesn't want to help us, fine. But at least they should have a wait-and-see attitude, rather than describing us as criminals who will create global conflict if we are allowed to function.'

'What about the bans on watching films and football?' I asked. 'People say you are going to restrict their freedoms.'

'All this is being exaggerated. In some of those cinemas, there were all sorts of X-rated movies being shown, often to small children who should have been going to school. And with the football matches, that became a problem because people were watching matches and fighting. We were getting calls from people in the neighbourhood, saying can you please send a court army to pacify the situation?'

He sounded like a metropolitan chief constable back in Britain, defending his force's robust handling of some public order situation.

'But some of these cinemas were just showing normal films,' I said. 'And there have also been reports of your militiamen beating women for not wearing the veil.'

'It is possible that some of the courts have made mistakes from time to time,' said Aweys. 'You must remember that they are not all co-ordinated yet, and some have maybe been too strict.'

We carried on for about half an hour, with me failing to elicit a single bloodcurdling quote of the kind that would excite the office back home. Having expected a living, breathing Bin Laden lieutenant, I left the interview feeling I'd been in the company of a Church of England vicar. If there was a single more gentle, reasonable-sounding terrorist on the US wanted list, I'd yet to meet him.

All the same, it remained to be seen whether Sheikh Aweys was ever going to get his chance to prove what a good egg he was. Having achieved the seemingly impossible in pacifying Mogadishu, some of the Courts' leaders had been invited to internationally-backed talks in Nairobi the following week. The idea was to explore ways of forging some power-sharing agreement with the TFG, fusing the Courts' popularity on the ground with the TFG's international legitimacy. But Aweys wasn't on the invite list, and not just because of his UN travel ban. Britain's Foreign Office, which was helping supervise the talks, said they could do business with 'more moderate' Courts members, but not him.

'The Courts have brought an element of stability to the country, but they offer a type of rule that is neither democratic nor pluralistic,' a spokesman told me. 'Sheikh Aweys is not someone we can work with. We have to be principled as well as pragmatic.'

He declined to say which particular principles Aweys offended. But when I mentioned it later to Abdullahi Mohamed Shirma, a local charity worker, there was a weary roll of the eyes. Principles, he said, were something the West only cared about when it suited them – and something that ordinary Mogadishu residents could no longer afford.

'If an Islamist militia whips an old woman, you in the West will be horrified. Here, people will say that is minor compared with the rapes by warlords. Why does the West only worry now, when it never cared in the warlords' time?'

9: Clan warfare

IT WAS MID-MORNING on Day 15. José and I were sitting out in a small, rocky hollow that led down from one side of the cave. It was our equivalent of a stroll in a prison exercise yard, in that it got us away from the gloom of our stony cell, while still reminding us there was no chance of escape. Steep slopes surrounded us on all sides, preventing us seeing or being seen by the outside world, and there would always be a row of guards watching us from a nearby ridge, staring down like a Somali version of Mount Rushmore. Like a pair of jail block trusties, it was one of the meagre privileges we'd earned for good behaviour, along with the knife, the fork and the tins of pineapple chunks. There was nowhere comfortable to sit, but it was a chance to bask in the sun, smoke, and get some distance from the noisy chatter of the gang, even if it was only 20 yards.

By this time, we were running low on things to talk about. We'd done work, politics, and girlfriends past and present. And we'd held endless seminars on favourite books, films and music, to the point where we'd had to introduce rationing. If we hit on a movie that we both had plenty to say about, we'd save it for the evening and expand it into a discussion about the entire genre. So far there'd been a Horror Night, a Western Night, and an Evening with Quentin Tarantino, one of the few film directors I'd heard of. José also heard a great deal of stories from my book on Iraq. Not because he particularly wanted to, but because he was a captive audience, of which I took shameless advantage.

'You might as well listen mate, as we've run out of other things to talk about,' I'd say.

'Not again. You never shut up about it.'

'It's a shame I don't have my book with me, I could read it to you.'

'You don't need to, bastard, I feel like I know it all already.'

'Anyway, as I was saying, one day there was a car bomb at the hotel I stayed at. And, afterwards...'

Luckily for José, that morning's particular episode of *'Once Upon a Time in Baghdad'* was interrupted by a group of the guards returning from an expedition into the surrounding valleys. They had their guns slung over their shoulders and carried small wicker basket in their arms, chattering gaily among themselves like a team of armed Red Riding Hoods. Skullface gestured at us to come and look. He and some of the other younger guards had begun to warm to us a little, especially after my triumph in the press-up contest at last week's Eid festival.

I peered inside Skullface's basket. It was brimming with pieces of torn-up bark, clinging to a thick white resin. He pointed to a tree growing halfway up a nearby cliff. It had a curious, stumpy trunk, bulging and grey-brown like a massive hunk of ginger, with a few spikey branches sprouting out of it. He made a chopping gesture.

'Parr-foom,' he said.

Parr-foom?

He held a piece of the bark to my nose. It had a strong antiseptic odour, like eucalyptus. It was the first clean-smelling thing I'd come across in weeks. Then I realised what Skullface was saying. *Parfoom* was perfume. Later, we would learn that it was probably either myrrh or frankincense, both of which came from trees found mainly in Somalia and Yemen. Until the invention of modern detergents, they had been in huge demand as fragrances, and were once more valuable than gold – hence the Three Wise Men bringing them as gifts to Jesus. To this day, they were still popular as aphrodisiacs and cure-alls in Chinese medicine. Our hosts were probably planning to sell the stuff next time they sent a party back to civilisation to buy supplies. It occurs to me that they were probably the only kidnap gang in the world with a sideline in aromatherapy.

At the time, though, I knew nothing of this, and so stuck a piece into my mouth, thinking it was some kind of gum. The Somalis guffawed. I flashed a grin all round, like a comedian breaking a winning gag with a tough audience. I didn't mind acting the fool. If it made us harder for them to kill, like a pair of cuddly rabbits, so be it. It was all part of a tactical double act that José and I had adopted to give us more room for manoeuvre with the gang. I was Mr Nice, the cheery, chatty one, who joked and smiled and led the English class, building up goodwill to earn us privileges like extra cigarettes. José was the quieter, sterner one, the Mr Nasty, or at least the Mr Not-Quite-So-Nice, who would then argue and complain if we didn't get them.

Yet as I sat back down to bore José again about Iraq, I noticed that one person in the camp wasn't sharing in the joke. It was Miro, the balding, older guy who'd led the original group that spirited us over the mountains. Rather than joining in the laughter, he was eyeballing us from the other side of the cave. He was clad in his usual get up of brown pleated slacks that were too short for him, and a bright orange tee shirt with a logo that said 'Golf Player'. With his narrow, yellowy eyes and slightly wizened face, he'd have been a perfect Hollywood cast for an evil, child-abusing grandpa. I'd seen him staring at us a couple of times before and thought it was just coincidence. Now I asked José if he'd noticed it too.

'Yes, I have, don't worry about it,' he said. 'He's just trying to play games with us, ignore him.'

'Why do you think he doesn't like us? The rest of them seem fine.'

'I think maybe it is because I argued with him over the water on the second day. Do you remember, when we were walking and we were both thirsty? He was the one I told to fuck off. I don't think he liked me challenging his authority.'

'You think it's just that?'

'Also, maybe he doesn't like us joking around with the younger guys. Remember, at first, he was like the big man, telling them all what to do? Now they are all smiling and waving at us all the time, he feels left out. Perhaps he's also worried that we will be befriend one of them too much and he will let us escape.'

'Fat chance. Fact is though, we've got Yusuf and the Guy of the Cigarettes on our side, plus all the younger guys. So he's on his own.'

The Old Bastard, as we nicknamed him from then on, had a Fagin-like relationship with his younger charges. He held court in a corner, dispensing wisdom, doling out pocket money, and telling jokes. Yet he didn't like them having fun in the cave if it didn't revolve around him. A couple of days later, during a particularly boring afternoon, Faisal and I were experimenting with a game of crazy golf, using a stick to hit a wizened lime into a series of holes dug in the ground. As we were negotiating the third hole, the Old Bastard got back from guard duty. He tutted officiously, confiscated the lime, and gestured at José and I to go back to our corner, like a pair of misbehaving pet dogs. Yusuf, however, had seen what had happened and decided the Old Bastard was being a spoilsport. He muttered something to him, and the lime was handed back to us with a forced smile. Faisal, watching from a corner, grinned at us and flicked a mock sergeant's salute behind his back

Pleasant though it had been to see him with humble pie smeared over his face, I didn't like the idea of having enemies in camp. It ripped a hole in the veneer of cordiality that allowed me to kid myself, most of the time at least, that this whole thing was manageable, and predictable. And it was clear that the Old Bastard did not appreciate being humiliated. From then on he started playing little power games designed to remind us who was boss. The eyeballing sessions grew more frequent. He also began bumming cigarettes off us, something none of the rest of the gang did as they knew we valued them too much.

'What shall we do if he keeps this up?' I asked.

'From now on, we'll tell him no,' José said. 'Otherwise he will be taking them from us all the time. Besides, he will probably respect us more if we stand up to him.'

José was probably right, although I suspected he had more of a stomach for a fight than I did. I was all for defending our dignity, but I was also anxious to avoid any running confrontation. My predicament made me think of all the court cases I'd covered over the years in which some middle-class professional had fallen foul of the law and ended up copping a jail sentence. As they were led away from the dock, handcuffed to a guard and looking terrified, I always found myself wondering how they coped once they reached prison. What did they do when some cellblock heavy came-a-calling? Did they stick up for themselves, and risk getting beaten up? Or did they just capitulate, reasoning it was best just to sit things out until they were free again? Most I suspected, probably just gave in. Sad as it was to admit it, my temptation was to do the same. Short of the Old Bastard turning 'sister' on us, discretion was probably the better part of valour.

On the other hand, I owed it to José to maintain a united front. And if we were going to be in here any length of time, maybe it was better that nobody saw us as soft touches. On the last phone call we'd had to Nick, a few days ago, I'd asked whether there was any progress on talks to free us. He'd said that there was, but that he couldn't go into details, and that in any event, it probably wouldn't be until after Christmas, by which time we'd have languished here a month. During that same phone call, Ali also told us the gang was about to issue new death threats, apparently incredulous that nobody had coughed up their $6 million yet. As we'd wandered back to the cave, the Old Bastard had sniggered and chanted *'Morto'*. My grasp of Italian probably wasn't much better than his, but from the way he drew his finger across his throat, I had a feeling it probably meant 'dead'.

A few days later, we were summonsed up the mountainside for yet another phone session back to London. As we scrambled up the slope, we noticed the Old Bastard sat beside Yusuf and the others, fixing us with his usual stare. It looked ominous. He didn't usually sit in on the phone calls. As Yusuf tried to reach Ali on the phone, the Old Bastard got to his feet, brandishing his Kalashnikov with a flourish. Then he pointed it at me, muttering angrily, and gestured that I came and sit right in front of him.

Oh my God, what is he doing...?

The Old Bastard ratcheted back the slide on his weapon, its banana-shaped magazine glinting in the sun. The Kalashnikov is a great weapon for theatrics. Its cocking mechanism involves a series of distinctive gear crunches, ideal for any bully who wants to gradually up his ante. Whether there was a live round in the chamber or not, I had no idea. But if I wasn't about to face a real execution, I was in for either a mock one or a beating with the barrel.

'Just ignore him, man,' muttered José, not looking up.

I sat where I was, gazing out across the valley as if I hadn't even noticed the snarling loon waving a gun in my face. If he was going to beat my head in, there wasn't much I could do. But I wasn't going to sit in front of him to make it easier. He gestured again.

Come on man, be strong. Don't piss your pants. This guy is just trying to frighten you.

I turned my eyes to the rest of the gang. They were sniggering nervously, like a bunch of kids watching a school bully. Then, just as I was bracing myself for a blow across the face, Skullface 2 and the Smoker got to their feet and said something to the Old Bastard. He snarled back, pointed angrily at me, then a scuffle broke out as they tried to grab his gun from him. Others joined in and started dragging him off down the slope. As they disappeared around a corner, two gunshots rang out, their echo journeying back and forth across the valley.

Christ, has he shot them? Or have they *shot* him*?*

Sadly not. I saw him standing further down the slope, hands tied behind his back, one of the others pointing his gun at him. The Smoker clambered back up, out of breath and nursing a cut to the ankle where he'd stumbled on the rocks.

Yusuf passed me the phone, expressionless. I took it, hand shaking. What the hell was going on? Part of me suspected this was all just pantomime designed to frighten me before I spoke to Nick. But that fight had looked fairly genuine. Surely they wouldn't fire guns in the air, and risk drawing attention to themselves, unless it was necessary?

Nick's voice came on the line, crackling via what sounded like Sunday lunch in Ali's sitting room.

'Hi, Colin, can you hear me? How is everything?'

I told him what had happened, adding that it might have been 'pantomime' and gambling that Ali wouldn't understand what it meant. For all that I didn't want to show the gang we were frightened, I didn't want them to think they had to scare us even more.

'Hmm. Okay. I think we may just be entering into a rather difficult stage in our dealings with them,' Nick said.

He was pointedly calm, as if briefing a boardroom on a last-minute glitch in a takeover bid.

'In a way, this is a sign of progress. It shows we're moving into a different phase.

'How do you mean?'

'I can't tell you too much. But be aware that we are talking to Ali every day now, in between talking to you on the phone. I'm sure they won't do anything bad to you. You and José are too valuable as assets.'

Assets? It wasn't a particularly reassuring choice of words. It made us sound like commodities, a container full of wheat stuck in a trading dispute, perhaps, or given the circumstances, maybe a shipment of cocaine. There was something dehumanising about it, as if as long as we were delivered in the end, it didn't really matter if some damage occurred in transit. Nick rang off, leaving me with Ali.

'Ali, why is this gang trying to frighten us?' I asked.

'You must understand, they are not happy. They are saying it has been weeks now. And still your friend Nick is offering them nothing.'

'Well, I can't help that. You know nobody is allowed to pay ransoms in my country.'

'That is not the only problem. These guys holding you, they are pirates. And they are angry about some news that they heard recently, about what your British Navy did. You are a journalist, aren't you? I think you will have heard this news yourself. A British ship killed two pirates. The clan of those two pirates now wants to kill a British person after what your country did. The men who are holding you now, they are saying that if Nick does not help them, they will sell you to these pirates in Eyl.'

I put the handset down for a moment, as if it had bitten me. This was not the way I'd hoped to be the first Western journalist to enter Eyl. I picked it up again.

'Come on Ali, I cannot help what my government does. I am just a journalist.'

'Maybe. But they are angry. And they are also angry at your photographer. He has insulted African people.'

'Eh? What do you mean?'

'There are pictures on the internet that he made. They show naked Africans, sitting in a hospital. This is very insulting.'

It dawned on me what he was talking about. José, like most photographers, had a website showcasing all his work. I'd looked at it before I met him. On it was a shoot he'd done in a run-down mental asylum in the Congo, including a picture of a naked inmate in a cell, staring loll-eyed at the camera. It was the kind of arty, madness-in-the-heart-of-darkness image that foreign picture desk editors love, and it had won him first prize in last year's World Press Photo Awards. But while it might have impressed some esteemed international judging panel, its finer points had been lost on Ali.

'It is exploiting African people, making them look like they are slaves,' he said.

'No it's not,' I pleaded. 'It's showing how people are suffering in a mental hospital. That's José's job. He is a photographer, he was trying to show that nobody was caring for these people. That is why he goes to these dangerous countries, to help. That is why he and I came here to Somalia too. And now look at what has happened! We have been kidnapped for trying to help!'

I was now sounding exactly like some of the more pompous colleagues that José and I had passed so much of our time denouncing. But right now, the 'missionaries of truth' card was the only one we had left up our sleeve. Not that it made any difference. Nothing I could say seemed to shake Ali from the conviction that José was some sort of pornographer-in-chief of African suffering. He rang off and we headed back down the slope.

'Are you okay man?' José asked.

'Yes, I think so,' I said. I was pleased with myself for not looking too scared when the Old Bastard had waved the gun in my face. But inside I was rattled. Either he really had developed a psychotic hatred of us, and they'd only just stopped him beating my head in. or it was theatre, in which case they were conniving with him, which wasn't much better. If they could do this now, what else might they have planned down the line?

As we neared the cave, I nursed the vague hope that we'd find him lying tied up in a corner, preferably with his head staved in by a large rock. But no: he'd obviously been untied and allowed to return. There he was, cheerfully holding court with several of his wrestling companions from earlier. Faisal was sat just behind him. I tried to catch his eye. This time, there was no reassuring glance to say 'Sorry, mate, this guy's an arsehole.' He just looked away, expressionless. Part of me felt stupid now for trying to curry favour with the gang by playing the fool. They hadn't been laughing with me, they'd been laughing *at* me, knowing all along that it was going to get ugly. Better to have been Mr Cool, like José.

'They are just trying to pressurise us, man, don't worry,' said José, as we flopped down on the mattress. 'You did well up there, you stayed calm.'

'I didn't feel calm, I can tell you. Weird, though, wasn't it, the way they just dragged him off? I mean, if they want to threaten us, why don't they all do it?'

'I think maybe they have different opinions. I think the Old Bastard is trying to say. 'Look, we have to show people that we are serious.''

I informed José about the bereaved pirates of Eyl, and the affront to African dignity caused by his World Press Photo victory.

'Bullshit,' he said. 'Ali has just been surfing the internet for things to frighten us with. He finds the Navy thing about you, and these photos on my website. Do you think these guys give a shit about people in the Congo?'

'No, not really.'

All the same, I couldn't help giving Ali's threat the benefit of the doubt. Frankly, Ali could have said I was going to be sold to white slave traders, and part of me would have believed him. In our circumstances, my mind was proving vulnerable to suggestion. My imagination rehearsed a vivid scenario in which a lorry-load of Eyl pirates came to collect me. I'd exchange farewells with José, and then be driven back to their village to face whatever the modern-day equivalent of walking the plank was.

What was genuinely worrying, though, was the gang's awareness that there might be other buyers out there for us. In Iraq, the practice of buying and selling hostages was why so many Westerners had fallen into Al Qaeda's hands. The minority of real Al Qaeda crazies, the ones who actually liked beheading people, didn't have the time or resources to go around kidnapping. But they hadn't needed to. All they did was put out word that they would pay good money for a foreigner, and they got half of Baghdad's underworld combing the streets on their behalf. The existence of the hostage market was one of the reasons that kidnapping had become such big business in Iraq. Whenever someone was kidnapped, there was always pressure to cough up a ransom as quickly as possible, before they were sold to someone far nastier. And the more readily ransoms were paid, of course, the more kidnaps there were.

We spent the rest of the afternoon on the mattress, making no contact with the gang at all. I barely dared to stick my head up, fearful of encountering the Old Bastard's gimlet stare. The gang ignored us back. As evening fell, we were offered nothing to eat, and we did not ask. We weren't exactly on hunger strike, but from now on Mr Grey was Mr Angry, or at least Mr As- Cross-As-He-Dared. There'd be no more English lessons. No smiles. No jokes. No more rapport-building, pretending everything was wonderful. And no more cigarettes for the Old Bastard, unless he extracted them at gunpoint. In a sense it was a relief. Having someone wave a Kalashnikov in your face did at least have the effect of clearing the air.

Later that night I scrambled out of the cave to take a piss. We had a designated patch of rocks just around the corner, overlooking a steep slope leading into a valley. Either out of respect for our dignity, or because they figured it was impossible for us to escape, the gang never bothered watching us while we performed our ablutions. It was the one time I would find myself completely alone. It always brought on a contemplative moment, as if one was stepping outside the whole hideous drama for a minute, addressing an imaginary audience like a soliloquising Hamlet, and saying, 'Look at this mess I'm in'. True, not even the most innovative Hamlet productions I'd seen had the Dane taking a piss as he did so. But like him, I found myself beginning to ponder the prospect of madness. I'd look outwards over the valley and inwards at myself, trying to assess my state of mind, wondering when I'd begin to crack up.

When, note, not *if*. It was, I feared, only a matter of time. I'd already developed a slight nervous tick, grinding my teeth a lot. If we stayed here for much longer, I'd have nothing left with which to chew our stringy goatmeat rations. And what if the Old Bastard began torturing us? I couldn't stop dwelling on it. What might he do? He couldn't exactly cut off an ear and mail it back to London, but there were all manner of other options if he wanted to convey his impatience to Nick. A thump in the balls just before I got on the phone, perhaps. A bullet fired right next to the ear drum. Perhaps he'd grab the straggly beard that was now sprouting on my chin, and yank the strands out. My mind explored all manner of lurid possibilities, although they were probably nothing compared to the tricks he might have learned himself over the years. The last couple of decades in Somalia had offered great career opportunities for sadists and psychopaths.

I finished pissing, looked out for a minute over a blazing, starry sky, and staggered back to the cave. The Old Bastard was holding court round the campfire as ever, supping a cup of goat fat and telling some tale, to much sycophantic laughter from the others. What was he saying, I wondered?

'There was this guy I tortured once, right, and you'll never guess what...'

I clambered into bed, trying not bump my head on the low rocks above me. The Old Bastard finished his tale, raised his goat fat smoothie in what appeared to be a toast to himself, and launched into some other anecdote. At least in the dark he didn't bother staring at us.

*****

One of José's favourite books was *The Outsider*, Albert Camus's tale of the Frenchman, Mersault, who cannot see the point of human existence. He shoots an Arab one day for little reason other than to watch him die, and is then sentenced to hang, losing any chance of clemency because he refuses to express remorse. Or something like that. I'd read it as an angst-ridden sixth former at school, hoping Camus would address my own inner turmoil, only to get the feeling that his messages were going rather above my head. As I confessed to José, listening to *The Smiths* was more my level.

Twenty years on from reading the book, the only thing that stuck in my mind that the main character, Mersault, spent most of his time on death row in bed. With nothing else do, he slept for up to 16 hours a day. I remembered thinking it would be impossible for anyone in such forced idleness to sleep so much, and yet now José and I found ourselves doing the same. Bedtime was typically when darkness fell, around 6pm, after which we would chat for a while and then drift off. Not all of it was proper sleep. I would doze, wake for a while, then drift off again. But even fitful semi-consciousness was still better than being awake. In our own little stony jail, it was the equivalent of lock-up time, safe from the other residents. Neither of us ever bothered stirring before 7 am, and I would have slept longer if I could.

On the afternoon of the threats from the Old Bastard, we went to bed at 4pm and did not get up until 8am the next day. By then my back was aching from lying down for so long. As we sat picking at a plate of rice and tomatoes, I couldn't help looking out the corner of my eye to see where he was, scanning the cave for his distinctive orange teeshirt. Yes, there he was giving us the stare already. Little was I to know that within a few hours, I'd be glad he was around.

*****

Throughout our time, we'd had a steady stream of visitors to the cave. They would drop past every few days, sometimes greybearded elders, sometimes kids in their mid-teens. We guessed they were either clan emissaries bringing in news from outside, or local herders who were being paid to turn a blind eye, and whose curiosity about the hostages had to be tolerated. Many would stare at José and me like a pair of zoo exhibits.

I'd barely registered our two latest guests that day, a couple of lads about Faisal's age. But as they got up to leave, voices were suddenly raised. José and I looked up to see an argument in progress, the visitors jostling with Skullface and the Mirror Man. Others joined in, shoving and shouting. Then a shot rang out, deafening in the confines of the cave. Someone, I couldn't tell who, had pulled a pistol and fired into the roof. José and I cowered on the floor as the pair were chased out of the cave at gunpoint. Other guards came running in. The bullet had hit the cave ceiling just above our mat and ricocheted several times, carving white bite marks in the beige rock. It was a miracle that the 'assets' hadn't been hit.

Outside the cave, there were shouts. Another shot rang out, echoing round the valley, followed by what sounded like return fire. The gang were grabbing their guns and rushing outside, leaving a few to guard us.

'My God, we are going to war,' José said, as the Smoker ushered us over to a bundle of boulders just to the left of the cave's entrance. He'd grabbed one of the belt-fed machine guns, the bullets coiled round his neck, Rambo-style. On a cliff top overlooking us, maybe 50 metres up, we could see the outline of a man with a gun. He fired a shot in our direction, kicking up dust right next to the mat where we had been sat seconds ago. José had said he liked Sam Peckinpah movies. Now he was in the middle of one.

We huddled down amid the boulders, which were also a spot we'd been using as a toilet, with coils of evil-smelling tissue littered everywhere. Further down the slope, the gang was fanning out, directed by the Old Bastard, who was sneaking along with his gun like a Somali John Wayne. He looked in his element. More shots sounded out, from where I couldn't tell. The Smoker was scanning the valley up and down, eyes darting around nervously, shouting to the others. Up above us to one side there towered another cliff edge. If the cliff top sniper reappeared there, he'd have a perfect vantage point.

Another shot rang out. I squatted down as low as I could, trying to avoid the filthy tissue. After a couple of minutes, it felt like one of those stress positions that CIA interrogators used. For the first time since we'd been grabbed in Bossaso, I began wondering if we might die here. I did a quick stock take of my life.

Colin Freeman, born in Edinburgh, 1969. Died aged 38. Had a semi-successful newspaper career. Owned a two-bed flat in Brixton, with half the mortgage paid off. Wrote a book on Iraq. Left behind a grieving girlfriend. On which note, it would have been nice to have slept with a few more women over the years, especially if José's record is anything to go by (sorry, Jane). But otherwise, not a bad life, really. Hopefully enough to make a few paragraphs in the Telegraph's obituaries section. And killed in a clan gunfight in Somalia. Not many people had that on their headstones. Assuming anyone ever found out, that was. If they did, they'd hopefully not mention that I took the fatal bullet while standing in a pile of my own shit.

I glanced at José, who looked – for the first time – as scared as I felt. Now, we were not only prisoners, we were being fought over. Like Poland during World War II. Assuming we got out of this alive – and with AK47 rounds zipping by that was not a certainty – warfare with some other clan could delay our release indefinitely. Which meant further weeks, months and God knew how long in the company of the Old Bastard. A feeling of utter despair took hold of me. Death, I began to think, would have its consolations. It would at least be a euthanasia, a way out of this misery. And preferable, almost, to being injured. A bullet-shattered leg or arm, with no painkillers or medicine at hand, would be horrific.

The gunfire stopped. We stayed crouched down for about 15 minutes, my legs now screaming from cramp. The Smoker uncoiled his chain gun and urged us back to the cave. The rest of the gang filtered back, yacking excitedly and tracing the various bullet grazes on the cave walls.

That afternoon, the gang convened what looked like some sort of council of war. They took turns to say their piece, the rest listening as each man spoke uninterrupted for ten minutes or more. We listened in too, straining to hear some recognisable nugget that might give us a clue as to what was going on. Most often it just made us nervous. '*Hubud*' or bullet, came up a lot, as did *mushkilleh* (problem), *sajarra* (car) and on one occasion, what sounded – to my hyper-sensitised ear at least – like the word 'Eyl'. Could the visitors be emissaries from the pirate clan, arguing over the price? And if so, how many more of their pals were lurking in the mountains?

Whatever was being discussed, though, I was surprised by how calm the gang seemed. At no point did anyone raise their voice in any way, nor was there any sign of tension or argument.

'It's weird,' I whispered to José, as the Hobbit squawked his high-pitched contribution to the debate. 'You'd think after something like this, they'd all be at each other's throats.'

'I know,' he said. 'Normally when I have worked with Somalis in Mogadishu, they are always arguing with each other, fighting. But here, not once.'

José reckoned that what we were seeing was the clan system at work. It was the flip side, he theorised, of all the quarreling and feuding that had torn Somalia apart as a nation. Just as members of different clans seemed born enemies, members of the same clan were predisposed to get along. It was true that we had no way of telling whether this particular bunch *were* all related. But it was hard to think of any other explanation as to how they all co-operated so well. It wasn't just about their behaviour when under fire. It was also evident in their everyday interaction around the camp. There were endless tedious jobs to be done: guarding, cooking, cleaning, fetching, yet not once had I seen any of the commanders ever telling Faisal or Skullface off for not making the tea or shirking stag duty. Never so much as a sharp word or raised voice between them. Most of the time we heard only chuckles and friendly banter. Cooped up like this, a bunch of Westerners would have been at each other's throats long before now.

*****

José and I were not the first foreigners to ponder the mysteries of the Somali clan system, and while our analysis was no more than educated guesswork other people had dwelt on it a lot longer and not got much further. Ever since foreign traders first set foot in Somalia hundreds of years ago, they had realised that understanding the clans was essential for business. Victorian adventurers like Speke and Burton had studied Somalia's different peoples in the same meticulous fashion as they recorded flora and fauna, noting each clan's characteristics with their usual fine disregard for political correctness. The Gudabirsi, for example, were 'inveterate liars' who were also 'turbulent and unmanageable', although though not as 'bloodthirsty' as the neighbouring Eesa, with whom they sometimes fought. A century and a half on from Speke's era, aid workers and diplomats in modern-day Somalia still sought to acquire much the same knowledge, even if they no longer used the language of the pith-helmet era. A UN official I knew, who had spent 18 months based near Mogadishu, had told me it was impossible to get anything done other than by operating within the clan network.

'You don't see it at first, because Somalis like to give an image of modernity to Westerners,' he'd said. 'But beneath the surface the clan structure is the only thing that counts. I first learned this after we rented a building from a certain clan who weren't the dominant people in that particular area. We got threats and all sorts of other problems.'

Like any conscientious aid worker, my UN friend did his best to understand how it all worked. He pored over social anthropology textbooks and spent spare hours grilling his Somali staff on their clan structures and histories. He found a world of endlessly shifting alliances and coalitions, based on marriages and feuds that could be traced all the way back to the dawn of Islam, when descendants of the Prophet Mohammed were said to have sailed across to Somalia from Saudi Arabia. Broadly speaking, there were five major clans – the Darod, the Dir, the Hawiye, the Isaaq and the Rahanweyn – all of which claimed lineage back to a single male ancestor from Islam's founding nobility. There was, however, according to Sir Richard Burton, a mischievous rumour that that the first Darod to leave the Prophet's homeland did so because he'd stolen a pair of Mohammed's slippers.

Like so much else in Somalia, the clan system was entrenched by the country's uniquely harsh landscape. Until the middle of the 20th century, it had supported little other than a nomadic lifestyle based around herding camels. Man and beast were constantly on the move, as drinking wells and pastures periodically dried up. As such, when two Somalis met, it was more meaningful to ask 'Who are you from?' than 'Where are you from?' The habit had stuck, and to this day, Somalis still memorised their clan ancestries by rote. My UN worker friend found that his local staff could recite their great-grandfathers' names back 20 generations and more.

Unfortunately, the way a clan defined itself by personal history, not geographical location, meant that feuds, when they erupted, were seldom truly forgotten. The very nature of nomadic life meant that disputes were common, as clans fought over access to scarce grazing lands and drinking water. But rather than simply being resolved, they would become part of a clan's identity, promoting vendettas that could fester for generations, and which could be invoked at any time to justify a petty quarrel. For all my aid worker friend knew, the animosity he'd stirred over his rented building could have been related to some squabble that started centuries ago. His local staff also told of him the famous Somali proverb which held that family always came first, whatever the right or wrongs:

'My brother and I against my father. My father's household against that of my uncle's. My father and uncle's households against the rest of the clan. The clan against other clans. And our nation against the world.'

It was this bellicose attitude, that blood was always unquestionably thicker than water, that had led to so much of it being spilt on Somali soil over the years. In my UN friend's various Somali textbooks, academics talked of it as 'tribal chauvinism', or 'racism without colour'. But few outsiders could master the clan system's inner workings enough to think of ways of solving its problems. After a thousand years of marrying, fighting and migrating, the sprawling genealogies of clans and sub-clan could have filled a dozen volumes of *Burke's Peerage*. Fathoming out the allegiances and enmities, working out the potential Montagues and Capulets in any given situation, was something only Somalis themselves could really do.

'It was incredibly complicated,' my UN friend recalled. 'I tried to understand the way it all worked, but in the end I had to just rely our local staff, which meant I was maybe manipulated quite a lot of the time.'

Like my aid worker friend, I was no social anthropologist. But Somalia was not the only part of the world I had been where clans seemed to be the working partners of ungovernability and lawlessness. In my experience as a reporter, you could draw a fairly accurate map of the world's dysfunctional states simply by picking out those where tribal authority still prevailed. In Iraq, the areas that gave the coalition forces the most trouble tended to be the rural neighbourhoods where clans were still strong. When American or British forces shot or arrested someone, they invited vengeance not just from one household, but thousands. Clans were likewise prevalent in Afghanistan and Chechnya, both of which had proved similarly resistant to the efforts of foreign powers to turn them into house-trained colonies.

Yet you didn't have to seek out distant warzones to see how clans could stick several thousand fingers up to authority. Back in the summer, I'd gone to the Greek island of Crete for a story about how shepherds in remote mountain villages had become mini-drug barons, growing vast crops of marijuana amid the olive groves. When the police had tried to raid them, they'd fought back with machine guns, prompting unlikely headlines that an island better known for its tourist tavernas was becoming 'Europe's Colombia'. It was a strange tale indeed, *Zorba the Greek* meets *The Godfather*, yet according to one weary local police chief I'd spoken to, there was nothing remarkable about it. Cut off from both the Greek mainland and the rest of Crete itself, the clans of the mountains had always defied outside authority, he said, for better or worse. In the 1700s, they'd fought off the Ottoman Turks, during World War II they'd led the resistance against Nazi occupation. Today, in much the same fashion, they resented attention from his drug squads. It was the same code of Omerta that still held good in places like Sicily and Albania – once again, places where the clan system still worked, and which still exported world-class Mafias.

Was it that same kind of solidarity, I wondered, that now bound together our captors as they held their council of war together that afternoon? The gunfight at lunchtime presumably threatened serious trouble for them. If the other clan didn't come back mob-handed, they might at the very least take revenge by giving our location to the police. Yet rather than panicking or fighting, like some bunch of amateur crooks, they were quietly discussing tactics, sounding as calm as Nick was on the phone from London. The problem was that Somali society only seemed to function well at this micro-level, of clans and gangs, of mini-mafias who had total trust in their own little circle, but were innately suspicious of anyone else. It was a disastrous sociological blueprint for nation building, but a perfect one for organised crime.

*****

That night, after dinner, I suggested to José that we say prayers before bed. They were for the gang's ear, rather than the Almighty's. I wanted them to be aware that we knew we were now in potential danger, and remind them, in case we were to be sold to new owners, that we were God-fearing souls. We knelt ostentatiously at the foot of the mat, as I said what I could remember of the Lord's Prayer and José mumbled some Catholic incantation. None of the gang paid the slightest attention, and we retired to bed feeling slightly foolish.

As I lay smoking a cigarette, though, I began to see why people might end up believing in God. It wasn't so much about the spiritual side, the afterlife and so on. It was more the here and now, of yearning to see that there was someone, or something, who represented justice and decency in the world. Back in Britain, we had at least had a functioning system of law and human rights, however imperfect people might say it was. Here, though, stuck between Old Bastard on one side and new gang of villains on the other, I was getting a taste, albeit a pretty mild one, of the misery that millions of ordinary people in Africa and elsewhere had every day of their lives. If you lived in a country with no decent government, where thugs ruled and evil deeds went unpunished, I could see why you might want to believe in some higher power at large, taking notes on who was behaving and who wasn't, and making plans for some judgment day. It wouldn't matter whether your divine being was God, Allah, or a voodoo deity, as long you could give yourself hope that people might get their just deserts. Life wasn't worth the bother otherwise. Atheism, surely, was a luxury for the comfortably-off, for that upper strata of the world where mankind did a reasonable job of standing in for God. I didn't think I'd ever become religious, no matter how long we spent here. My atheistic instincts were far too strong. But after 24 of the most unpleasant hours of my life, I began to wish that I could, although the benign, forgiving Almighty of my Sunday school years wasn't quite what I had in mind. Right now I wanted a vengeful, angry God, an Old Testament type who'd move in obvious rather than mysterious ways, who'd melt the Old Bastard with a blast of righteous hellfire in front of all his pathetic buddies. Just as well I wasn't cooped up with Terry Waite.

10: All in the mind

TIME IS THE hostage's immortal enemy. No matter what ways are devised to kill the hours, days, weeks and months, an infinite number still stretch ahead – infinite, because there is no telling when or if freedom will come. A prisoner serving a fixed jail sentence can make a slow, but sanity-preserving countdown to freedom. A hostage relies on the whim of his kidnappers. Early on in our captivity, I thought of chalking the days up on the cave wall. But I decided not to bother, even though it could be done without stirring from the mattress: without a fixed date to get to, an ever-expanding grid of crosses and strokes would indicate only how much time we'd done, not how little there was left to go.

To give ourselves a sense of perspective, José and I would talk about other hostage cases. It was a reminder that things could be a great deal worse. The case of Brian Keenan, the Irish university lecturer held hostage by Islamic militants in Beirut between 1986 and 1990, stood out above all others. I'd watched Keenan reading from his book, *An Evil Cradling*, when I was a journalism student, little thinking that I would ever be in a position to compare experiences. Not that I was, really. Keenan's ordeal was infinitely worse than mine on every front. He spent much of the time alone, chained up in basements and cellars, fighting off not just the onset of madness, but also his guards, who often beat him for standing up to them. No doubt he would have found our cave pretty comfortable by comparison, and the Old Bastard nothing more than a mild nuisance.

Many of the kidnaps we talked of involved people I knew personally. The Baghdad foreign press corps had a long roll call of reporters who'd been abducted, and while none of them had spent anything like as long in captivity as Keenan, the prospect of ending up in an Al Qaeda snuff movie gave it a horror all of its own. Jill Carroll, an American fellow freelancer who I'd shared a hotel suite with at one point, had been kidnapped by a Sunni militant group that shot her translator dead during the abduction. She'd been held alone in a house for weeks by supporters of Abu Musab al Zarqawi, the leader of Al Qaeda in Iraq, fearing she might be beheaded like so many of his other victims. For much of the time she'd been guarded by a man who wore a suicide vest, ready to blow the place sky high if anyone tried to storm it. She was released three months later for no obvious reason, amid reports that Iraqi insurgents had decided that it hurt their image to take women hostage. Whether that was true or not, I had no idea, although I remembered thinking that it would not be much use to me in the same circumstances.

Then there was James Brandon, a young reporter just out of university, who'd been my occasional stand-in as the *Sunday Telegraph's* stringer in Baghdad. While covering for me in August 2004, he'd been sent down to Basra, where a group of Shia militants had snatched him from his hotel. They released him 24 hours later, but not before parading him on a video released to al Jazeera, in which they held a gun to his head and threatened to kill him unless US forces immediately halted a major operation against Shia insurgents in the city of Najaf. Watching the footage from my flat in London, I was convinced James was going to die. It also occurred to me that had I taken my holidays at a different time, it might well have been me starting out from the video.

It was a similar tale with Georges Malbrunot, a French reporter living in the hotel room next to mine, whom I often accompanied on out-of-town trips to split driving costs. He and his colleague were kidnapped by an Al Qaeda group as they drove to cover the fighting in Najaf, and held for four months. Once again, when I'd seen his face staring out from a hostage video, I couldn't help thinking how easily I could have been sat in their car with them. From what Georges told me after his release, it was just as well I hadn't been.

'The guys holding us were real extremists,' he said. 'They told us that because the French had no armies in Iraq, they would spare our lives. But they said if we'd been British or American, they'd have killed us straightaway.'

One of the more bizarre cases José and I discussed was that of Ulf Hjertstrom, an elderly Swedish businessman who'd spent many years living in Baghdad. In 2006, he'd been kidnapped by Sunni militants and held in a cell that doubled as an execution chamber for hostages that couldn't afford to pay their ransoms. During his time in captivity, eight or nine Iraqi captives were shot dead in front of him, the execution squad turning the TV up in the room next door to hide the noise. Hjertstrom himself, however, was freed after 67 days and returned to Sweden, where he gave an extraordinary press conference.

Given that he came from a country known for its devotion to peace and diplomacy, the expectation among the assembled press pack was that he going to use the occasion to extend a message of forgiveness to his captors, to say it was all part of the ugly business of war and so on. Far from it. Instead, he announced that he'd made a few calls to old pals in Saddam's intelligence services, and had hired a gang of Iraqi hitmen to hunt his captors down.

'I have now put some people to work to find these bastards,' he'd growled to the astonished hacks. 'I invested about $50,000 so far and we will get them, one by one. I don't care if they arrest them or kill them, as long as these criminals are taken off the streets. It is not revenge. It is just common sense.'

In choosing Charles Bronson rather than Mahatma Gandhi as his role model, Hjertstrom had confounded not only the peace-loving image of his fellow countrymen, but also their contribution to one of the classic aspects of hostage psychology – Stockholm Syndrome. This was the famous – though now largely discredited – condition in which hostages supposedly ended up bonding with their captors. It was originally identified among a group of bank clerks taken prisoner during a robbery in the Swedish capital in 1973. Not only did the clerks tell police negotiators to let the robbers go free, one of them refused to testify in court and became friends with one of the robbers after he left jail. An American psychiatrist named Frank Ochberg later defined Stockholm Syndrome as 'a primitive gratitude for the gift of life'. His theory was that through the simple act of not killing their prisoner straightaway, a hostage taker effectively becomes a life-giver in their captive's eyes. The hostage's natural desire to distract themselves from their tormentor's darker side also means that the slightest kindnesses assumed undue proportion. A pack of cigarettes, a kind word, or even just the loosening of an uncomfortable ligature can seem more significant than threats or beatings, or indeed the act of imprisonment itself.

Stockholm Syndrome supposedly struck again in 1974, in the photogenic form of Patty Hearst, the heiress to the American Hearst newspaper empire. A student at California's Berkeley University, she was abducted by the Symbionese Liberation Army, one of the many eccentric militant groups that sprung up as flower power began to wilt in the early 1970s. What started out as a straightforward tale of drug-crazed hippies kidnapping a nice middle-class girl took an unfathomable twist when, two months after her abduction, a tape-recorded message was released in which she announced that she'd joined her captors' cause. She then helped the gang carry out a bank robbery, becoming an icon of urban guerrilla chic when the police released security camera footage of her holding a rifle. Hearst later served 22 months of a jail sentence for bank robbery, but was granted a full pardon by President Bill Clinton in 2001.

Since then, though, relatively few further stories have surfaced of hostage-kidnapper love-ins, to the point where many psychiatrists now believe it is the exception, rather than the rule. It was, it seems, just a fashionable theory of the counter-culture period, when there was a ready audience for stories about people choosing to side with outlaws rather than The Man. The case of Ulf Hjertstrom and his Iraqi hit squad wasn't the first to call it into question. In 1999, an FBI study of hostage victims over the previous 25 years had concluded that Stockholm Syndrome had been 'over-emphasised, over-analysed, over-psychologised, and over-publicised.'

All the same, I often wondered whether José and I were showing signs of it. During the gunfight, I'd experienced the odd sensation of being impressed at how the gang had fended off the interlopers. It was as if we'd been part of the clan, protected from other, possibly nastier, foes in these lawless mountains. The belt-fed machine guns that had once seemed so threatening were a source of reassurance, as was the calm manner in which they'd held their council of war afterwards. If trouble broke out again, then we – sorry, they – would be ready for all comers. Then again, José and I were not exactly your typical hostage case study. The people our kidnappers were fighting were not the police, after all, but another armed gang, not something that happened during your average kidnap case in Sweden or California. If we ever got out, maybe the shrink that psychoanalysed us could write some paper on Bossaso Syndrome.

My own theory was that as a hostage, you came to prize the status quo above all else. Knowing that things could take a turn for the worse at any moment – as they had with yesterday's gunfight, and the Old Bastard's threats the day before – bred an instinctive fear of change. Hence the nerves whenever we scrambled up the mountainside for a phone call, or when a new face joined the kidnap gang, or when pretty much anything else happened that broke our mind-numbingly tedious routine.

Just how strong this feeling was I only realised as dusk fell on the day after the gunfight, when the gang stamped out the fire and began tidying away all traces of our presence. We were on the move again. As José and I gathered our few belongings – the mat and blankets, the chess pieces, the cigarettes and lighter – I felt my teeth grinding more than ever. What was happening now? Couldn't we just stay where we were? Never had the devil I knew and despised so much seemed so good.

On previous journeys, the gang had always carried everything for us, but now we were no longer such privileged guests. The Old Bastard handed us a couple of sticks, and showed us how to knot our blankets around them, Dick Whittington-style. To my surprise, he beamed approvingly as we raised them to our shoulders. We waited in the hollow as a scout party headed off up the mountainside, a whistle sounding out that the route was judged clear.

Yet once we began marching off towards the nearest ridge, I began to feel not worse, but slightly better. As I settled into a rhythm, trying hard as ever not to stumble on the rocks, I realised it was actually just relief at getting out from the cave. It struck me now just how tense the last few days had been. Having previously dreaded all change, now I was all for it.

Or was it just that the Old Bastard had smiled at me for once? Much as I hated to admit it, that too was one reason why I now had rather more of a spring in my step. Maybe Stockholm Syndrome did exist after all.

*****

Three hours later, we entered a canyon that cut a long, winding groove into a hillside, ending in a rocky cul-de-sac. Once again, we were perfectly hidden. A bulge in the canyon walls made it impossible for anyone at the top to see right down to the bottom. After camping out for the night, at dawn we were on the move again. A narrow track that climbed halfway up one side of the canyon led into the mouth of our next hideaway. Whereas the other places we'd stayed in were mainly rocky nooks and overhangs, this was what might be termed a 'proper' cave. It was a huge rock tunnel with an entrance the size of a house, stretching back 50 yards into the hillside. We nicknamed it Tora Bora, after Bin Laden's mountain complex in Afghanistan. Its insides were of smooth volcanic rock that had cooled into uneven contours, like frozen rapids. Staring into its mouth felt rather like inspecting the throat of some huge, long-fossilized dragon. It was easy to imagine dinosaurs or sabre-toothed cats roaming around inside millions of years ago. As I scanned the walls, I half-expected to see cave paintings by ancient Somalis, no doubt clubbing the hell out of each other.

Overall, it looked almost comfortable by cave standards. If nothing else, we'd have proper shelter if it rained. Closer examination, though, revealed that we were not the only residents. In a small crevice in the rock, I noticed, was a funnel web of tightly-woven gossamer. Then I noticed another. And another. And several more. There were hundreds of them. José poked one with a long stick.

'Did you see anything?' I asked.

'Something moved inside, but I couldn't see what it was,' he said.

If the beasts lurking within were what I thought they were, we'd be sharing bedspace with one of the deadliest creatures in the world. Funnel web spiders were one of the very few that could kill grown adults: I'd written stories about the Australian variety, which occasionally terrorised back gardens in suburban Sydney. Unless the Somali variety was its harmless cousin, we'd be in big trouble if we got bit. My imagination, responding creatively to a crisis as ever, also flashed up a helpful image of the Old Bastard threatening me with one.

José probed around in a few more holes. To my immense relief, nothing came scuttling out to take him on. Perhaps they were all hibernating. Or maybe they only came out at night. Either way, we were going to be around to find out. The gang was busy making their sleeping arrangements around the cave, fashioning mattresses out of twigs torn from nearby bushes. The Old Bastard, who now bizarrely seemed to have appointed himself as our personal footman, made one for José and me, just at the cave's entrance. He located a flattish spot in the rocks, laid the twigs in a criss-cross pattern, topped it off with bunches of wild grass, and rolled the mat on top. Then he urged us to try it out. Thanks to the pliancy of the bush twigs underneath, the mat felt surprisingly buoyant – the caveman's answer to a waterbed. The Old Bastard beamed at our approving looks, like a Habitat salesman dealing with a pair of newly-weds. Why was he now being so friendly, I wondered? It was almost as unsettling as him eyeballing us all the time.

*****

Early on in our kidnapping, when our spirits were still strong, I'd vowed that if we were stuck here for weeks or months, I would use the time constructively. Daylight hours would be one long round of self-improvement. As well as mastering the basics of Somali, I would ask the Teacher to help me with my Arabic, and José to drill me in Spanish. I would keep fit with press-ups, and devote allotted times to careful, structured discussion with José about the great issues of the world. Combined with the mental exercise of regular chess matches, such a routine would keep us occupied, focused and healthy. When eventually freed, we would emerge fit, erudite and multi-lingual, modern-day Renaissance men who'd triumphed over our primitive circumstances.

It wasn't quite working out like that. Instead, three weeks in, we seemed to be getting closer to the cave man way of life, not further from it. The English-Somali lessons had stopped due to dwindling interest on both sides, and playing chess had become too much like hard work. So too, increasingly, was just making basic speech. Unable to think of new things to discuss, we spent growing amounts of time in listless silence. Over lunch one day, I watched José gnaw a goat's bone and then chuck it over his shoulder into the bushes outside the cave. With his matted hair and beard, he would easily have fitted in among whichever early humanity might have dwelt here thousands of years ago. And they, at least, would have had to turn in an honest day's graft as hunter-gatherers. We, by contrast, were turning into Stone Age couch potatoes, waited on hand and foot. I fretted that without purpose or stimulation, our minds would begin to rot, as if struck by some mild form of Alzheimer's disease. I was mindful of a tale told to me by a young dissident I'd interviewed a few months before in Belarus, known as 'Europe's last dictatorship' because its unreformed, Soviet-style government. He'd told me that during his frequent spells in the local KGB prison, he could feel his mind deteriorating for lack of things to do.

'After a couple of weeks, you find you can only read and think about half as quick as normal,' he'd said. 'Your brain slows right down.'

My own listlessness, I suspected, was due partly to focusing so much mental energy on simply remaining calm. There were certain times – mainly the mornings, when the rest of the day stretched ahead with all its uncertainties – when I felt particularly queasy, and the yearning for it all to just end became particularly intense. I'd never expected the kind of inner tranquility that hostages like Brian Keenan seemed to have found to come easily to me. Back home, I was the kind of person who would curse if the bus or Tube was late, or be cast into a gloom for days if the paper spiked a piece I'd written. Here in the cave, however, tantrums and despair were an indulgence one couldn't afford. It reminded me of the tactics that my old surfing instructor had taught me for coping in 'wipe outs', when a wave held you under water and spun you round like a washing machine. The trick was simply to relax and trust that you would eventually float back up the surface. The moment you started to thrash or struggle, you ran out of oxygen and it became unbearable.

As ever, I tried to cope by thinking of others worse off than myself, although as time went on they had to be very unfortunate indeed to make me feel better. I gorged myself on other's sufferings, abandoning all sense of perspective in my attempts to get perspective. Poor old Brian Keenan, stuck in his cellar for five years, was no longer enough. I thought of people with terminal illnesses, prisoners on Death Row; my grandfather's generation, who'd fought in WWII; the inmates of Auschwitz and Belsen. Anyone, anywhere, as long as they were worse off than me. Listening to the BBC World Service, I found myself taking a new interest in stories about prisoners, people in Guantanamo Bay, and anyone else deprived of liberty. Similarly, non-incarcerated people in the news seemed to belong in a different world, their freedom defining them above everything else. On one occasion I listened to a US economics pundit talking for ten minutes without taking in a word of what he was saying. All I could think was: 'You got up this morning, did this interview, and then you were *free* for the rest of the day. *Free* to do whatever you want.'

Of our own kidnapping, we still heard nothing, although we did hear a broadcast on the BBC World Service in which other hostages compared experiences. It was presented by Alan Johnston, the BBC's former Gaza correspondent, who'd been abducted for four months in 2007. He was talking to the politician Ingrid Betancourt, who'd spent six years as a hostage of the Left-wing FARC rebels in Colombia.

José and I listened intently as they swapped notes, nodding knowledgeably at bits we recognised. There were, it seemed, certain concerns that were common to all hostages: the guilt for the worry caused to others, the joy of messages from home, and the issue of toilet access (Johnston had en suite; Betancourt, to her huge embarrassment, had to perform her ablutions in front of her guards). Like us, they also had radios to keep in touch with the outside world.

'It's just possible that in a makeshift prison in Colombia or Iraq or Afghanistan right now, there may be a kidnap victim in a cell listening to us on the radio,' said Johnston at one point. 'What would your message to him or her be?

José and I put our ears up to close to the speakers. *Finally, someone on the radio was talking about us*. Even if they didn't know who we were, or where.

'Don't be hard on yourself, just love yourself,' replied Betancourt. 'And always forgive yourself and know that whatever has been wrong you can do it the next time better. And don't be afraid of death – it's just a little step.'

Don't be afraid of death? That was not advice I hoped to have to heed at any point. Johnson's counsel was rather better.

'Whatever you do, try and act in a way that you will feel proud of afterwards,' he said. 'It's about waiting and believing. If you wait long enough, the door's going to open.'

How long though? Three weeks, as we'd now done? Three months? Three years? One would require a great deal of inner strength to last that anything like that long. And on current form so far, I suspected I was no Brian Keenan.

11: A sea dog's tale

'Seems like that thing about sending you to Eyl was bullshit, then.'
'Yes, thank God.'
'You missed out on your exclusive, though, to be the first British guy to go there.'
'Do you know what, I don't actually think I would have been. There was another Brit who beat me to it. A sailor who was hijacked earlier this year...'

THE LOUNGE OF Colin Darch's house on the north Devon coast had looked like just the sort of place a veteran sea captain might enjoy a comfortable retirement in. Through the large bay windows, there was a fine view out towards the Bristol Channel, while mounted on the walls was a collection of memorabilia from over half a century at sea: old maritime charts, photos of him in uniform as a young man, a cluster of baffling sailors' knots on a plaque. Also in the lounge were his saxophone and oil painting easel, two hobbies that his wife Barbara, a leading light in the local brass band, hoped would now keep him sufficiently occupied in retirement.

It wasn't that the band particularly needed extra players for its horn section. To discover the real reason she didn't want him to going back to sea, you had to look at one of his art works that hung on the wall. It depicted a wall of imposing cliffs, rising steeply up from a beach and indented with a cove that was dotted with a few tiny houses and boats. At first glance, it could have been somewhere on the Devon coast, but the caption below, written in Colin's neat handwriting, read: '*Gabbac, Somalia*'. Gabbac was a village in the Eyl district, about 20 miles north of the town of Eyl itself. Colin had recreated every detail of its soaring headlands from memory, having had plenty of time to study them. In early 2008, he had spent nearly seven weeks moored just a mile offshore, after the boat he was commanding, the *Svitzer Korsakov*, became one of the early catches of the piracy boom.

Since his release, Colin had become something of a local celebrity in Devon, as probably the first local sailor to fall victim to pirates since the 1600s, when the West Country had been Britain's answer to Puntland, crawling with buccaneers of every sort. His ordeal had made for a rather pacier-than-normal read in the local paper, the *North Devon Journal*, and he'd presided over the opening of a local village flower show. But that wasn't the only reason I'd picked him out to talk to. By then there were hundreds of sailors around the world who'd languished as pirate hostages off the Somali coast, many of them for months at a time. Finding ones willing to talk on the record about their experiences, though, was not easy. Since most had been party to the ransom negotiations, the shipping firms they worked for were reluctant to let them talk to the media.

Colin was different. Now retired, he was free to say what he wanted, and could recollect his experience in vivid detail, with the aid of a ship's log that he had kept through all 47 days. When I rang him out of the blue one evening, he promptly invited me to down to stay with him and his wife down in Devon. The man who picked me up from the train station had a tanned, weather-beaten face, snow-white hair with salt-and-pepper eyebrows, and a respectable sailor's thirst. He told me his story over a hot summer's afternoon and evening, starting with tea and biscuits in his lounge, moving onto to ales in his local pub, and finishing with glasses of rum back in his kitchen. Like all the best tales of disaster at sea, it began with a premonition that the trip would go wrong right from the very start.

After going to sea at 16 and spending much of his life in the merchant navy, Colin had ended up as a freelance captain, contracted by a Dutch shipping company to deliver ships and cargoes all over the world. In December 2007, he and a colleague had taken a contract to deliver two brand-new Russian tug boats from a shipyard in St Petersburg to the island of Sakhalin in Russia's Far East, where they would service oil platforms. It was a journey of some two months in all, starting out in the icy waters of the Baltic in mid-winter, heading down through the Mediterranean and the Gulf of Aden, and then across the Indian Ocean to Singapore, where a new command would take over.

On this occasion, however, it became clear that the journey was going to be difficult before they even set sail. When Colin and his Irish engineer Ted turned up at the docks one bleak, wintry morning in St Petersburg, they were met by a crew of four Russians who seemed hand-picked to fit all of the worst stereotypes of Russian men. The first mate, Sergei, a huge, bald guy to whom Colin would have to trust half the sailing, reeked of vodka much of the time. The two able seamen, Dmitri and Vladimir, were surly, disorganised and barely able to speak any English. When they finally set sail on December 16, having eased their way through the Russian port bureaucracy with a vodka party for various dock officials, Colin discovered something even worse about his new sailing companions. None of them could cook. Instead, they simply kept a large pan on the stove all day, containing water, scraps of cabbage and lumps of meat and bones, from which they would ladle a portion at any time. Colin and Ted nicknamed it 'Gulag soup'.

They headed into the North Sea and several rough days of sailing, walls of green water crashing over the bow. Such was the pounding that by New Year's Day, technical problems with the other tug, the *Svitzer Busse*, forced them to dock again in Holland. That night found Colin sat in a local bar, downing a few beers in a bid to cheer himself up. Not only had he not eaten properly for days, his bunk had worked loose from its fittings so that it slid around in the cabin, making it impossible to sleep. Short of an entire flock of albatrosses dropping dead on the deck, it was hard to imagine a more ill-omened start to a voyage.

'There is nothing I like about this ship,' he wrote that night. 'Is she jinxed?'

The two ships continued south into the Mediterranean, and then into the Red Sea via the Suez Canal, known as 'Marlboro Country' because of the amount of petty bribes required to ensure smooth passage. At that point, the other tug had to divert to Oman to fix a problem with her air-conditioning system. Colin continued on towards through the Gulf of Aden, thinking himself fortunate for avoiding further delays. In fact, his bad luck was just about to begin.

By the afternoon of February 1, the tug was almost through the Gulf, sailing 70 miles north of Cape Gardafui, the very tip of Puntland's north east corner. The Somali coastline was not even visible, not that Colin was particularly concerned about the threat from pirates. Back then they were deemed a relatively minor risk, attacking only vessels that strayed directly toward their shores.

'The wisdom was that as long as you stayed more than 60 miles from the coastline, you'd be fine,' Colin told me. 'We were 70 miles off, so we were complying. Obviously, 100 miles off would have been better, but then you are using more fuel, and that is not on.'

Then, around 1600hrs, Colin saw a white fibreglass skiff approaching from the starboard side, bumping over the waves at high speed. Inside it were five men, heads swathed in white rags. One was manning a powerful outboard engine, another was holding a tall grappling ladder. The rest were clutching Kalashnikovs.

The *Svitzer Korsakov* did not surrender straightaway. With a maximum speed of just 12 knots, and a deck clearance of just six feet, she was potentially easy prey for the pirates, but there was still plenty her crew could do to fend them off. They locked the steel main deck doors from within, put out a general Mayday call, and pressed a secret alarm button connected to a control centre in Britain that would activate a tracking device. Colin then started evasive manoeuvring. The tug might be slow, but it was not ungainly. Designed to tow far bigger ships around in a confined harbour, it was the marine equivalent of a 4x4, equipped with two 3,000 horsepower thrusters that could allow it to turn and reverse on a sixpence. As the pirates came level with the ship's stern, Colin gave one of the rear thrusters full power at 90 degrees, hoping to slam the pirate skiff with his rear flank, like a wildebeest batting off a lion. The pirate vessel dodged just in time, circled around and came back, only for Colin to force it out the way a second time.

'By this time the adrenalin was rushing through us all, the ship's alarm was sounding and we were shouting and swearing at the tops of our voices in English and Russian,' Colin recalled. 'I was gaining in confidence that I could keep them off, but in case I actually hit and sank them, I got Ted to take pictures to prove they were armed, not innocent fishermen. On about their third attack they started firing the guns, and you could hear these shots going "crack, crack crack".'

After the third attack, Ted shouted that the pirate with the grappling ladder had fallen into the water. As his friends paused to fish him out, Colin thought they might be giving up. Then a second skiff with another four gunmen lurched into view. They now had pirates either side.

'Deep down we knew we were doomed at this point, but I was suddenly really furious and hoped to ram one boat so that they would then have to stop and rescue their mates. I really was determined to kill them by that time. You get so much adrenaline, you no longer feel afraid.'

The pirates came at the tug again, firing sporadically. Colin threw the ship from side to side, thrashing up a welter of white water. Then, just as he thought he might have swamped the pirates in the tug's wake, he heard a shout from Ted.

'They're aboard!'

Colin stopped the engines, and the waters around them became calm. There was no point in resisting now. From outside the wheelhouse they could shouts in Somali, more gunshots, and the clatter of footsteps on steel walkways. The crew fell silent, wondering what sort of treatment they'd get from men they'd just tried their best to drown.

*****

The pirates piled into the wheelhouse, shouting, glaring and wild-eyed. One of them, a stocky figure who spoke some English, introduced himself by the unlikely name of Andrew. Andrew asked who the captain was and, when Colin identified himself, pointed to a big, hard-looking accomplice stood next to him. 'This is Omar, our captain,' Andrew said. He announced that 'Captain Omar' was now in command, and then launched into a long diatribe about the dire state of Somalia, and how with no government for 17 years, the only way to survive was by hijacking and ransoming. There was no reason for Colin and his men to be harmed as long as they did what they were told, he promised, although if they tried to get in the way, blood would be shed. The rest of the pirates looked on menacingly.

'They are angry because you fight them,' said Andrew.

'Me, fight?' Colin protested. 'What with? You have the guns!'

'No, no, but you try to sink our boats!' Andrew replied.

'As the captain of this ship, it is my duty to prevent armed robbers from boarding,' Colin replied.

To his surprise, the pirates seemed to accept that as fair play, and moved onto other business. Andrew ordered the crew to use the tug's crane to lift one of their skiffs aboard, during which it slipped loose, disgorging ammunition, engines and luggage into water a mile deep. 'Never mind!' said Andrew breezily, as Colin and the crew braced themselves for a beating. 'We didn't need that, full ahead!'

Three days later, they were anchored off the coast of Eyl, after one of the most perilous journeys Colin had ever undergone. Captain Omar, who was more of a soldier than a sailor, had insisted on sticking close to the shore the whole way, so that if a foreign warship tried to intercept, it would be easy to disembark with the hostages. Colin had spent the whole time fearing they were about to hit a rock or the rusting remains of a sunken wreck, a prospect made more likely by Captain Omar forbidding the use of lights. The tug had no paper charts for the unscheduled detour down the coast, and a set of electronic charts that Sergei had acquired were far from reliable. He had bought the entire set for £100 on the black market in St Petersburg, and they were years out of date.

There was little to see at Eyl. The town itself, a nondescript, flyblown hamlet of crumbling villas, was up a creek inland, and the pirates chose to keep their hostages on the ship, where they had access to its satellite phone and radio. The only real sign they were in pirate territory was the presence of another hijacked vessel anchored offshore, a trawler from Singapore that the gang proudly described as 'one of theirs'. By later in the year, as the piracy business really began to boom, there would sometimes be half a dozen ships in the bay, languishing like catches in an angler's keep net. Yet even now, a buzz of excitement went around town as the *Svitzer Korsakov* came in, just like it did when there was a new qhat delivery.

Suddenly the sleepy, sun-roasted alleyways were full of people: clan elders, middlemen, negotiators, armourers, suppliers and all the others hangers-on who now lived off the ransom dollars. Several skiffs motored out to greet the tug, bringing with them a dozen more pirates and a mullah dressed in a robe and white cap, who led prayers. Also on board came supplies of food, including two live goats, and several bundles of qhat. By that evening, the ship's deck was soon covered in discarded qhat leaves, although Colin was relieved to note that it seemed to make his captors relaxed rather than aggressive. The hostages were allowed to wander freely around the boat, and Andrew, the English-speaking pirate, became chattier. In between mouthfuls of qhat, he explained why he and his friends had become pirates.

'He said they were doing it because they were fed up with people plundering their fish, and dumping toxic waste in their seas,' Colin recalled. 'They didn't actually call themselves pirates, they called themselves a militia. There was about 200 of them in all, apparently, operating in teams of ten. At first they'd just confiscated fish catches, but as some of the foreign trawlers began arming themselves, they found it easier to just grab any passing ship and hold it to ransom.'

The next morning, Colin was allowed to ring his boss in Holland on the ship's satellite phone. He in turn gave him a number for a man in Copenhagen, David White, whom would act as the intermediary. The gang issued a $2.5 million ransom demand, threatening to shoot the entire crew if it wasn't paid in three days' time. Colin doubted the threats would be carried out, or that the owners would refuse to pay a ransom. But one thing did worry him. When White had asked for details of a middleman to whom it might be paid, the pirates had looked blank.

'These guys were obviously doing this for the first time, and it was clear they had no bank accounts or intermediaries to receive the cash,' Colin said. 'They told me they wanted the cash actually delivered on board, so I had to patiently explain that nobody from Copenhagen could fly into Somalia with suitcases of dollars, and come trotting over the desert on donkey or camel, without being robbed along the way. It occurred to me that even if they wanted to pay the ransom, there was no obvious way of getting the money through.'

*****

Fast forward two weeks, and pirates and hostages alike were feeling the strain. There was no tangible progress on finding a way to pay the ransom, and the shipping company was refusing to pay more than a fifth of $2.5 million the pirates wanted. The once-brand new ship was now a mess, covered in qhat leaves and stinking from housing so many people for so long. The pirates had ransacked the crew's cabins, and appropriated company teeshirts and boiler suits to replace the clothes they lost when their skiff sank, giving them the odd impression of being part of the crew. Colin was particularly annoyed to see the pirate's cook, a young, slightly-built fellow, wandering around in his newly-purchased Cotton Traders tracksuit bottoms. He did concede, though, that the cook's goat spaghettis and risottos were much tastier than the Gulag soup.

Tensions were also high among the hostages, with Ted and Colin beginning to tire of the Russians' constant surliness. The St Petersburg men made no effort to hide their disdain for the pirate 'monkeys', to the point where Colin feared one of them might end up getting shot. To his horror, Ted then reported to him that the Russians were planning to jump three of the pirates for their weapons, and then using them to kill the rest. When Colin had asked him if this was true, Sergei nodded. It was the only way out, he insisted. Vladimir Putin, Russia's hardman leader, 'would not pay one rouble for a Russian life,' he said. Sergei was only persuaded to drop the plan after Colin explained that it was the ship's insurers, not the Russian government, who would pay any ransom. He added that a botched escape attempt would also backfire on all the hostages together.

Nerves were further frayed by the presence of the USS *Carney*, an American destroyer serving with the anti-piracy fleet, which was monitoring the hijack from a few miles away. Colin had initially been reassured to see it, but was now wishing it would just go away. Rather than attempting any kind of rescue, all it did was sail in close occasionally to take a look, at which point the pirates would hustle Colin and the rest of the crew into the wheelhouse at gunpoint, shouting: 'Soldiers of America, go 'way!' Whenever resupply skiffs sailed out from Eyl, the warship would open fire, churning up the sea around them with high-calibre shells, but most of the time they still got through. It seemed that whoever was commanding the USS *Carney* was authorised only to fire warning shots at the skiffs, not blow them out the water. Nor did the barrage prevent the tug being moved around. After a few days in Eyl, rough weather forced them to sail to a more secure anchor further up the coast at Gabbac, where they now were.

The view that Colin would later recreate in his living room in Appledore was not one that tested his brushwork skills very highly. Stretching as far as the eye could in either direction was a narrow strip of sandy beach backed by a wall of towering red cliffs, which formed the edge of a desert plateau. The only break in an otherwise uniform geography was a deep *wadi*, or river valley, which had carved a winding path down to the sea over the centuries. Pitched on the right-hand slopes of the *wadi* were eight bright orange tents, which formed the pirate's camp. The locals, who lived in a huddle of round, thatched huts on the plateau, seemed well set-up to cater for them. In the radio in the tug's wheelhouse, the gang were in constant touch with a radio operator in the village. Most of the time, Colin noticed, the voice of 'Radio Gabbac' seemed to be a woman.

By this time, the hostages had got to know their captors well. Conversations over tea revealed snapshots of their previous lives, usually with some unfortunate twist of fate that had led them into taking the pirate coin. One pirate, a beetle-browed fellow nicknamed Anthony Quinn for his resemblance to the actor, had had a job in Dubai as a chauffeur. Working long, unregulated hours, he fell asleep at the wheel one day and ploughed into another car, killing its occupant. He was jailed for 21 days, stripped of his licence and visa, and then deported, leaving him unable to cater for his three wives and many children. Two other pirates, one called Ahmed and another nicknamed Sammy Davis Junior, had both served in the now-defunct Somali coastguard, while Captain Omar claimed to have fought as a paratrooper in Barre's army, and had a series of white scars across his leg where he'd been wounded in battle. Others came across as just common thugs, in particular one called Mohammed, whom even the other pirates seemed scared of. 'Nobody ever went near him,' said Colin. 'Ahmed once told me, 'That man, killer!''

Fortunately, Captain Omar generally ran a tight ship among his men, including a disciplinary code and corresponding punishments. On two occasions, the hostages wandered out on deck to find Sammy Davis Junior and Andrew chained up in painfully contorted positions, sweltering in the fierce sun. What they had done to incur Captain Omar's displeasure remained a mystery, although when Ted wandered past the unfortunate Andrew with a pailful of toilet water, he was urged by the rest of the gang to chuck it over him. Indeed, the pirates often warned the hostages that there were scoundrels among their number, men who could not be trusted. When Colin complained one day that his watch had gone missing from his room, Ahmed launched his own criminal investigation, eventually returning it a few hours later. 'Captain, you must be careful,' he counselled in a low voice. 'Some of these men are t'ieves!'

*****

Soon it became clear that Andrew had fallen out of favour for good, when a tall, gowned figure with all his top front teeth missing clambered on board and pronounced himself as his replacement as translator.

'I am Mohammed Abdul Ali,' he said. 'I am a respectable schoolmaster, not one of these bandits! They have forced me to work for them as an interpreter to help obtain the money and your release.'

Colin shook his hand. 'How much are they paying you, then?'

'Five thousand dollars,' he replied promptly.

Eager to practice his English, Mohammed told his story. He was 29, unmarried, and ran a school for 150 fee-paying students. He spoke in a slightly effeminate manner, leading Ted to speculate that in a less macho society, he would have been gay. Mohammed fretted that his students would be without a teacher until the hijack was over. He urged Colin to persuade the owners to increase their offer, suggesting that the educational needs of his untended pupils should be the priority for all parties.

A couple of mornings later, after Colin had finished a breakfast of cornflakes and camel's milk, David White got in touch again to increase his initial offer of $258,000 to $427,000. His concession, though, seemed to anger rather than encourage the pirates, who said it was still insultingly low. Mohammed the schoolteacher grabbed the satellite phone and yelled at White.

'You have three days to find the money or we start to shoot the crew. Now put that in your pipe and smoke it!'

The language was quaint, but judging by the atmosphere on board, it felt like the threat was becoming serious. Imagining the crew being put before a pirate firing squad, Colin and Ted's thoughts turned to escape. Days of observing their routine had revealed possible weak spots that might be exploited. In particular, Ted had noticed that none of the guards ever accompanied him down into the engine room. It was dark, noisy and hot down there, a claustrophobic maze of machinery linked by cramped, narrow passageways. That meant they were unfamiliar with its lay-out, in particular the lockable steel hatchway that led to the large hydraulics chamber at the stern. Colin and Ted realised that if the crew could sneak themselves in there one day, it could serve as a 'safe room' for them to hide in while the Marines on board the USS *Carney* stormed the ship. The hydraulics room had watertight steel walls; anyone inside would be reasonably well-protected from stray bullets. To make it hard for the pirates to work out where they were, they could wait until night time and then cut all the lights on the ship, plunging it into darkness and giving a go-ahead signal to the USS *Carney*. The only question was how to alert the

Americans to their plan without letting on to their captors. A few days later, Colin dropped a coded message into a satellite phone conversation with David White.

'Before discussing the ransom, I would like to say how it comforts us to know that all parties have our welfare at heart,' he said. 'The ship owners say our lives are their main concern; the warship says their main interest is safeguarding the lives of the hostages; and the militia promise us we will not be harmed if the ransom demands are met. As Master, I promise to protect the lives of the crew. If something nasty like a *blackout* should occur, the crew will be *tucked away safe behind steel doors come what may!*'

The last sentence of the message aroused no suspicion from the pirates. Colin had spoken faster than normal, gambling that Mohammad the schoolmaster, who was listening in, would rather pretend he'd understood than admit that his English was inadequate. Discreet preparations got underway. One by one, the crew removed all the starting switches for the emergency lights, which would normally come on in the event of a power failure. It meant that when they cut the power, the windowless engine room would remain in pitch blackness, making it hard for the pirates to locate the hatch. A five-litre drum of drinking water was sneaked down there as well, and spare cigarettes, in case of a lengthy siege.

By the night of February 11 everything was in place. Ted and Colin had heard nothing back from David White to indicate either way whether the Americans were aware of the plot, but they decided to go ahead while they still had the chance. Just before midnight, the crew sneaked down to the engine room, where they shut down various fuel valves to starve the electricity generator. Ted added in a couple of booby traps, greasing the engine room stairs with oil and tying a trip rope across the bottom step. As the lights began to dim, they entered the hydraulic room and closed the watertight door, lashing it down to hinder anyone opening it from the other side. It had all gone perfectly. Colin and Ted congratulated each other, the Russians lit cigarettes in celebration, and a sense of comradeship that until now had been entirely missing from the whole journey took hold.

'We had a good old chuckle as we thought of all the confusion and panic that would be going on up above,' Colin said. 'We knew the ship was in total darkness, and we could picture the pirates coming down the stairs, slipping on the oil, falling, breaking arms legs or necks, and accidentally shooting each other. From then on, it was just a case of holding out for a few hours until the Marines came.'

Sadly, the bad luck that had dogged the *Svitzer Korsakov* ever since it left the shipyard in St Petersburg struck again. Or, to be more precise, the bad workmanship. Each of the emergency lights around the ship were supposed to be marked by a prominent red blob; one of them, however, had been overlooked by the ship's fitters, so that when the crew had gone round switching them off, they hadn't spotted it. It was now shining brightly, illuminating the ship's engine room, and making it easy for the pirates to hunt their way around. Down in the hydraulics room, Colin and the crew were none the wiser. They sat for a full hour, wondering when battle might commence, and then heard banging on the other side of the door. The sound of the accompanying curses suggested it was not the liberating hand of the US Marine corps.

Thinking it was just a case of buying extra time, the hideaways backed into an adjacent compartment, once again closing the hatch behind them. When the pirates began breaking into that one too, they climbed through yet another hatch into what would be their last line of defence, the salt water ballast tank. This was a place that not even a people smuggler would have considered hiding cargo in. A ribbed chamber about 40 feet wide and 12 feet high, it was equipped with ducts into which sea water could either be sucked in or pumped out to adjust the tug's weight in different conditions. Climbing in was like plunging into a pitch dark, enclosed swimming pool, in which the water sluiced up and down as the ship tossed in the waves.

'The water was roaring and crashing back and forth, rising to about six feet at times, and the noise of it made conversation impossible except in short snatches,' said Colin. 'We found some ledges to sit on in a corner, and then just waited there like hunted animals, hoping to hear the sound of gunfire that might mean we were about to get released.'

The hours passed. The dial of Colin's watch, glowing in the dark, told him it was now dawn outside. Briefly there was the sound of the pirates banging on the escape hatch, but they failed to break through its stout steel door. The Russians sat smoking until their cigarettes became too damp to light, while Colin swigged from a bottle of water, peeing through his trousers, wondering if the pirates might try to blow the escape hatch open with an RPG. Still he thought the Marines must be on their way. Perhaps such assaults just had to be planned very carefully beforehand. He contemplated them dragging him blinking into daylight, hailing him a hero, giving him food, clean clothes, and Bourbon by the pint.

By 4pm, however, he began to accept that no Marines were coming. Colin would later learn from the officers on the USS *Carney* that they received no details of the signal from David White in Copenhagen, and that even if they had, nothing would have happened. American servicemens' lives would not, generally, be put at risk to rescue a group of non-US citizens. After a brief discussion, the fugitives in the ballast tank agreed to give themselves up. Quite apart it being pitch-dark and utterly disorientating, Colin reckoned the watertight chamber held no more than about 24 hours of oxygen. To their horror, they found the hatch wouldn't budge. The pirates had done the bolts up on the other side, leaving them imprisoned in what might become their own watery tomb.

'At that moment I felt utter panic,' Colin said. 'We tried knocking on the hatch, but we heard nothing back. For all we knew, the pirates might have decided to leave us in there for a day or two as punishment, by which time we'd have asphyxiated.'

Then, around 7pm, after some 18 hours in the tank, they heard the sound of a spanner working on the nuts outside. There were Somali voices, a sudden shaft of light, and then a shout of 'Captain Colin come out!' The pirates brought the crew to the bridge, where they stood, dripping wet, in front of Captain Omar, who stared at them as if presiding over a court martial. What kind of punishment might they face, Colin wondered? A few hours chained to the deck, in the manner of Sammy Davis Junior, would be getting off lightly.

Luckily, Captain Omar seemed to have respect for a worthy adversary. He grinned, shook Colin's hand, and pointed to a corner of the wheelhouse. 'Sil-leep!' he said.

Colin lay down, shivering with cold until Captain Omar placed a heavy blanket on him. Outside the USS *Carney* was still cruising up and down. 'Useless bastards,' he thought.

*****

Fed up with the slow progress of the negotiations, Ted took matters into his own hands. During a convivial chat with Anthony Quinn one evening, he said bluntly that there was no chance the pirates would ever get anything like $2.5 million. To his surprise, Quinn agreed, but pointed out that for Captain Omar not to lose face, they would at least have to recoup their expenses on top of the $427,000 already offered. Ted took a sheet of paper and made a list:

2 x skiffs lost in the initial attack

ammunition and fuel

wages for pirates

loss of earnings from other employment (due to failure of shipping company to pay ransom immediately)

Goats

Cigarettes

Qhat

The list went on and on, and with Anthony Quinn's generous costings, took the final ransom price to some $900,000. But it was a far more realistic sum than $2.5 million. To Colin's astonishment, it was put to a pirate committee the next day and approved. David White came back with a counter-offer $678,000, which the pirates eventually agreed to. However, the gang said that none of the Somali businessmen they had approached in Bossaso, Djibouti or Dubai were willing to get involved in receiving the ransom. Nor were various Somali money wire agencies, who suspected straightaway that the nominated recipients were not who they said they were. As Colin noted in his ship's log, it was as if the hijackers had won the National Lottery but could not find their winning ticket.

*****

Eventually the ship owners came up with a solution. Rather than relying on some unreliable pirate middleman, they would simply deliver the cash direct to the boat. A launch carrying the entire ransom would set sail from either Dubai or Mombasa, and rendezvous with the tug at sea. To be safe, the delivery boat would stay several hundred yards from the tug while just a couple of pirates sailed out in a skiff to collect the cash. The gang approved the plan, although they counselled against any delivery from Mombasa, which would involve passing through waters controlled by the Shabab, rather than 'ordinary, simple pirates'.

Finally, on March 16th, a call came to say that the ransom boat would arrive the following day. The hostages were asked to answer a few final proof-of-life questions. To everyone's amusement, the Russians had trouble answering the questions set by their wives, such as 'What is the name of your wife's best girlfriend?' and 'What was the number of your apartment when you were first married?'

Shortly before 5am, the delivery boat, skippered by a man named only as 'Martin', pulled up about half a mile away. Chaos then ensued, however, as the locals in Gabbac spotted what was going on and tried to get in on the action.

'The people ashore sensed something interesting was happening and came out in several boats, waving AK47s and circling the delivery vessel like Red Indians round the wagons,' said Colin. 'I got a distressed radio call from Martin, asking which gunmen should be given the goods. Fortunately our lot managed to muscle their way in, keeping the other wolves at bay.'

As Colin sighed in relief, Ahmed appeared beside him, all smiles, 'Captain, you are free!'

*****

Stashed in bricks of $100 bills, the package of $678,000 came sandwiched in a wooden pallet a square metre in size. The bricks were wrapped in tape, and took several hours for the gang to count in the mess room. The pirates hid the cash about their persons, tucking it in trousers and jackets. Most disembarked that evening, but Captain Omar and six others asked for a 'lift' up to Beyla, some 70 miles north, where they would feel less at risk of robbery once they reached land.

Colin's heart sank at the prospect of yet more time with them, although Captain Omar said they would guard the ship against attack by other pirates. The USS *Carney* had been nowhere to be seen for the last day or two: Colin suspected it did not want to be party to a ransom handover. By 7pm, the *Svitzer Korsakov* was finally on the move again, the remaining pirates posted as look-outs on deck. Sure enough, when they reached Beyla, Captain Omar and his men headed ashore. Completing his captain's log that night, Colin found himself laughing at the final entry, a surreal finish to a strange journey: *'Pirates on piracy watch.'*

12: Christmas in the cave

OUR PHONE CALLS to Nick took place roughly once every five days and lasted about half an hour, depending on how often Ali's phone connection broke down. To keep our spirits up, Nick got our friends to compose brief messages for us, to be relayed from London to our mountain top, via Ali's sitting room. Rather like people entering competitions on cereal packets, they would spend hours coming up with pithy, inspirational slogans, only for the punchlines to be shredded into to patchy gibberish by the poor phone connection.

'Colin, your friend Mark asks, do you remember the time when you ******?' Nick would say. 'Anyway, he says that whatever you do, don't ******!'

The few that did pass through intelligibly, though, were good morale boosters. Jane got one through saying she was looking forward to taking me again to Planet Angel, a nightclub we'd had many happy times at together. José, true to his image as the cave lothario, got messages from no less than three different women claiming to be his girlfriend, in Ethiopia, Spain, and Australia respectively. It cheered him up no end, although some of the spicier messages were not the sort of thing that Nick felt particularly comfortable reading out. One message, from 'Maria' in Spain, instructed him to call José 'Marmalade', to praise his 'sexy voice', and to promise 'some very pleasurable physical activity' when he returned. Worried that Ali might disapprove – and perhaps also fearing that he'd sound like a telephone sex-chat line – Nick censored it. 'Maria says she is thinking about you a lot,' he told José.

I was dreading our first call from Tora Bora. Much as we were anxious to get back in touch with London, to tell them about the gunfight and the threats to sell me to the pirates in Eyl, I feared it would also be the moment when the Old Bastard started playing up again. This time he might inflict some proper damage. On about the third day in our new location, the Sherpa gave us the signal once again to follow him out the cave.

'Telefon. London. You'.

As we scrambled up a steep, perilous slope to a flat stretch of hillside, I was scared stiff. This could be it, our first taste of torture. Rather than hoping it didn't happen, I tried to pep-talk myself into coping with it.

Don't worry mate, it's all just part of the game, nothing personal. They won't kill you, just a few cuts and bruises. Brian Keenan had months of it, and he's all right now, isn't he?

Er, is he?

Come on, see it as a test of how much you can handle. What was it that Alan Johnston said on the radio? 'Whatever you do, try and act in a way that you will feel proud of afterwards.'

Can't we just admit that I don't want it to happen?

I flopped down beside Yusuf. The hillside beneath us stretched down into a picturesque flood plain, patches of beige scrub criss-crossed by dried-up river beds full of washed grey stones. I stared out like a landscape artist captivated by his subject, pretending not to see the Old Bastard, who was squatting like some malevolent coyote under a thorn tree in the near foreground. As Yusuf waited for Ali to call, he wandered up to listen in.

Nick came on the line. Previously, both José and I had been at pains to stress that we could hold on for a while longer if needs be. Now, though, I laid it on fairly thick. Much as we didn't want to cause too much worry, I didn't want them thinking they had all the time in the world. Then for the first time in three weeks, I heard good news.

'There are grounds for optimism that you might not have to be there much longer,' said Nick.

He wouldn't go into details, and stressed it was all proving 'incredibly complex'. But if things went according to plan, a man called 'Mr David' would hopefully be flying into Bossaso soon to pick us up. He was aiming to arrive within coming days, and with luck, we might even be out before Christmas. Nick then read me out a few messages from well-wishers, although once again their hard work was squandered. All I could think of was what he'd just said. *We might actually get freed!* The mere possibility of it, the warm glow it suddenly lit inside, made me realise just how much I'd abandoned hope.

Back at the cave, we had a celebratory cigarette each. Never before could anyone have felt so good smoking a Business Royal. I was even looking forward to dinner – which, judging by the smell from the cooking pot that Skullface was stirring, was a repeat of the Goat Surprise we'd had for breakfast, lunch and dinner the night before.

'This is good news, something is finally happening,' said José, as Skullface tossed the unwanted remains of the goat's hind quarters into the canyon below. It flew past our heads and landed with a crash in the bushes.

'Yes, thank God, we needed it.'

'Who do you think this Mr David guy is?'

'No idea. Didn't sound like Nick wanted to say. Someone from the British Foreign Office, perhaps? Or maybe from a private security company. I guess they need to make sure that if we are freed, there is someone who can make sure we get out okay and don't get just kidnapped again.'

'Anyway, maybe another five, ten days and we will be free. We can manage that okay, I think.'

That night we stayed up talking until late. Suddenly, we felt like we had a future again. I immediately announced plans to return to this cave in some future decade when Somalia was safe again, to do a TV documentary about my kidnapping. Perhaps I could locate Yusuf or Faisal, hopefully by then rather older, wiser and gentler, and interview them. There were lots of things I'd love to know. Why exactly had they'd kidnapped us? What impressions did they form of us? And what was that gunfight about?

There were also shorter term media engagements to think about. We'd probably be in the news when we got freed. We started a running joke about giving a post-release press conference, the tone of which suggested we were yet to acquire the dignified air normally expected of former hostages.

'I will say that it was fine, except for being stuck with some British asshole who was talking about Iraq all the time...'

'And I will say that you were scared and crying all the time, asking me to cuddle you.'

'And I will say that you offered the whole gang your sexual services, just to get extra cigarettes.'

'And I will say that you offered the same thing first, but they turned you down.'

By the end of the evening, a cave in the wilds of northern Somalia was once again full of schoolboy giggling. Staring out of the cave into the stars, I felt strangely alive, the mirror image of the near-death experience during the gunfight a few days before. For a brief while, it really did feel like it was just one big, weird adventure.

*****

Nick's phone call was a huge shot in the arm for cave morale. We then suffered severe withdrawal symptoms when the hope it brought promptly faded again.

'I'm afraid we're having some difficulties getting our man, Mr David, into the country to pick you up,' he said in a phone call three days later, on about December 17 or 18.

'How do you mean?' I asked, my heart sinking.

'I can't really go into details, but as I said before, it's proving extremely complicated. He's having difficulty getting a visa, for one thing. The authorities in Puntland are proving rather difficult to deal with. It's very frustrating – we'd been hoping to have you out by Christmas.'

'Any idea how much longer it will take?'

'Sorry, impossible to say.'

There being little else to discuss, Nick rang off, wishing us a Merry Christmas in case we didn't speak again until afterwards. I told him to ask Jane's parents to look after her on what I was sure would be a difficult day.

We wandered back to the cave, shoulders slumped like a pair of cons after a failed parole hearing. The fact that Mr David, whoever he was, couldn't even get a visa was surely not a good sign. It meant he either didn't have good local contacts, or worse still, someone within the government was actively getting in his way. I'd put myself under strict orders, when we'd had that first chink of light a few days before, to heed Nick's warning that there were many hurdles yet to go. But impatience was now knocking at my door, and it did not want to be kept waiting. Our next phone call would now not be until after Christmas. Not only did that mean several more days of infernal tedium, they were days in which something could go wrong. The people we'd fought the gunfight with might come back mob handed, for a start. The gang, I'd noticed, had remained jumpy ever since we'd relocated. Whenever they heard unfamiliar noises outside the cave, José and I were ushered back into its further recesses.

The following days dragged by at glacial speed. Little in them marked one from another. Even our captors seemed bored, spending much of their time stripping the two belt-fed machine guns into their component parts and then re-assembling them. It was a kind of military Rubik's Cube exercise, and could take nearly all afternoon, depending on how clueless the person doing it was. There were no longer any visitors, save for the odd flock of passing goats and a pack of baboons that we would hear barking from the other side of the valley, but never see. Sometimes I'd imagine a huge pack of them coming to our aid, overrunning the kidnappers and tearing the Old Bastard to pieces. Who, to be fair, was continuing to treat us well. One morning, he brought us a breakfast of fried goat's liver; on another, he even gave José a cigarette.

All the same, I still regarded him as a threat. Rather like the spiders lurking behind the funnel webs, just the knowledge that he was around made me slightly uneasy. I couldn't help looking up every now and then to check where he was. One day, after one of the minions gave him a haircut with a pair of hand-held clippers, I sneaked over and picked up a few tufts from the floor, hiding them in my wallet.

'If ever we get out here, and the Old Bastard gets arrested, I will give the police these hair samples so that they can do a DNA test,' I told José.

He laughed. 'You think the cops around here have DNA equipment?'

'No. But if these guys are ever put on trial for kidnapping us, the British police might offer to help prepare evidence.'

'You have been watching too many movies, my friend. These guys will never be caught, and even if they are, there will be no proper trial. They will either be sentenced straightaway, or let out after paying a bribe.'

There was no harm in trying, I said. Although thinking about it, I wasn't actually sure how I'd feel about giving evidence against them. For the crime of kidnapping, the penalty would no doubt be severe. Execution, quite possibly, or 20 years in the communal pen in Bossaso Central. How would it feel, to be standing up in court and putting them all away, watching young Faisal and Skullface stare back from the dock? After all, weren't juvenile delinquents like them just as much victims as José and I, doing what they had to do in a land where crime was one of the few activities that paid? You didn't have to be a *Guardian*-reading liberal like Jane to agree that the average Somali teenager had more excuses than most to drift into crime. On the other hand, with the government here so weak anyway, the short arm of the law had to make examples of the few crooks it got hold of. Having some Westerner pleading for clemency would send out precisely the wrong message, and ensure further guests in places like Tora Bora.

'What would you do?' I asked José. 'Personally, I think I would blame the senior guys like the Old Bastard, and ask for the likes of Faisal to be spared.'

'I used to think I'd want them all to be let off,' he said. 'But after all the time these fuckers have kept us in here, I have changed my mind.'

*****

Five more days went past with no phone call from Nick. The only good news was that the Old Bastard had left the cave the day before, sporting his sharp new haircut, and hadn't been seen since. As we lay in bad that evening, there came a sudden shout in the dark.

'Yella! Yella!'

It was the Sherpa, standing over us, shouting the Arabic for 'Let's go'. We were on the move again. Unlike the exodus from the previous cave, where all traces of our presence had been carefully tidied away, this time we were leaving in a hurry. Minutes later, we were scrambling along the slope out of the canyon, trying to not to drop either ourselves or our blanket bundles in the darkened abyss to one side. Could the other gang be on our tail? Or could this even be us getting released? After the torpor of the last five days, any activity was welcome.

We exited the canyon and headed out onto open ground, silent except for the sound of a dozen-odd pairs of trudging feet.

'Do you see that?' José whispered. 'A car.'

He pointed to two red pinpricks glowing in the distant gloom, perhaps a mile away or so. They looked like the brake lights of some kind of vehicle, but as suddenly as they had appeared, they vanished again.

'Are you sure that was a car?' I said, a few hundred yards later.

'Definitely.'

'Where's it gone then?

'Must have driven off.'

'No way, we'd have heard it. You can hear a pin drop round here.'

'I am telling you, it was a car. How much do you want to bet?'

'A pack of cigarettes. No, sorry, better make that one cigarette.'

'Done.'

The car did not materialise, but we did eventually hit a track, the first sign of civilisation we'd seen since the lorry journey on Day Three. The track then intersected with another, where the rest of the gang was waiting. Looking around, I now saw nearly every single face that had come and gone in the last three weeks. People greeted each other like it was some kind of reunion. Skullface 2 seemed genuinely pleased to see me. The only person absent was the Old Bastard. With any luck, this was all a move to cut to him out the deal.

Yusuf's number two, the Guy of the Cigarettes, now seemed to take charge. He divided the group into two, counting in Italian, and issued instructions in a low voice to each party. Something was obviously happening for which a co-ordinated, disciplined, full-strength turn-out was required. Could we really be getting released? The gang seemed upbeat and excited, and their mood was infectious. As we set off again, the walk along the track a pleasant stroll after all those days stumbling over rocks, I almost felt a sense of camaraderie, as if I was part of the team. All the players were here – Faisal, Skullfaces 1 and 2, The Trekker, the Hobbit, The Mirror Man, The Smoker and all the rest, these men and kids I'd come to know so well and yet so little, plus the dozen or come-and-go guards on the periphery, who never did anything so good, bad or interesting as to deserve a nickname.

We set off in single file, the Guy of the Cigarettes up front. The track wound on and on, meandering up and down through low-rise hills, the moon growing ever higher and brighter. Soon José's wager came good. In the distance, where the track headed over the brow of a hill, the beams of a pair of car headlamps shone up from the other side, like two suns rising from behind a mountain. From the top, we looked down to see not one car, but three. Behind the glare of their headlamps we could make out about a dozen people standing around, another group of shadowy travel companions ready to take us on to whatever the next stage was in this strange adventure.

'Shit, I think this might be it,' whispered José. *'This might actually be the handover'.*

The faces waiting to greet us loomed into view. I looked for some white ones among them, a sign they were from the other side. There was none. Still, perhaps we were heading back to Bossaso, or somewhere near, as a pre-cursor to being released. They bundled us into the rear seat of one of the SUVs and took off, about 15 people to a car, some crammed inside, the rest clinging to the bumper, the roof, the sideboards. Skullface's head appeared upside down through the rear passenger window, yacking away with Faisal over the roar of the engine.

We drove for about 40 minutes, slowing down at one point in a clearing where yet another large group of Somalis were waiting. The headlights briefly lit them up – there must have been at least another

25 of them, all heavily armed. Our convoy went straight past them, and who they were, we'd never know. But it set me thinking. How many other large gangs were there, I wondered, crawling around places like Somalia and other lawless parts of the world at night, trafficking hostages, refugees, drugs, weapons? It was the kind of thing you could spend a lifetime as a foreign correspondent and still never glimpse. The only other Westerners who got to see this kind of activity would be mercenaries, top-end international crooks and maybe the odd CIA ground agent.

To our disappointment, we pulled over again long before I saw anything that could be mistaken for the wink of Bossaso's lights. We headed off on foot with Yusuf, the Mirror Man and Skullface 2, bedding down on open ground next to a tree. I still felt optimistic. They wouldn't leave us with just these three guarding us, surely, if this was a permanent arrangement. They weren't even carrying their Kalashnikovs. Maybe they had an agreement that only a few of them would be involved in the final hand-over, unarmed. We lay on the mattress looking up at the stars. With no glare from street lights around to get in the way, we had what was probably one of the best views of the galaxy anywhere on the planet. Yet despite having spent much of the last month staring up at it, we still hadn't got very far in mapping out the constellations.

'You see that one, there?' I said. 'The one that has three stars in a row and then a kind of square shape at the end? That's the Plough.'

'No, it's not. It's the Cart.'

'The Cart? There is no such thing as the Cart.'

'Yes there is. We have it in Spain.

'But it doesn't look anything like a cart! Unless it's a cart with square wheels.'

'Well it doesn't look like a plough, either.'

'Yes it does. Well, a bit, anyway. But that's not the point. None of the stars look anything like the names they're given. The Bear doesn't look a bear, the Pan doesn't look like a pan, and so on. It's a like a crap game of join-the-dots.'

'I am telling you, its name in Spanish is the Cart.'

'It's not! And anyway, who cares what its name is in Spanish? The galaxy is British.'

'Okay, we shall make a bet on all these things, my friend. Whoever loses shall buy the other a dinner in a good restaurant when we are freed. Speaking of which, you owe me a cigarette now from that last bet. There was a car after all.'

'I will give you it when we are free.'

'I won't need it then, bastard! I will buy a whole pack for myself.'

'Maybe by tomorrow night you'll be able to. Sitting in a bar somewhere.'

It was not to be. Just as we'd climbed under our blankets, Yusuf roused us again and we headed off up a slope nearby, stopping at a yet another cave. This one was just a large piece of flat rock with a space under it, from which came a rich, earthy smell. I was about to spread our mattress out, when the Mirror Man grabbed my hand and shone his flashlight inside. What I had assumed was just nice, springy earth was in fact a thick, black carpet of goats' droppings, stretching in every direction.

'So much for ending up in a hotel tonight, now instead we are living in a goat's toilet,' José lamented.

As dawn broke and lit up the surroundings, it became clear we were just as much in the boondocks as ever. Mountains and hills stretched around as before. We moved twice the next day, making camp at what I figured was now our sixth – seventh? – cave. Now experts in such accommodation, we sized it up like a couple of estate agents. Again, it was up a narrow gulley that cut into a hillside, a recess with a small hollow that was guarded by large boulders and frankincense trees. It was smaller than most of our previous hang-outs, and the roof was a lot lower. To get inside involved crawling on hands and feet. It felt dank rather than dry, and as dusk fell there was the odd whine of a mosquito. Most depressing of all, though, was the sight at one side of the cave of several bulging white hessian sacks. Some were of rice, others – nearly as big – were of sugar for the teapot. They had re-supplied, a sign that they expected to be here a while.

*****

We settled reluctantly into our new abode, finding the least uncomfortable spot to lay the mat and locating a suitable patch of rocks to use as a toilet. It was December 23. We should also have been hunting for some kind of shrub to serve as a Christmas tree, on the not-very-Christian basis that the more we made a ritual of it, the better our chances of scrounging extra cigarettes. But neither of us felt in the mood. All thoughts of Christmas were dominated by what it would be like for our families, sat at home going through the motions of celebration, while trying to ignore the empty place at the table. I wondered if Jane and my family had bought me any presents. It must be a horrible choice to make. To buy something would invite worry about clinging to false hopes. Not to do so might seem a step towards giving up hope altogether. Dilemmas like that were probably cropping up for them every day, little emotional booby-traps stitched into the gaps where my life had been ripped out of theirs.

Christmas morning arrived. José and I briefly grunted the compliments of the season to each other, and failed to follow up with a joke. I had no idea whether the gang knew what people normally did on Christmas Day, but looking at us, they would have assumed it was a pretty austere affair, characterised by long, contemplative spells of silence. It made their modest Eid celebration look like the Rio Carnival. Nor was it a time of plenty. We'd smoked our last Business Royal on the way over from Tora Bora, in anticipation of getting released, and since then, the Guy of the Cigarettes had not been around to act as Santa.

To add to the gloom, the weather – until now almost constantly sunny – turned cloudy and drizzly. Even the BBC World Service had an off day. I tried to get the Queen's Speech, but found no signal at all. It reminded me of one Christmas in my distant childhood, when I'd been sent to my room for misbehaving, the injustice of it made all the more greater because it was supposed to be the happiest day of the year. As we went to bed, I joked weakly to José that I would have given him a Christmas stocking, were it not for the fact my socks stank. Then I tried the radio again, finally picking up a strange, high-pitched rendition of *O Come All Ye Faithful*, sung by an Indian choir broadcasting from Delhi. Never before had I felt more cut off from the world.

13: Mission Impossible

ON HER MOBILE phone, Jane had saved a photo she'd taken of us sitting up in bed one morning. It showed us with our heads together on the pillow, grinning like a pair of teenagers in a photo booth. I called it our 'Beauty and the Beast' shot. She looked sweet, while I seemed to wear the slightly smug expression of a man who thought he'd snared a mate considerably more attractive than he. Jane, bless her, thought I looked rather handsome in it, but as I've said before, our opinions differed on most things. This, at least, was one point where I chose not to lecture her on how wrong she was.

In the weeks since I'd vanished, that photo had become the focus of a ritual that she would go through as she went to bed. She'd put out the lights, switch on the phone and stare at our faces on the screen in the dark, reminding herself of happier times. At first, it helped, as something to look forward to before the long, sleepless night that usually lay ahead. But as the weeks passed, the face that smiled back seemed to become less that of me, more that of some stranger. In a 'kidnap diary' she'd started keeping, she noted the change. 'I feel like I'm losing my grip on who you are,' she wrote. 'I've worn out the photos I have of you by looking at them too much, so now they don't look like anything.'

Whether I'd come back alive or not wasn't the only question on her mind. The *Telegraph* crisis team had done their best to reassure her that my release was only a question of when, not if. What they couldn't tell her was whether I'd still want to be with her. Yes, the team had passed her messages from me saying that I loved her. But was she to take them at face value, or were they just to keep her morale up? All kinds of things might be going through my head as I sat in that cave, she figured, to make me change my mind about her yet again. And if I had done, I was hardly going to send her a break-up message via Nick and Ali.

Jane had started the diary on the suggestion of a psychologist from Hostage UK, a charity set up by Terry Waite, the former Beirut hostage. It didn't get involved in individual cases, but it could offer independent advice to families so that they weren't dependent for information purely on the Foreign Office or an employer. While Jane felt reasonably certain that the *Telegraph* had my best interests at heart, it was good to have a second opinion. The diary was a way of dealing with things a day at a time, and allowing the worst days to have the page turned on them. No day had been easy. Nearly every entry talked of anxiety attacks that welled up from nowhere, panic attacks, and exhaustion due to inability to sleep. The first five days, before the proof of life call, had been the worst. At the back of her mind, Jane had been convinced I was already dead. 'My greatest fear was that you'd simply disappeared,' she noted in the diary. 'That perhaps someone had tried to take you, and something had gone wrong, and that we'd just never hear from you again.'

The news that I was alive had come to her in one of the daily phone calls she now received from Nick, who was in charge of liaising with both her and my family. Every day, usually around late afternoon, he would ring to give them an update, even if it was just to say that nothing had happened. Jane's hands would tremble whenever his number flashed up on her phone, especially if he rang outside the normal time, which would make her fear something had gone wrong. His calls were long on reassurance, short on facts. On the advice of Mark, the security expert, Nick could disclose only basic information: that I was passing the time by playing chess, was a little bored, but was getting on well with José. The intimidation from the Old Bastard, the gun battle, the threats to sell us to the pirates in Eyl – all were kept quiet.

Keeping next-of-kin in the dark is standard policy among professional hostage negotiators. It reduces the risk of sensitive details being leaked by family members, and stops them going mad with worry when things don't go to plan, as they frequently don't. More importantly, it relieves them of any role in operational decisions. Calling a kidnapper's bluff, as is occasionally required, is far harder if it is your own loved one that has the gun pointed at them. The down side of the policy, from a family's perspective anyway, is that it prevents much scrutiny of the negotiating team's performance. If they are trying the wrong tactics, or just not trying very much at all, the next-of-kin is none the wiser. Try as they might, neither Jane nor my family could quite banish that thought from their minds. It wasn't that they didn't trust Nick or Mark. It was more that they simply didn't know what to make of the whole thing. They'd been flung into an unfamiliar world, one they knew from spy novels, not real life. There was always that nagging feeling that I'd been secretly written off all along, hung out to dry as part of some shadowy deal they'd never learn of, that maybe not even the *Telegraph* knew about.

*****

For those who knew no better, Room N-17 of the *Telegraph* building at Victoria looked like it might be the nerve centre for some particularly sensitive news investigation. Set back from the rest of the vast open-plan news floor, it was one of a row of offices used for meetings and presentations. N-17, though, was the only one fitted with a door entry pad and keycode. It was where the *Telegraph* crisis team worked from every day, and in an office full of people who were paid to be nosey, information was kept on a strictly need-to-know basis. Led by Adrian Michaels, the foreign-editor-in-chief, the team was advised by Mark, the security expert, and also included David Wastell, the *Sunday Telegraph's* foreign editor, and Nick. They'd been relieved of all other duties, leaving the rest of the newspapers' foreign desk to cope on a skeleton staff. Newspaper journalists like to pride themselves on being able to cope with stress, but this was in a different league. While Mark, the security expert, could afford to see me as just another case, to them I was also a colleague – an annoying one at times, yes, who argued a lot and who seldom got the teas in, but whose fate they still felt a personal stake in. As a result, every minute of every hour felt important, every decision potentially crucial. And unlike their more regular work for the *Sunday Telegraph*, with this particular project there was no chance to start all over again after a bad week.

The first days and weeks had been an abrupt crash course in Somalia and its political players. Mark, the security expert, had worked on several piracy cases in Somalia, but a kidnapping on land was a different matter. Piracy cases were a relatively straightforward dialogue between a boat owner and kidnappers: any negotiations were mostly just financial, and could be conducted out at sea, via a ship's satellite phone, without interference from Somalis on the mainland. Kidnapping cases on land were much more complicated. Politicians, religious leaders, clan chiefs and others might all want to stick their oar in – some helpfully, some not. The team tried to build up as accurate a picture of life in Puntland as possible, although reliable information was hard to come by. Everyone they spoke to – be it fellow journalists, Somali businessmen, politicians or academics – all seemed to say different things. People recommended as potential allies by one source would be named as villains by others, and vice versa. As news of the kidnapping spread on the Somali grapevine, the team were also approached by a number of dubious 'middlemen', whose offers to act as go-betweens to the kidnappers invariably involved 'introduction fees' of several thousand dollars.

All of which meant that for every occasional day of progress, there were normally five days of hitches, delays and setbacks. To keep things focused, the team stuck to the same routine every day. The recorded transcripts of every phone call to Ali were written up and analysed. An update on all proceedings, and any decisions taken, were circulated twice daily to the paper's senior management. The company's insurers, legal and personnel people were kept in the loop. And a PR strategy was put into place, both to maintain the news black-out and respond to any unexpected turns of events. Outside media interest remained intense, especially in Spain, where many newspapers and TV stations took a great deal more persuasion to heed the black-out request. Fiona Macdonald, the *Telegraph*'s PR chief, fielded calls day and night on her mobile, and spent much time ringing foreign editors to ask for their continued co-operation. She also had to craft, in advance, a series of official 'response lines' to various scenarios, including what would happen if José and I did not come back. In one grim moment, the crisis team also discussed what would happen if called to give evidence at an inquest.

The prospect of it ending in tragedy weighed most heavily on David. As my direct line manager, it was he who had made the fateful suggestion that I went to Somalia in the first place. Like most sensible foreign editors, David never pressurised his correspondents into going anywhere dangerous against their will. The rule was that final decision on whether a risk was acceptable or not was always a call for the person who was actually going to be taking it. I could easily have told him that the pirate story in Somalia had looked a bit too dicey, thanks, without fearing the slightest repercussions. But that same sense of caution that made him a responsible foreign editor prevented him absolving himself entirely. Should he really have asked me to go there in the first place? Should he have insisted that I take longer to check it out first? If I didn't come back alive, he'd be one of the main witnesses at any inquest, possibly facing hostile questioning from a barrister representing my family. They'd been fine until now, but their attitude might well change if things went wrong. The foreign desk's every action would be picked over with the benefit of hindsight, with the kind of attention to detail that no one could afford when working to newspaper deadlines.

Yet as time went on, a sense of team spirit gradually took hold in the incident room. No longer did they feel like amateurs in a cloak-and-dagger world, as they had in the early days, when they'd turn up for work and realise they'd forgotten the code for the door entry pad. Soon they had built up a detailed intelligence dossier on Puntland and its key players, illustrated by photos that adorned the wall like suspects in a murder inquiry. Linked by clan and affiliation, it was a gallery of ministers, police chiefs, warlords and middlemen, showing who might be involved, who might be helpful, and who might be somewhere in between. Neither Nick, Adrian nor David had ever done anything like it before, and while there were often setbacks, arguments, and times of utter despair, they also found it exhilarating. For inspiration, they took to starting each day by playing the theme tune to *Mission Impossible*, the TV drama about a team of elite secret agents who tackled international criminal masterminds. Not that Ali and the gang seemed quite of that calibre. Nick found that during the afternoons, Ali was often so stoned on qhat that it was impossible to get any sense out of him. On one occasion, after some sort of falling out between himself and the kidnappers, he'd also confided to Nick that some of the gang were 'stupid jungle bunny people'. At such moments, the *Mission Impossible* theme music seemed entirely appropriate.

*****

For all the team's efforts, though, not everyone was convinced that the *Telegraph* was doing all it could. Instead, as news of the kidnap went around the journalist grapevine, rumours spread to exactly the opposite effect: that the paper had secretly washed its hands of us, and was leaving José and me to rot in the cave. Jane learned of the *Telegraph's* alleged skullduggery through an email from a friend alerting her to a Facebook page. It was called 'Free Colin Freeman', and already acquired several hundred members.

'Colin has been kidnapped in Somalia along with photo journalist José Cendon,' it read. 'Like many before them, they are striving to tell the world of events happening in our global community. Let's join together to offer support to their family and friends, and appeal to the captors to return them to freedom.'

She read it with alarm. The site seemed well-intentioned, but clearly ran contrary to the *Telegraph's* theory that, by raising our profile, José and I would appear more valuable to the kidnappers. A few of the blog postings linked to the page also seemed motivated as much by a suspicion of the paper as any desire to see 'The *Telegraph* Two' freed. One blogger was particularly critical.

'The *Telegraph* has remained oddly in the shadows about kidnapped reporter Colin Freeman,' he or she wrote. 'Where are the *Telegraph* headlines? The daily pleas for his release? I'm still looking. If anyone can tell me the *Telegraph* is actively working for Freeman's release, I will gladly post the welcome news.'

The bloggers – none of whom, as far as anyone could tell, actually knew me – were particularly suspicious about the fact that all my articles had been removed from the *Telegraph* website. The crisis team had done this because they feared that something I had written over the years might inadvertently offend the gang – which, given the way they'd claimed to take offence about José's photographs from the Congo, was not an unreasonable concern. But certain internet scribes took it a sign that the paper was pretending I'd never worked for them.

Adrian had emailed the Facebook site, pointing out the risks of publicity and asking them to observe the news blackout. Other newspapers and TV stations had all co-operated, knowing that one day they might have to ask such a favour for one of their own staff. The web, however, was different. Many bloggers have a near-evangelical pride in the internet as the world's last great unpoliced frontier, free from all censorship. Adrian's request simply reinforced their impression of a cover-up.

'I don't think the *Telegraph* has Colin's interests at heart,' remarked one. 'They seem to think that Somali gangsters chewing qhat in the mountains are able to peruse the internet looking for stories on Colin... I suggest ignoring the *Telegraph's* moral blackmail – possibly motivated by its own desire to avoid bad publicity – and its pathetic attempts at censorship, and publicly campaign for his release.'

Some entries on Facebook page came to Adrian's defence, pointing out that the *Telegraph*, which regularly sent correspondents to dangerous places, might be best placed to judge whether a news black-out was appropriate. They also noted that while the 'blackout or not?' issue might be an interesting intellectual debate, it might be better discussed once the kidnap was over, when the rights and wrongs of any media strategy could be viewed in light of whether we were alive or not.

To their credit, most of the Facebook contributors took that point on board, and the posts eventually ceased. Yet for Jane and my family, the web campaign had already tapped into a growing sense of worry. They, more than anyone else, were having to take the *Telegraph* in good faith. Reading the blogs and Facebook entries, they couldn't help feeling a nasty frisson of doubt. What if the bloggers were right? In the absence of much solid information about what was actually going on behind the scenes, they had no way of judging. It was now four weeks into the kidnap, and there was still no sign of José or me being freed. Did the *Telegraph* really know best?

It was my younger brother, Richard, who asked that question most. To the surprise of the rest of my family, he'd been the one who'd taken the news of my disappearance hardest. My junior by eight years, we'd led pretty much separate lives as kids and barely saw each other in the years after I'd left home. It was only in the last decade that we'd started to become friends and really got to know each other, and this was perhaps what had made the prospect of losing me yet again all the harder. While I was sat in the cave worrying about my parents having heart attacks, it was Richard who'd been the most stressed. At one point, he even volunteered to go to Somalia to campaign on my behalf, an offer that caused alarm among the crisis team. One hostage in the Freeman family was enough, they warned.

What they didn't mention was that they had already sent someone to do just that, with disastrous results. In early December, they had engaged the assistance of an American security expert based in Kenya. This was the mysterious 'Mr David', the man who'd tried and so far failed to get a visa for Puntland. Ahead of his trip, Mr David had sent a Somali fixer to Bossaso to do some discreet inquiries as to who was holding me and why. The fixer, a young man from Mogadishu, had been in town only a couple of days when he was arrested by the security minister, Samatar. Hearing that there was a stranger wandering around asking questions about José and me, they'd accused him of being involved in the kidnap itself in some way. After five days of fraught negotiations, Mr David had finally sprung him from jail. This was what Nick had euphemistically described to José and me as 'difficulties with the Puntland authorities'. Privately, the crisis team suspected that the Puntland government knew all along what Mr David's fixer was doing, but that elements within its ranks did not want us released, or not yet anyway. Exactly who and why, nobody knew, but it would also explain why Mr David was having such trouble getting a visa.

It was a complex, gloomy picture. Yet as Christmas went and New Year beckoned, the crisis team prepared themselves for the fact that they would eventually have to let my family in on it. Sooner or later, they feared my parents' sense of patience would soon wear as thin as my brother's. Plans were laid to give them a fuller briefing on what steps had been taken so far, and why things were not going as quickly as might have been hoped. If nothing else, it would show they had been trying.

14: Betrayal

LEFT TO ITS OWN devices for so much of the day, my mind tended to disappoint me. I'd hoped that one of the few benefits of prolonged incarceration might be the chance to really think about the world and my place within it, to dwell on those knotty subjects that normal life never left time for. Instead, the questions my brain chose to wrestle with would not even have qualified for a pub quiz.

1. Name, in chronological order, and by colour and make, all the cars your father drove between 1975 and 1988.

2. Can you remember the name of your English teacher in Third Year at secondary school?

3. Name, from north to south, all the pubs on Lothian Road in Edinburgh.

This was one of the tougher exams, as well. As time wore on, my brain would devote time to questions such as: *'Rank, in order of attractiveness, every woman in the Telegraph newsroom'*, and *'Heineken is a better beer than Stella. Discuss.'* Yet increasingly, anything more complex felt too much like hard work. I could waste anything up to an hour retracing some pub crawl through Edinburgh, or remembering every single person in my old journalism class from 1993. It wasn't exactly a ringing endorsement of a university education, nor did it suggest that any of the books that lined my shelves at home had had any impact whatsoever. But it was still mental exercise of a sort – even if, intellectually speaking, it was roughly equivalent to counting sheep.

In my more cerebral moments, one book that did come back to me time and again was Gerald Hanley's *Warriors – Life and Death among the Somali people*. It was one of just a handful of books written by outsiders about Somalia, and had spent many years out of print, but was now considered a travel literature classic, up there with Wilfred Thesiger's account of the Marsh Arabs of southern Iraq. Hanley served here as an Army officer during World War II, when the British had taken over the running of neighbouring Italian Somaliland. *Warriors* was his account of his time stationed in isolated military outposts, where foreign peacekeepers once again had the thankless task of stopping bloodshed between Somalia's warring clans. While most of his fellow officers detested it here, Hanley was seduced by the sheer harshness of the country's territory and the fierceness of its people, describing his unlikely romance in elegant, haunting prose. On the back of my own copy, dog-eared from reading and re-reading, was a testimony from Ernest Hemingway.

The Somalia that Hanley came to love so much sounded very different from the one we were marooned in. Mogadishu he knew as a city of fleshpots and Italian restaurants, a place to enjoy a cold ale at the officers' club after long stints up country. Eyl he loved for its springs of good drinking water, free of the gypsum crystals that gave soldiers the dreaded 'desert clap'. Most of his book's action, though, took place in what British soldiers nicknamed the Shag – the vast, empty Somali interior, where officers like Hanley were often stationed alone for months on end. British servicemen doubtless endured tougher postings in the war years, but in terms of isolation from the rest of the world, and lack of creature comforts, the Shag took some beating. With only Somali conscripts for company, and little to do all day except get in the way of inter-tribal slaughter, nearly every officer feared for his sanity after a while. Hanley, an aspiring author, saw into his own deteriorating state of mind, wrote about it, and produced a masterpiece. Many of his comrades had no such coping mechanisms. During his time out there, no less than seven committed suicide, draining the last of their precious booze rations on some despairing night and blowing their brains out with their service revolvers. At least 15 more went mad, as traumatised as victims of shellshock. As Hanley remarked: 'It is almost impossible to describe the malaise, the very special weariness of spirit which isolation among fierce tribesmen brings.'

Could José and I end up going mad out here in the Shag ourselves? To be fair, we were here together, not alone, and we'd only done a month so far, which was nothing like the time that Hanley did during each Shag-stint. But as each day passed, we talked to each other less and less, to the point where whole mornings and afternoons would pass in silence, the two of us lost in what was left of our own thoughts.

During those times, unable to think of anything to say to each other, we were already in solitary of a kind, or so it felt. We had no fixed return date for heading back to civilisation, and no distractions whatsoever: no work to do, no games except chess, and no reading matter of any kind. Hanley too had suffered shortages of books – at one point he was reduced to a copy of an ancient Victorian tome called *Engineering problems in Paraguay*, which he found too boring to read even in his dire situation. Personally, I think I would have given it a go. It would have had words, diagrams, maybe even pictures – most likely rather dull, but still capable of transporting me to another world that was not Somalia. My fear was that, as the weeks and months continued, I would simply run out of things to think about, that a time would come when even the thoughts of bygone pub crawls, favourite beers and childhood stories would run dry, when memory lane would simply come to an end. The mind was not the place of limitless sanctuary I had imagined it would be.

Not knowing when it would all end was the hardest thing. It made it impossible to pace oneself, to know whether the marathon was nearly over, or whether there were many more days yet to go. The next phone call we had, on Boxing Day, was typical. Nick told us that Mr David, our mystery saviour, was now hoping to get his visa soon, but there was still no real idea of when it would happen, or even if. As we staggered back to the cave that afternoon, my mind felt as ragged and threadbare as my clothes. Eating yet another unappetizing goat risotto that evening, I wiped my metal spoon clean and glanced at the greasy reflection within it. Staring back at me was a dirty, tousle-haired figure, with a scraggly Ben Gunn beard and a haggard expression. It was the sort of look, I imagined, that Hanley's fellow officers took on before they killed themselves.

It seemed unconceivable that having nothing to do could be so punishing: Dante had surely missed a trick by not including 'Boredom' as one of his nine circles of hell, a place where sinners simply sat around idle for the rest of eternity. There was something uniquely life-sapping about a routine where you woke up and then spent the rest of the day doing nothing, moving only for ablutions. It was pointless, which made the effort required to get through each day seem all the greater. During mid-afternoon, when each day was drawing to a close, José and I would still usually make a point of talking. If we stuck at it long enough, we might find a topic of conversation that might kill half an hour, and might even make us laugh. Increasingly, though, it felt like more effort than it was worth. If I ever got out, I figured I could solve Britain's prison overcrowding crisis overnight. Remove all books, TVs and newspapers from convicts' cells, end association time and visiting hours, and you could cut most sentences to a fraction of what they were. Six weeks would seem like six months, six months like six years, and so on. Judge Freeman also knew, though, why such simple-sounding solutions were no longer used in the civilised world. Mankind is a social animal, and even the most anti-social man is still socially created, his own identity shaped by the people around him. Put anyone in solitary for more than a few months and they begin to lose their sense of who they are, and with it the moorings that keep them sane.

Occasionally, as discussions between Nick and the gang seemed to drag on without conclusion, José and I wondered whether other options were being considered. Could the British government be considering some plan to send in a special forces unit to free us? I knew they'd tried it in a few cases in Iraq, although mostly for kidnaps involving terrorist gangs. I had no idea whether José and I would be considered sufficiently important to rescue, much less whether they had some kind of satellite imagery that could pinpoint where we were. But either way, I couldn't see how an assault team could get anywhere near the cave without giving themselves away. The gang had lookouts all over the mountains, and on the rare occasions when we heard a plane somewhere near, they would scan the sky suspiciously. Pulling it off, as far as I could see, would require a plan of the sort normally only found in Andy McNab novels. The rescuers would have to parachute down far from earshot, hike through the mountains disguised as goatherds or suchlike, 'slot' each of the kidnappers on guard duty, to borrow McNab's vernacular, and then creep up on the cave while the rest were asleep. It was hard to see the British government authorizing that just to rescue a pair of hacks like us. And besides, much as I was sure the SAS might relish such a challenge, I didn't actually like the idea of anybody being killed to save our sorry skins. When pondered for real, the mere thought that somebody might die because of my decision to come to Somalia – even if it was the Old Bastard – would be a hard one to live with.

Our only other chance was to hatch another escape plan. I'd personally long given up on that idea, but José hadn't. While I'd been busy trying to remember who'd taught me maths in 1985, he'd killed much of his time thinking about different ways to abscond, like Steve McQueen during his stints in the 'Cooler' in *The Great Escape*. About a mile from our new cave there was a track running through a valley, and a few times a day we would hear a car going down it. For José, it was a tantalising sound.

'If we could get down there, we could hide up and wait for a car to come along, or follow the road down until we find someone,' he'd say. 'Then we just need to ask to borrow their mobile phone, or take us to someone who has one, and we can call for help.'

'Yeah, but it's a big gamble. And anyway, how do we get out of here in the first place?'

'You see how these assholes are getting lazy. Sometimes only one or two guard us in the afternoons now. They even leave their guns lying around. I keep thinking that if we could grab one, we might be in with a chance…'

'Do you know how to fire a gun?'

'No, that is the other problem. But you tried one once, didn't you? Can you remember how?'

I doubted it. It was true that I'd once fired a Kalashnikov. It was one of the few stories from Baghdad in which José had shown any interest. My driver, who'd served as a weapons instructor in Saddam's army, kept several AK47s hidden under his bed for 'self-defense' purposes. Set on fully-automatic, it had taken just a couple of seconds to empty an entire 30 round magazine. But there was a difference firing one into the sky and firing one into a person. Besides which, while the Kalashnikov was supposed to be the world's simplest-to-operate machine gun, with just 17 moving parts, I couldn't remember how you either loaded it or took the safety catch off – fairly crucial parts of the jigsaw. And even if I could, it would have been a major gamble. Nick and everyone else in London would be horrified if they got a phone call from Ali saying we'd vanished. They'd assume the gang had killed us.

In a way, it was just as well that the odds were so obviously stacked against us. José, being a little less placid than I, might well have been tempted by any half-reasonable chance, which could have led to tensions between us had he chosen to take it. If he'd threatened to go it alone, I'd have had to argue that it would put me at risk of reprisals from the gang. Especially since sometime on the afternoon of December 28th, we saw a familiar-looking figure in an orange Golf Sports teeshirt wandering into the cave.

'Hey, look,' said José. 'It's your friend again. The Old Bastard.'

He swaggered in, uncocked his rifle, and fell straight back into his role as camp sergeant, poking the fire, stirring the goat stew and generally setting the cave to rights. There was also a lengthy eyeball in our direction. Just like the old days. Watching him, I felt a sharp stab of fear. His return, after a week of blissful absence, made me realise just how frightened I was of him. I also felt humiliation. It would have been one thing to have been petrified of some big thug of a bloke, of which there were a few around the camp. The Old Bastard, however, looked just like a little old man, not the sort of person that any self-respecting adult should have swaggering through his nightmares.

'I hoped I'd never see that guy again,' I said.

'Ah, don't worry. I think maybe it's a good sign. Perhaps he is back because he knows we are about to get released.'

'Where do you think he's been?'

'Maybe he's been off making all the arrangements. Or you never know, maybe he's been off seeing his wife.'

'You think there is a Mrs Old Bastard?'

*****

It seemed the Old Bastard had indeed turned up for something special. On December 30, there was another phone call from Nick.

'Hello Colin, has Ali told you anything?' he asked me.

'Eh?'

'I'm pleased to say that arrangements have been made for you and José to be released.'

'Yeah? Great! That's brilliant news. Fantastic.'

'Have they not said anything to you about it already?'

'Er, no...'

'Are you sure?'

'Yes. Nothing at all.'

'Oh... okay. That's a bit odd. Well, anyway, it will probably take place sometime in the next couple of days. I can't go into too much detail right now, but it has all been arranged. You will be taken to some other location, maybe by car, and then handed over to some Somali intermediaries. Then you will be taken back to the International Village Hotel in Bossaso. At the handover, you may meet a Somali who you already know. As ever, it has been extremely difficult getting all this sorted out, but we hope this time there should be no problems.'

'Er, right. Got you. Terrific.'

Back at the cave, José and I tried not to get too excited. It wasn't that hard. It did seem odd that nobody at our end had mentioned anything about it. If our release was imminent, I'd have expected a few farewells from the gang; the odd offer, perhaps, from the likes of the Mirror Man and Faisal to exchange email addresses, or to look his sister up at her college in *Leeva-pool*. Yet they were all behaving pretty much as normal, apart from the Old Bastard, who'd disappeared off again.

Sure enough, the next two days came and went with no sign of movement. There were no further phone calls either, nor was anyone packing up the camp. Instead, sometime in the early afternoon on New Year's Day, we heard the sound of new arrivals. Looking out, we saw the Old Bastard again, frog-marching another prisoner to cave. As he steered the newcomer towards our corner, poking his

Kalashnikov in his back and snarling at him, I suddenly recognised a face that I hadn't thought about for a long time.

It was Ahmed.

*****

He came towards us, crouching down to get under the low cave ceiling. After the misery of the last few weeks, including our stint working together, he was another person I'd hoped never to lay eyes on him again. Especially not in these circumstances. I stared at him, struggling to work out why he was here. For a moment, I thought of what Nick had said on the phone a couple of days before? *'At the handover, you may meet a Somali who you already know.'* Was this it? Was he here because we were about to be freed?

It didn't seem like it. The Old Bastard stood over him, jabbering away in a threatening manner. He'd covered his head with a chequered Arab keffiyah scarf that left only a slit for his eyes, which somehow looked even more vicious when minus the rest of his face. Ahmed knelt down, drawing frantically on a cigarette.

'Ahmed,' I said. 'What happened to you?'

'I h-have been a p-prisoner, j-just like you,' he said. His stutter was on fully automatic, just like it had been when we'd chewed qhat together that Saturday night. 'I t-tried to run away, but they t-took me in a different car.'

I listened to him aghast, feeling a rush of guilt unlike anything that had hit me so far. So Ahmed and Mustapha had had nothing to do with it after all. And we'd now got them into big trouble. Serious, serious trouble.

'So w-what happened to you and José?' Ahmed asked. 'Are you both okay? D-did they hurt you in any way?'

'We are fine, Ahmed,' I said. 'They have not been too bad to us. Do you know who these people are? Why have they kidnapped us?'

'Understand one thing, I do n-not know who they are. They are some kind of m-militia, just living around in these m-mountains. I heard of these kind of groups before, but I never s-saw them.'

'Where have they been holding you?'

'In a cave near to here. Mustapha is a prisoner also.'

'Where is he now?'

'In another cave, not the same as me. He is injured.'

'How?'

'There was a fight between two groups of militia. But I think he is okay.'

To my shame, I realised that I'd been so wrapped up with my own problems that I'd never really wondered what had happened to Ahmed and Mustapha. What fate would they face now? The harsh reality of kidnaps in countries like this, I suspected, was that not all hostages were born equal. José and I, as Westerners, would be seen as the important assets, the ones who were worth more alive than dead. The British and Spanish governments would probably focus their limited resources on finding us, and us only. Any locals unfortunate enough to be scooped up alongside us might well be deemed expendable. I could think of numerous kidnaps where journalists' fixers, drivers and translators had ended up dead by some roadside, or simply never heard of again. Ahmed and Mustapha would have to hope someone in Puntland cared enough to lobby for them, which probably wasn't very likely. True, nobody had forced them to come and work with us. But they were just ordinary Somalis, trying to earn a living, and perhaps unaware of the temptations that two visiting foreigners might present to their fellow countrymen. It could be argued that it was as much our fault as theirs. If they died, I'd have it on my conscience for the rest of my life.

'Ahmed, what have they brought you over here for?' I asked.

'You know this man called Ali, who is your interpreter when you m-make phone calls? The gang have replaced him with m-me,' he said.

'Why. What is wrong with Ali?'

Ahmed pointed at Yusuf. 'You see that man there, Yusuf? He is the friend of Ali, the interpreter. There is an argument b-between them and the rest of the m-militia. The militia are unhappy. They have spent all this time in the cave, but your friend Nick, he has not offered anything. The m-militia say that Yusuf should no longer be the l-leader and Ali should no longer be the interpreter. That is why I am here now as interpreter.'

'Er... right. And so what do they want you to tell us?'

'They say that the plan to let you go is cancelled.'

'What? Why?'

'I do not know. I am only interpreter.'

'But why? Why?'

'They will not tell me this. But understand this one th-thing. There is some kind of p-problem between them, you can see for yourself.'

I looked over at Yusuf. He was stood on the far side of the cave, seemingly taking no interest in the proceedings. If there'd really been a coup against him, it was a very gentlemanly one by Somali standards. I'd have expected him to be executed on the spot, or at least banished from the cave at gunpoint. But if it was true, it was a disaster. So much for clan solidarity. A split in the gang could leave us stuck here forever.

The Old Bastard jabbed Ahmed with his gun butt and snarled something.

'What is happening now, Ahmed? Can you translate?'

'This man, Miro, he is the new leader,' Ahmed said.

Oh, great.

'He wants you to call to London, to tell them not to listen to Ali any more, and that they will not be letting you go.'

We gathered our shoes and set off up the hill to find a place to call.

'That fucking lying bastard.'

It was José, whispering in my ear. Ahmed was up ahead, out of earshot.

'Eh?'

'Ahmed.'

'What do you mean?'

'Did you not see his clothes? His shirt is clean white, and his trouser still have creases in. He has not been in a cave, like us, no way. He has even had a shave. He is fucking involved in this, I tell you.'

'Do you think so?'

'Of course, man! This is a fucking set-up!'

I hadn't even looked at what Ahmed was wearing, nor had it occurred to me to take what he said at anything other than face value. So much for my skills of journalistic inquiry. Now, thinking about it, I realised José had a point. Unless Ahmed's cave had an en suite wardrobe and bathroom, he was remarkably well-groomed for someone who had been sleeping rough for five weeks. His face and hair looked clean. His goatee was as short and neatly-trimmed as it had been when we'd first shook hands at the airport. José and I, by contrast, looked like a pair of street bums.

Come to think of it, other strands of his story didn't add up either. Why would the gang be holding him and Mustapha in separate caves from us, given all the extra manpower it would involve? And why, more importantly, hadn't he asked, among his first questions, whether anything was being done to get him out? He didn't actually seem that frightened. If I'd been him, I'd have been a complete gibbering wreck after so long on my own. Then again, was I jumping to conclusions because it meant I could blame Ahmed, rather than myself, for all this mess? The idea of him getting us into the shit, I could live with. The other way around was less easy.

Either way, what little hope there had been in our world was now vanishing. Someone handed me a mobile and told me to call Nick direct, flicking the handset on speakerphone so that Ahmed could hear as well. There was no calling any middleman first, to decoy the signal. That was a bad sign in itself. It suggested they were getting careless, and if they got careless, they might get dangerous.

Nick's voice answered. He sounded surprised to hear me.

'Hello Colin, is that you? Is everything alright?'

'Er, no, not really. There has been some kind of disagreement with the gang. They say the agreement to release us is finished.'

'What? What do you mean?'

I launched into a convoluted explanation about Ahmed's arrival, the squabble with Yusuf, the sacking of Ali, and the apparent coup by the Old Bastard, while also trying to insinuate José's theory that

Ahmed was lying his head off. I hoped Nick, or whoever was there with him, was taking notes. In my rattled state, I explained it in a rambling way that would probably only have been properly understood with an accompanying flow chart. Once again, whatever journalistic skills I had were letting me down. How many times had I filed, to deadline over the phone, stories explaining, in easy-to-understand terms, some complex coup or palace intrigue in some far-off foreign land? Now, when it mattered most, I was spouting gobbledygook.

Nick seemed to get the main point, though. For the first time, he actually sounded angry, his voice booming out the phone speaker for all to hear.

'So we don't have an agreement any more? Well that's a big problem, *a really big problem*. What the fuck are they playing at? Where is Ali?'

'Er, like I said, Nick, they are not using Ali anymore, they don't trust him. Ahmed wants to speak to you in fact, here he is.'

I handed over the phone.

'Hello, this is M-Ahmed. I am the new translator for this m-militia. Understand one thing, I...'

'Sorry, who is this?'

'This is Ahmed...'

'Who are you? Where is Ali?'

'What do you mean, who am I? I am M-Ahmed! I was translating for these g-guys! I am also in the custody of this m-militia! I have been here for four weeks! It is the fault of your j-journalists that I am kidnapped!'

'Well, I am sorry, but I don't really know who you are, Ahmed. Ali is the person we have been talking to, and his friend Yusuf. We cannot just start talking to new people. This will mess everything up. Our representative, Mr David, is due to arrive in Bossaso tomorrow. He is supposed to be coming to collect Colin and José. This has all been agreed!'

Nick was clearly calling Ahmed's bluff. Maybe whoever was advising him suspected that this whole 'split in the gang' business was just a ruse to pile on pressure, just like the threats to send us to Eyl.

Then again, if this was all yet more theatre, why the hell weren't they making it look a bit more convincing, with a properly staged fall-out with Yusuf? As ever, none of it added up. Was the coup real? Or was it theatre? Or, more confusingly, was it theatre, but acting so bad it looked like it had to be real?

'Please Mr Nick, understand one th-thing,' said Ahmed. 'This militia is saying that Mr Ali and Mr Yusuf are no longer important. There are new p-people in command now.'

'Well that's no use,' said Nick. 'We have spent a lot of time talking to Ali and Yusuf, and we trust them now. We don't know these new people. What do they want? Do they want to stay with Colin and José in those mountains forever?'

Nick asked to speak to me again.

'I am sorry Nick, I have no idea what is going on,' I said.

'Is Yusuf still there? Have you seen him?

'Yes, he's here at the moment.'

'Have you seen any signs of tensions within the gang?'

'Not really, no. What do you think's happening?'

'We're not sure. It may be theatre, or just some last-minute wobble at their end, some petty squabble. They are probably all very tense at the moment. Maybe Ali will ring us later. If you speak to Ahmed again, try and get him to make the others see sense.'

He rang off. I sincerely hoped he was right about this all being a bluff. If it was, though, the gang were playing it too. As we got up to wander down the hill, the Old Bastard said something to Ahmed and pointed at us.

'He is saying, u-understand one thing,' said Ahmed. 'He will keep you here for a whole year if he needs to.'

*****

Ahmed was dragged off in a different direction while José and I returned to the cave. We were done for now. Screwed. Two days ago, when we'd been told we were about to go free, I remembered thinking that if all went ahead without further incident, we'd probably just about get back home with our sanity intact. But to start again from scratch now, to wait another six weeks, maybe more, that would have me knocking at the door of the funny farm. And if the Old Bastard was in now in charge, there was no telling how long we'd be here. He was a good soldier-sergeant, but didn't strike me as having much of a brain, unlike like Yusuf or the Guy of the Cigarettes. For some reason, though, I didn't feel panic. It was if the burden of hope had been lifted, and we could now just give up. Not that that was a good sign. Abandoning all hope of ever getting freed was probably not, on the whole, good for maintaining a positive mental outlook.

Yusuf turned up along with the Guy of the Cigarettes, and sat by the campfire. José, feeling he no longer had anything to lose, gave him a piece of what little was left of his mind.

'What the fuck, Yusuf? What is going on? We go home, or not, eh? What is this fucking problem now, eh, my friend? What is this fucking *mushkilleh*?'

He shrugged and wandered off, giving nothing away. José and I turned to each other. We'd had no cigarettes for days, which wasn't helping our mood.

'Okay, so you were probably right about Ahmed,' I said.

'Probably? How do you mean? Certainly, no?'

'Well, we don't know for sure, do we?'

'Are you kidding? The guy is definitely involved.'

'Well, you never know. I mean, he might have been given clean clothes by the gang for some reason. Perhaps they were less worried about the police looking for him, so they just kept him hostage in a house, or something, where he could wash.'

'Are you kidding? It is all bullshit, I tell you. I have thought it all along. Ever since we were kidnapped.'

'I suppose so. All I am saying is that this whole thing is so weird, we can't be certain of anything really.'

'I don't understand you, man! I don't see why you even wonder about this. That fucking pair, they are involved.'

For the first time since this whole nightmare had started, José sounded annoyed with me.

The next day, Ahmed was brought back to the cave. This time, I inspected his clothes more closely. Sure enough, they looked pretty clean.

'Understand one thing,' he said. 'There is some new information. A high committee has been f-formed. They are to decide whether to let you g-go or not.'

'A high committee? What do you mean?'

'A high committee of this militia.'

'Who's on it?'

He gestured to the Old Bastard. 'This man here, and some others. They will meet this evening.'

I remembered what Nick had said about using Ahmed to put our case to the gang. We might not get another chance.

'Listen Ahmed, you need to tell the high committee that they must let us go now. There will be big problems if they don't. We don't all want to be stuck here forever, do we? They must see that, surely, as much as we do?'

'Maybe. I cannot tell.'

As a very last resort, I tried flattery.

'They must not have arguments, it is not professional,' I said. I pointed to the Old Bastard. 'Tell him, Ahmed, that José and I have been very impressed so far with everything. They are very clever kidnappers, the way they took us, the way they have everything organised, the caves, the food, the cigarettes and everything. They have been very professional. Never an argument, never even a small bad word to each other. It is amazing! You would not see Westerners able to do this. So why are they fighting now? That is what amateurs do, not professionals. And these guys are professionals, right! Make them understand this one thing!'

I broke off to let Ahmed translate. I'd become quite impassioned, like some kind of motivational speaker. Any more, and I'd have probably added: 'You've let me, down, you've let Nick down, but worst of all...'

Ahmed relayed my rant to the Old Bastard. He listened, nodding occasionally, as if testimonies to his work were only to be expected.

Then he marched Ahmed off down the slope and was not seen again that day. Nor were Yusuf and the Guy of the Cigarettes. Perhaps the 'high committee' was in session. Not only had we been kidnapped by amateurs, it seemed, we'd been kidnapped by amateurs with delusions of grandeur. Right now, though, appealing to their sense of self-importance seemed about our only chance.

15: Back to Londonspain

IF I WAS GOING TO spend the next year sitting staring into space all day, I was going to do it properly. Richard, my friend who'd caught malaria while teaching in Africa, had become a full-time Buddhist during his years of convalescence, and had often recommended meditation to me. It was supposed to be all about emptying the mind, of thinking about nothing whatsoever. Given that I was running out of things to think about anyway, it had to be worth a try. As José and I waited for the worthies of the 'high committee' to deliver their verdict, I made myself as comfortable as I could on the mat, and stared at a crack on the cave ceiling a few feet above.

For someone who had nothing much to think about, thinking about nothing proved surprisingly hard. Thoughts kept creeping in. What would lunch be? Would we ever get any more cigarettes? Was that strange clicking noise in the corner the sound of a gecko, or something more dangerous?

But after about an hour, things began to settle down. There was no emptying of the mind, *per se*, but the thoughts that did come in became calmer, more rational, more soothing. And they were proper thoughts, too. Instead of shabby old pubs and shabbier old teachers from my past, I thought about Richard and his friends in their Buddhist commune in Manchester. I imagined them all talking to me, telling me not worry, to try to let go. Soon, my own inner voice was doing the same.

Okay, so you are in trouble here, and you are worried how everybody else will be feeling at home. But there is no point in feeling guilty. It wasn't your fault that you got kidnapped.

Really?

No. You were just doing your job. And you are very lucky to have such a job, travelling the world. Remember why it was you got into this line of work. It was to seek experience, was it not? Some experiences are good, some are bad, but all are valid. You will learn from it, and if you stay calm here, you will get out of here one day, stronger than you were before.

What if we don't get out?

That is fate. So why be worried about it? Face it head on, be strong. Then you will at least die happy.

It felt good, as if some calm, totally unflappable character had taken up residence inside me – even if he did talk rather like Obi Wan Kenobi from Star Wars. And this was just the beginning. Richard said that the more meditation you did, the better it got. He often went on special Buddhist retreats in the Welsh mountains where everyone meditated in silence for up to a month at a time. They'd love it here. Maybe I could try to be like them. I had no handbooks or proper knowledge on how to meditate properly, but I'd just have to improvise. The Buddha, Obi Wan Kenobi, or whoever, would hopefully guide the way.

Then, just as I was on the verge of discovering everlasting inner peace, my karma was shattered by the clunk-click of a Kalashnikov being cocked just above our heads. I looked up to see the Sherpa staring down at me. Then I realised he was smiling. Cocking his gun at us was his idea of a joke. What a card he was.

'Telephone, you!' he said. *'Londonspain!'*

Had the High Committee adjudicated? Minutes later, we were up on the top of the hill waiting for a phone call again. This time, it was the Guy of the Cigarettes in charge. And this time, everything felt very different. His big, wolfish face cracked a grin of broken teeth, and he uttered two words in the fractured Arabic that was the only mutual language we had.

'Al yom,' he said. Today. He pointed a huge hand towards the valley, as if gesturing in the direction of some imagined Londonspain.

Something in his manner told us that he meant it this time. A few minutes later, a phone call from Nick confirmed that the plan to release us was back on. This time, there was also a second phone call from a man called Ian, who had a South African accent. He asked us some proof of life questions, and said that he and Mr David were waiting for us in Bossaso. This was it. *This was really it.*

The Guy of the Cigarettes had no cigarettes with which to celebrate, so I stared out over the valley, savouring the mountain skyline for what might hopefully now be the last time. The keel-shaped peaks were bathed in the rich late afternoon sun, huge slabs of blood orange rock with tiny clouds scudding overhead. We weren't free yet, but already a feeling of joy, that rare happiness one only gets very occasionally in life, was surging through me.

Remember this moment, and this view, until the day you die. Which may now be rather further away than you thought.

We went back to the cave and sat around drinking tea, wondering would happen next. It didn't cross my mind to meditate again. We were going to get released. Nirvana could wait.

*****

The next morning, as the first greyness of dawn peeked into the cave, we were on the move. The gang reloaded their Kalashnikov magazines from a large grey Russian-issue ammunition tin, a thing the size of a shoe box with a peel-off metal lid like a can of tuna. Yusuf picked up the black laptop bag in which he carried his Koran and two hand grenades. We bade the geckos in the cave goodbye and headed down to the dusty track where cars occasionally passed. We were a full turn-out, about 20 in all. The instructions for our release were the same vague ones we'd had before. Someone would come to meet us, but who, when and where we had no idea.

We marched for an hour, the moon still large, and then rested up behind a rocky knoll, away from the road. Someone made tea and we sat drinking, wishing we had cigarettes. Then, from somewhere in the distance, there came a quick bark of gunfire, three short sharp shots. A single shot followed in reply.

I looked up, alarmed. Was another gun battle underway? Not for the first time, I entertained visions of the handover ending in a bloodbath. Like drug deals, one of the most likely moments where kidnaps tended to go wrong was the handover. Lots of people with jumpy trigger fingers, no trust on either side, and fears that it might all be a police set-up. The Trekker looked at me, smiled and pointed to his watch. About a minute later, there was another identical gunfire exchange. It was some sort of signal.

Seconds later, the Guy of the Cigarettes appeared on the brow of a nearby hill, waving us forward like a Somali Hannibal. Marching back to the road, we could see other armed groups coming in from other parts of the valley. An SUV appeared from out of some bushes with about ten men, one of them clutching a rocket-propelled grenade launcher. A rusting technical roared up in a cloud of dust, a man in a red-check keffiyah and sunglasses standing behind its anti-aircraft gun. More cars and men kept arriving. Soon there was a small, Mad Max-style army about 50 strong. José and I were ordered into the back cabin of a rusting yellow lorry, driven by a grizzled-looking clan elder type. He'd dropped by the camp a few times in recent days, a man with a distinctive mole where his right cheekbone cragged out over his grey beard.

We headed along a track that wound through the floor of a wide mountain valley, a route so bumpy the lorry seldom got out of first gear. In the SUV in front of us, the man with the rocket-propelled grenade hung out of a rear window, his weapon's diamond-shaped head pointing skywards. Our captors clearly didn't have much faith in whoever it was we were meeting. As the road ahead climbed out of the valley to a high mountain pass, the convoy stopped and four men got out, taking up positions behind some boulders nearby. Another four did the same thing again halfway up the pass. If anybody tried to chase us, they'd be heading straight into a series of ambushes.

At the top, we halted. Ahead, a valley peered down onto the plains that led to the coast. The wind whistled through the lorry's cabin. Hundreds of feet below, at the bottom of a steep, winding track, we could see three white SUVs, presumably belonging to whoever had come to pick us up. After a wait of about half an hour, and numerous phone calls, The Guy of the Cigarettes, the Sherpa, the Old Bastard and half a dozen others formed an advance party. They ordered us to start walking down the hill, and followed just behind. I felt very exposed. If anyone started shooting on either side, we'd be right in the middle. The rest of the gang brought up the rear, fanning out either side of the track, guns at the ready like infantrymen, eyes scanning the valley for threats. It felt like a Somali version of the Checkpoint Charlie handovers of the Cold War.

We neared the SUVs. I'd expected a white face or two, but the men standing around were all Somalis. A few clutched guns. Two of them walked towards us, a pair of old men dressed in poorly-fitting suits and trainers, and with not many teeth between them. Were these the intermediaries, the trusted clan elders? They didn't exactly look like pillars of the community. Then again, it probably took a certain type of ducker and diver to be trusted by a kidnap gang in delicate matters like this. The Grandpas looked at us, inspecting the goods, and then exchanged words with the Guy of the Cigarettes. It sounded tense, but cordial. Who knew, perhaps they met like this every week.

One of them urged us to come forward. We turned and looked at the Guy of the Cigarettes for confirmation. He nodded. For a moment I wondered what to say to him. What was the appropriate etiquette for bidding farewell to someone who'd kidnapped you? One half of me wondered whether to shake his hand, to say it had been an interesting adventure, that I'd been impressed by his professionalism, to wish him all the best in his future kidnapping career and so on. The other half, the sensible half, knew that was stupid, and that he might see it that way too. Instead, with just the briefest of nods, we parted company forever.

'Hello, you are now free,' beamed one of the elders, leading us to the cars. 'Everything is okay, don't worry, you are coming back to Bossaso.'

'Have you got a cigarette?' I asked.

*****

The journey back was only about an hour, and passed without incident. Save, that was, for a blazing row that erupted among our Somali intermediaries just before we drove off, in which one of them pulled a gun on the other. For a few moments of abject horror, we watched as our saviours snarled in each other's faces. Just as I began fearing it was some decoy tactic, a prelude by the gang to snatch us back again, the others pulled them apart. One of the two Grandpas shot us a reassuring smile, as if to say, 'Don't worry, they're best mates really'. Perhaps waving a gun in someone's face was just a way of making your point. José and I exchanged weary glances.

As we drove off, I looked through the rear window. The gang were heading back up the valley, off to do whatever it was they did when they weren't kidnapping. Soon they disappeared altogether, as our convoy headed over the brow of a hill and into the plains. We picked up speed, driving under cloudless blue skies. One of the Somalis made a call on his mobile.

'We have the hostages,' he said.

We passed a tiny hamlet in the middle of nowhere, just three or four mud huts, scorched brown earth fused with corrugated iron and clumps of straw. It was the first human habitation we'd seen in weeks, yet it felt like hitting Broadway. Even so, I still felt tense. Until we were back in Bossaso – in fact, until we were actually on a *plane*, looking down on Somali soil from 36,000 feet – I'd fear some other convoy suddenly blocking the road and grabbing us again. And what exactly did we face now? I had no idea. Only that Mr David, international man of mystery, was waiting to pick us up in Bossaso, and that we'd probably be flown out to Nairobi. But what else awaited us? Could Nick have been engaging in a little news management when he'd said Jane and my parents were doing fine? And even if they were okay, would they be angry at me? And what would the office have to say about all this? Would they feel we'd blundered into this one like a pair of idiots? Were we in for an official dressing down, like Speke and Burton after they limped back to Aden 150 years ago? José and I reckoned we'd taken all reasonable steps to be careful. But it might not look that way from the outside. For all I knew, one of the first things this guy Mr David might be tasked with would be reading us the riot act, just to make sure we never did such a daft thing again.

At the hotel we drove straight into the rear of the compound, where there were some detached villas. The ostrich was there waiting for us, as were three white men. They wore khaki fatigues and hiking boots – the 'combat-casual' look favored by all ex-military men who work for private security companies. One of them, a slim figure in sunglasses who looked like he might have been the CIA's point man in Bossaso, stepped forward and offered his hand.

'Colin and José, right?' he said in an American accent.

Mr David, I presume?

'Yes, that's us. You must be Mr David,' I said.

'That's me. Welcome back. How are you feeling?'

I thought for a second.

'Absolutely fine. No problems at all.'

'Come with us up to this villa. Don't worry, it's very secure. We're going to be leaving very soon, but you've got time to have a shower. We've brought you a change of clothes too. We have a medical kit with us too. If you have any kind of injuries, any other problems, just say.'

'No, none at all.'

He led us up a flight of stairs and into a lounge. On the table were some bottles of water, and an envelope each for José and I. They had the *Telegraph* logo on them. Inside mine was a printed letter from Adrian Michaels, the foreign-editor-in-chief, and a hand-written note from my immediate boss, David. Luckily, neither of them also appeared to have enclosed a P-45. They both congratulated José and me on our release, reassured me all was well, and said everyone at the paper was looking forward to seeing me again.

Mr David briefed us on what would happen next. We weren't staying in Bossaso a moment longer than necessary. The Spanish ambassador to Kenya, who'd also been working to secure our release, would be arriving on his private jet in about an hour's time to fly us all back to Nairobi. The jet would make a refuel stop at an airport in Hargeisa, another Somali town, where we'd have a chance to call our next of kin. By then, they would have been told that we'd been released. Then we'd fly to Nairobi, where my boss, David, had already arrived from London and was waiting for me. The only thing we had to do before we left was a quick press conference with some Somali journalists.

'A press conference?'

'Don't worry, it's just for diplomatic reasons, to please the Puntland security minister. I think you met him when you got here? A man called Abdullahi Said Samatar?

'Yes, I remember him. He made me write him a letter asking for permission to get into the country.'

'That's him. We are kind of here with his permission, so we can't really get out of it. The journalists will come to the villa here, but there'll just be a few. I would just say as little as possible, and it hopefully won't last very long.'

I went to take a shower. Mr David gave me two plastic bags, one with some new clothes in, the other to dump the old ones in. I peeled off the garments that I'd hiked in, lived in and slept in the past forty days. The trousers, a pair of brown linen slacks, had lost all their colour for some reason and were now an army green, while the thin white stripes on my blue short-sleeved shirt were so dirty as to be almost invisible. The clothes weren't exactly fragrant, but on the whole, I was surprised by how little I smelt, not how much. I'd expected Mr David to be holding his nose.

I looked in the mirror, my first proper glance at my post-kidnap face. My teeth were a dull yellow, but otherwise I didn't look that bad. My skin was tanned, my cheekbones prominent, and the bags that I usually had under my eyes had gone, the result, no doubt, of sleeping 14 hours a day. I'd also lost at least a stone in weight. My beard, though, was a living, growing insult to the very notion of facial hair. While José had grown a thick, long black number that had earned him the nickname Bin Laden from the kidnappers, mine was a dreadful patchy thing, spreading unevenly like mange. Instead of sideburns, I had a cluster of strange whiskery patches around my jawline, like some Edwardian adventurer gone wrong.

The shower had no hot water, and despite shampooing, my hair seemed to have retained some kind of perma-grease which meant it spiked up, Johnny Rotten fashion, when I dried it off. I put on my new clothes, a pair of brown slacks and a white checked shirt, and emerged from the bathroom to see that José had been given exactly the same. We appeared for the press conference looking like the Proclaimer Twins.

A handful of Somali journalists had turned up along with the Security Minister. He delivered a long statement about Puntland being committed to assuring the safety of all foreign visitors, and then all eyes turned to us.

'I don't want to say much, just that José and I are both very happy to be released, and looking forward to going home,' I said, as the hacks brandished little digital cameras.

'Did they torture you?' asked one reporter brightly.

Good operator, I thought. Straight to the point.

'No, I am pleased to say that they generally treated us pretty well.'

His face assumed an expression I knew all too well myself, that of a journalist quickly losing all interest in the story. Sure enough, he and his colleagues asked a couple more questions for the sake of form, then headed out.

We were introduced to the Spanish ambassador Nicolas Martin, a cheery, white-haired fellow who'd been here on a similar mission the year before, when a Spanish aid worker had been kidnapped. He knew Somalia well, and was therefore anxious to get out as quickly as possible before anything untoward happened to his private jet. We clambered into a convoy of cars and headed off to the airport, that same ten minute journey we'd tried and failed to make six weeks before. This time, Bossaso police really did have us surrounded. Several trucks of armed men escorted us all the way to the runway and up to a ten seater-plane, its engines already running. We took off, and soon the shoreline of the pirate coast appeared below us. Then sandwiches were handed out. They were nothing special, tuna on white bread with a little salad dressing, but after six weeks of cave cuisine they were a starburst of novelty flavours, as if Heston Blumenthal had done the in-flight catering. Mr Martin also made the welcome announcement that as we were on a private jet, normal international aviation rules did not apply and we could smoke. In the space of a few hours, we'd gone from Stone Age men to rock stars.

José leaned forward and gave me a cigarette from a new carton of Marlboro Lights.

'Hey look, I have my own entire pack of smokes,' he said. 'No more begging to the Guy of the Cigarettes.'

I took one off him and we lit up. It tasted fantastic. Who said smoking was bad for you? And better than the tobacco rush, better than qhat, better than 100 per cent pure cocaine, I could feel the sense of freedom really kicking in.

As we smoked, ate, and smoked again, Mr David filled in some of the gaps in what we knew about our own story. It was hard to know where to start. The operation to release us seemed to have involved a cast of thousands. We learned of the *Telegraph* crisis team, of the professional negotiators, and of all the countless other players who had helped: diplomats like Mr Nicolas, foreign intelligence officials, politicians, other journalists who'd put their own contacts books at the *Telegraph's* disposal. Plus, of course, Mr David, who worked as a security advisor to aid agencies operating in Somalia, and was well-connected throughout the country.

José and I had a bet to settle.

'So, tell us,' I said to Mr David. 'Were Ahmed and Mustapha involved in our kidnapping?'

He smiled. 'Yes, we think so.'

'Really? How do you know?'

'Just various information that we've picked up in the last few weeks. We think they may also have been involved in three or four other incidents where foreigners were kidnapped in Bossaso over recent times. Did you do any checks on them beforehand?'

'Not really. There was no time. To be honest, I'm not sure we'd have found out much if we had. You just have to work with whoever you can get in some parts of the world.'

'They saw you coming, I'm afraid. Probably had it planned out all along. Do you remember that day when they took you to that hotel in downtown Bossaso. A place called the Hotel Juba?'

I did. We'd stopped there for a soft drink one morning, while Ahmed and Mustapha chatted to various people. They'd claimed the owner was an influential businessman, who might be able to help with our attempts to get access to the pirates in the jail. It hadn't made much sense at the time, but not much ever had in Bossaso. We'd just put it down as yet another sign that Ahmed and

Mustapha didn't know what they were doing. According to Mr David, they'd known exactly what they were doing. Waiting at the hotel that morning had been representatives of the kidnappers. Ahmed and Mustapha had brought us there as proof that they had us in the palm of their hands, that they could deliver us whenever they wanted. All that time we'd sat there drinking tea, impatiently wondering when we were going to get a move on, we'd been on display like goods in a shop window.

It was not a pleasant thing to learn. Mr David was smiling as he told the story, but my professional pride was smarting. And it meant José had won our bet. At least he'd had the sense to smell a rat.

'Where are Ahmed and Mustapha now?' I asked.

'We don't know. They've not been seen at all.'

'Are you sure they weren't kidnapped themselves?'

'Pretty much, yes.'

'Do you think the police will ever catch them?'

'I doubt it.'

'I can't believe we were stitched up like that. And I never saw it coming, at any point.'

'Don't worry about it. We got you out, that's the important thing. How are you feeling, by the way?'

'Fine, really. Absolutely on a high. It will take a little while to adjust, I guess, but I can't see any lasting problems. Just so glad to be out.'

'Take it easy. There is always a come-down after something like this. You have been under more pressure than you realise, and for a long time.'

'We'll see, I guess.'

'Take it from me, it will happen.'

We touched down to refuel at Hargeisa, a tiny airport in the back of beyond. Someone produced a satellite phone and told me I could make some calls. Jane and the office were waiting to hear from me, they said. First I rang Jane's number. As I heard the ringing tone over the hiss of static, I realised I was half-expecting Ali's voice to come on in the background.

'Is that you Col?' Jane's voice came on the phone, warm and close-sounding despite being bounced through space via a satellite.

'It's me hon. I'm out. I'm fine. And I'm really sorry.'

'Don't worry about that. God, I can't believe it's your voice. Are you really okay?'

'Yes, I am. Really, I'm fine.'

'Listen, your office has offered to fly me to Nairobi to meet you. Do you want me to come? I thought I might make an exception to my no-flying rule this time. I can get a flight this afternoon, be with you tomorrow morning. But only if you want me there.'

'Yes, please do. There's lots to talk about.'

That was an understatement. There was, however, no time to talk about anything right now. The plane's engines were starting up again.

'Listen, I've got to go. I've got to speak to the office as well before we take off again. I'll call you later. Tell everyone I said hello.'

Next up was my boss, David. He was his usual businesslike self. He solicited briefly as to my welfare, expressed how pleased everyone was to hear me alive, and then, as ever, got straight to the point.

'Listen, we will have a great catch-up later, but I need to talk shop for a minute. Unfortunately, you have been released on the worst possible day from the point of view of the *Sunday Telegraph*.'

'Eh?'

'Perhaps you've lost count of the days, but today *is* Sunday. Which means we've got another six days before our next edition. The reports of your release are already all over the news, and by next Sunday, it's going to seem a bit old.'

'Right...'

I could sense what was coming.

'So what we were wondering... only if you are up for it, of course... was whether you might thinking about writing a big first-hand account for the *Daily Telegraph* instead. Not for tomorrow – it's too late in the day now for that – but maybe for Tuesday's paper? You know the sort of thing. My ordeal at the hands of kidnappers etc.'

'Er, right, let me think about it for a minute.'

It wasn't quite what I'd been intending to do on my release. My tentative plan with José had been very simple – to check in at some hotel, find the bar, and spend the next 48 hours getting blind drunk. On the other hand, I owed my employers one. From what Mr David had been saying, they'd worked seriously hard to get me out. The very least I could do was make sure they didn't miss out on their own world exclusive. Plus, I grudgingly conceded, it was what being a professional journalist was supposed to be all about – filing your story, no matter what the circumstances. True, in any other profession, asking anyone to do even a stroke of work after what I'd just been through would invite some sort of negligence lawsuit. But that was one of the things I liked about my job. It wasn't just any other profession. The normal rules didn't apply. Which was why you got to go to places like Somalia. And get kidnapped.

'Okay. I'll do it.'

'Excellent. About 1500 words, maybe? Have a think about what you might want to write and we'll talk later. And I guess we should also think about saving part of your story up for Sunday as well.'

'Eh?'

'Well, I'm sure we'd still like something for then too. Some different angle maybe.'

'Er, yeah, whatever, sure.'

I could feel my teeth grinding again. The prospect of any bar time with José at all was fast disappearing.

'Oh, and just finally, there's also the website to think about. It would be really nice just to have a quick piece from you to put up there as soon as we can. Maybe about the moments leading up to your release today, how it all felt and so on. We can also use it in tomorrow's paper.'

'Ah, well that might be a bit difficult, because I'm just about to get back on the plane.'

'Okay. Well, can you borrow a pen and paper off someone? Then you can start writing during the flight, so you can have it ready to file when you get to Nairobi?'

'Bloody hell, man! I've just been released!'

'Fine, no, sorry, don't worry about it. As I said, it's only if you want to do it. No problem at all.'

'Dah... Okay, go on then.'

'Excellent! About 800 words?'

*****

If José and I had thought we were going to be left to our own devices when we got back to Nairobi, we were mistaken. We touched down to find ourselves treated like visiting dignitaries, with all our moves planned out for us, and very little time earmarked for getting rat-arsed. At the airport we were met by Rob Macaire, the British High Commissioner, and then ushered into the VIP lounge where David, my boss, was waiting along with Olga Craig, one of the *Sunday Telegraph's* senior feature writers. She'd been flown out as an emergency 'ghost writer' in case I was in too much of a state to pen any account of my ordeal myself. Luckily, I'd hit reasonable form on the plane and arrived bearing 800 words ready-scribbled on a jotter. We spent the next 40 minutes filing it over the phone, stretching the patience of the waiting press pack in the arrivals lobby outside. By the time we finally emerged, they'd gone home, depriving me of my once-in-a-lifetime chance to wander into a blaze of flashbulbs and say 'no comment'.

In Nairobi we spent the night at the Spanish ambassador's residence, a handsome old colonial pile where Robert Redford had stayed while making the film *Out of Africa*. It had a tennis court that had been built especially just for him, a swimming pool, oak paneled drawing rooms and old-fashioned, white-gloved catering staff who struggled to keep up with our demands for strong drink. Eventually they just gave José and me a bottle of rum and let us get on with it. We sat up drinking until about 2am, and then went to our bedrooms, wondering how we'd cope sleeping without each other.

Waking up hungover the next morning, I heard a gentle knock on the door. It was Jane, just arrived in from Nairobi airport. The last time I'd looked into her face had been a grey morning back in

London in early November, when we'd split up. Now, nearly two months later, we were meeting in mid-summer on the other side of the world, and about to plan the rest of our lives together. It was very weird, and very good. We hugged each other long and hard, she cried just as she'd done when we'd parted, and I wondered why I'd ever had any doubts. We chatted for a couple of hours, which wasn't near long enough to even make a start, and then I had to start work again. Much as I would have preferred to be sat by the poolside, the writing was good therapy. Not only did it keep my mind occupied, it was a chance to take control of my life again. After six weeks in which so many other people had worked on my behalf, here was something I could do on my own account.

That evening, just before we went downstairs for dinner with the ambassador, Jane used the laptop I'd borrowed off David to play a song she'd downloaded on her iPod.

'I want you to listen to this, it's very special to me,' she said.

'Who is it?'

'A band called Razorlight. You know how I was telling you about that first phone call I had from Nick? The one where they got the first proof of life from you?'

'Yeah?'

'Well, when I got the call, I was in a pub with some of your friends. They'd taken me out for Sunday lunch to try and give me a bit of support. Very nice of them. I was in a bit of a state at the time. Five days, and no idea what had happened to you. Anyway, the phone rang and I saw it was Nick's number. I could hardly answer the phone, my hand was shaking so much. Nick told me that they'd heard from you, and I just felt this amazing glow of relief all over me. Okay, you'd been kidnapped, but at least you weren't dead. So I went over to tell everyone, and at that moment this song came on. It's called *America*. When I got that home that night, I downloaded it to cheer me up.'

I listened carefully. It was a mellow indie-pop, like a collaboration between REM and The Strokes. It wasn't really my thing.

'Do you like it?' she asked brightly.

I looked at her.

'Honestly? No, not really.'

We giggled. Clearly, there were some things we'd still be disagreeing on.

*****

The next few days I threw myself into work. I wasn't quite on a par with Captain Speke, who, having been nearly killed in Somalia, immediately volunteered for the Crimean War. But I did churn out more than I ever normally wrote in a single week. After the 1,500 word piece for Tuesday's paper, I wrote a 4,500 word epic for the Sunday edition. It was about twice as long as anything I'd ever written for the paper before, but the Editor, recognising that it wasn't every day one of his reporters was taken hostage, cleared extra pages so that we could run every word. José likewise filed a long piece for a Spanish newspaper, *La Vanguardia*, complete with reference to 'El Viejo Bastardo' (the Old Bastard), and we also did a number of radio and TV interviews. Asked by one reporter how we coped, I said: 'Goat meat, rice and Rothmans', which later made Quote of the Day on some newswire service. Alas, my much-hoped for offer of a £100,000-a-year sponsorship retainer from Rothmans failed to materialise.

That week turned out to be one of the happiest of my life. The daytime was spent working, and evenings spent drinking the Ambassador's excellent Rioja, and catching up on messages from friends and colleagues. There is nothing like vanishing off the face of the earth for making people want to get in touch. My email inbox was jammed with greetings: pals both close and not so close, acquaintances I hadn't heard from in years, even soldiers I'd met out in Iraq. One of them breezily invited me to visit his unit in Baghdad as soon as I was ready. There were also numerous calls home to my family. On the advice of the *Telegraph's* hostage negotiation experts, they'd agreed it would be best to allow me to have some 'decompression' time on my own with Jane rather than flying out *en masse* to meet me.

It meant I wouldn't be seeing them until the end of the week, but when I first rang them I could already hear champagne corks popping in the lounge. It was, I would later find out, a welcome change of medication. During some of the harder times in the previous weeks, my mother and brother had been taking prescription tranquillisers to help them sleep. It was an indication of just how stressful the whole thing must have been. Just like Jane, though, they'd all managed to pull through without any lasting effects. My Mum's only complaint was that in one article, I'd written about my fears that her or Dad might suffer a heart attack. 'You made us sound like a pair of decrepit old pensioners ready to drop dead at any second,' she said.

Jane met José, someone who now knew me almost as well as she did. They compared notes on what I was like to share a bed with, sharing what were clearly long-festering complaints about my snoring. We also had a health check-up at a private clinic in Nairobi, where an expat Italian doctor issued an unexpected demand for on-the-spot urine and stool samples. For nearly an hour José and I paced up and down impotently, attempting to coax our bowels into doing the right thing, but all the process brought forth was the lowest in caveman humour.

'A shame the doctor can't just go to those rocks outside the cave, he could got as much as he wanted.'

'Or you could have just given him the underpants you wore all that time.'

It was only when the doctor said that the alternative was to wait overnight, and have the specimen jars couriered down to his clinic, that I finally found the necessary incentive to perform. Much as I was enjoying being waited on hand on foot by the embassy staff, there were some things you really couldn't expect other people to do for you. His request finally granted, the doctor filled out a few forms and gave us a preliminary all-clear. Our cave diet, he said, appeared to have done us no harm, despite drinking water from a diesel can.

'Diesel is quite good at killing bacteria, actually,' he said. 'It probably helped keep you clear of infection, although I wouldn't particularly recommend it long-term. Now, one final question. Did you suffer any violence, beatings or sexual abuse during your captivity?'

We shook our heads. He smiled, scribbling in his note pad. 'So you had a pretty boring time then, eh?'

As we left his office, my eye was caught by a newspaper clipping on a noticeboard, showing a photo of what looked like a smiling face in the night sky. For some reason I couldn't quite fathom, it looked familiar. I took a closer look. It was a report from a Kenyan newspaper from a few weeks before, about something called a 'conjunction of the moon with Jupiter and Venus'. It was some one-off alignment in the heavens, in which a crescent moon forms the 'smile', with Venus and Jupiter as the eyes above. Looking at the photo, I suddenly remembered where I'd seen the face before. It had been grinning down at me one night back in early December, when I'd staggered out of the cave for a piss in the middle of the night. Such was my distraught state of mind that I'd barely even registered it at the time. All I'd thought was something to the effect of 'even the bloody moon looks funny here in Somalia'.

The headline above the photo read 'Next showing, 2014'. At least, when it came around again, we wouldn't be watching it from a cave.

*****

That weekend, José and I flew home to very different welcomes. Because the Spanish media had largely ignored the news blackout throughout the kidnapping, José returned to his family to find himself a national celebrity. The plight of the good-looking freelance photographer stuck in the cave on Somalia's pirate coast had been a huge human interest story for the past six weeks, and his phone rang non-stop with requests for interviews. He was recognised in shops, bars and on the streets, and a Spanish cable channel even asked to do a made-for-TV movie about the drama. Much to my disappointment, he turned them down.

'They are a downmarket tabloid channel, they will not do a good job,' he told me.

'So what?' I said. 'It would be a laugh.'

'I am telling you, it would be a disaster. They will not try to make it realistic. They will use Moroccans as Somalis, or something.'

'Better still, it will be hilarious. I would love to see a Spanish version of myself. They will probably have me wearing a moustache and a pith helmet.'

My own return was rather more low-key. Jane and I flew back together after five days in Nairobi, arriving back at my parents' house on a freezing cold January evening. They hadn't been 'doorstepped' once, not even since my release, somewhat to my Mum's disappointment, who was rather excited about the prospect of appearing on BBC Newsroom South East. Instead, celebrity came in more minor ways. My sister's seven-year-old daughter Josie wrote about me for a school project on 'Someone who is famous', declaring that her previously intended subject, a newly-elected president by the name of Barack Obama, was 'a bit boring'. My mum, who was studying Spanish at night-school, had a conversation class devoted to the topic of her son's *secuestredo* (kidnapping). She also asked me for a copy of José's article for a translation class, a request I quietly overlooked after learning that it included such charming colloquialisms as *'Me cago en tu puta madre, hijo de puta.'* It was what José had told the Old Bastard when he'd been pining with thirst during our marathon walk. It translated roughly as: 'I shit on your whore of a mother, you son of a bitch.'

Meanwhile, my close friends rallied round in the way that only close friends can do, by taking the piss mercilessly. No aspect of my ordeal was sacred. The six weeks I'd spent sharing a bed with José prompted much gleeful speculation that there might have been some 'Brokeback Mountain' moments. And the headline on my first article about our release – '*Telegraph* man's walk to freedom' – drew inquiries as to whether I now compared myself to Nelson Mandela.

At the office, I was welcomed back by the team that had worked to get me out. Seldom had I seen my colleagues in such a good mood. It was, Adrian joked, 'the perfect team-building exercise'. They showed me around the crisis room, with its maps, photo galleries and piles of documentation. On the wall, next to the montage of different Somali faces, I also noticed another set of photos, of various film stars. They were the people that the team had decided would play themselves in *Crisis Team – The Movie*. At the bottom, alongside pictures of Daniel Craig, Michael Caine and others, I noticed a picture of Danny DeVito.

'What's Danny DeVito doing there?' I asked.

There was a pause, and a few sniggers.

'Er... that was you.'

'Have you been speaking to José? Did he tell you I looked like Danny DeVito?'

'Eh? No. We had this up since before you were both released.'

For the record, *I do not look like Danny DeVito*.

*****

For all the *esprit de corps* that the rescue effort generated, the *Telegraph* was anxious to ensure they never had to do anything like it again. I had a long debrief from Adrian and Mark about what went wrong. Could we have done more to check out how dangerous Puntland was beforehand? And could we have done some checks on Ahmed and Mustapha before hiring them?

My own answer to both questions, self-serving as it might sound, was and remains no. True, we later found out that we had visited Puntland at the worst possible time. The government was losing control, there'd been a spate of assassinations of local officials and politicians, and many of the security forces had been unpaid for months, creating ready recruits for piracy and kidnap gangs. With political turf wars also brewing ahead of the elections, it was not a good moment for two foreigners to pitch up in town and start nosing around. We also unearthed a report on a Somali news website saying that Mustapha had once been arrested in connection with the kidnapping in 2007 of the French journalist, Gwen Le Gouil. He'd apparently visited Le Gouil in the cave where he was held, claiming to be an 'intermediary' between the kidnappers and the French government. The authorities had accused him of colluding with the kidnappers and chucked him in jail for a few weeks.

All the same, I am not sure that being better briefed on the pitfalls of Puntland and its resident fixers would have stopped us going there. Most, if not all, assignments to foreign trouble spots are undertaken in the face of official advice to stay away. If journalists heeded every single warning they got, places like Iraq, Afghanistan and Somalia would go largely unreported by the Western media, other than through officially sanctioned 'embeds' . Likewise, for all that Mustapha's previous brush with the law might sound highly suspicious, in countries like Somalia, it is not unknown for journalists to mediate in kidnap cases, and, indeed, for officialdom to then chuck them in jail for no good reason afterwards. Sometimes, all it suggests is that a particular fixer has the confidence of some rather dodgy people, which is often exactly what foreign journalists are hiring them for.

There is also a limit to what due diligence can be done on any fixers in advance. I have lost count of the number of times I have been warned that one fixer or another is dishonest or untrustworthy – most often by rivals who proved little better. True, with extra time to do research we might have found reliable sources to warn us off Mustapha. But that would probably have meant postponing the trip for another week, by which time rival papers might have beaten us to it. Having said that, another foreign correspondent for *The Sunday Times* did look into going that same week as we did, but was advised by her fixer in Nairobi, a British freelance, that it would be too dangerous. That same freelance journalist, Rob Crilly, later told me how he'd feared he would be in big trouble with *The Sunday Times* when they saw my piece from Bossaso that first weekend.

'I was expecting a phone call from them asking 'why the hell did you tell us that place was dangerous?" he said. 'Then a few days later I heard you'd got kidnapped. I was torn between feeling sorry for you and feeling pleased that I'd been proved right.'

Since my release, I have also often been asked if I know why exactly we were kidnapped, and what led to our release. Who did it? Was it political or financial? And was a ransom paid? My answer is that I would be doing a disservice to all the people who helped get us free if I were to reveal any details of what hand they played. Nearly all hostage situations are essentially games of high-stakes bluff and double bluff, and it is through such tactics that negotiators persuade kidnappers that their best interests lie in freeing their captive. For that reason, the poker face must never, ever slip, and the tricks of the trade, the hidden aces up the sleeve, cannot generally be disclosed.

More importantly, I would be jeopardising the prospects of the many other poor hostages who are still stuck out in Somalia and elsewhere. As I write, there is a British aid worker kidnapped down near Mogadishu who may soon be spending his third anniversary in captivity. A Canadian freelance journalist and an Australian freelance photographer have also just been released in Mogadishu, having spent 436 days as hostages. What I can say about my own case is that a senior figure in the Puntland government, whom I cannot name, allegedly commissioned the kidnapping. He did so much to the anger of others, who know the damage that hostage taking does to their country's prospects, be it on land or at sea. But exactly how my own case was resolved is a secret that will have to remain – unlike me, thank God – in those mountain caves forever.

16: In Search of the Ladder Salesmen

'The taking of pyrates...is but a dry business, unless they catch 'em by extraordinary good fortune, with a prize fresh in their mouths.'
(The frustrations of early pirate hunting, *Queen Anne's Navy in the West Indies*, by Ruth Bourne)

'I MUST SAY, it looks quite nice from here.' Squinting to avoid the dazzle of the mid-morning sun on the water, the Royal Navy officer on HMS *Cornwall* cast his eyes towards land. There, squatting in front of a range of sepia-coloured mountains, was our first sign of life in nearly a day's sailing along an otherwise barren coastline. From three miles out to sea, Bossaso was just a flat smear of urban grey, with dock cranes, mosque towers and palm trees faintly visible amid the sprawl. To a sailor, perhaps any stretch of land begins to look tempting after a time.

'Take it from me, it's not very nice up close,' I said. 'You see that bit over there?' I pointed towards the west side of town. 'Somewhere round there is where they grabbed us, on the way to the airport. And you see those mountains? Somewhere in there, don't know where exactly, that's where we spent the next six weeks.'

My companion smiled, staring down into the foam-flecked emerald waters, where earlier, a school of porpoises had held a friendly race with the ship for several nautical miles.

'How does it feel, seeing it now?' he asked.

'Strange. Didn't think I'd ever see this stretch of coastline again.'

I certainly hadn't. It was September 2009, nine months on since my release from the land on our starboard bow. Life had more or less returned to normal. Jane and I were still together, and I was back at work, having suffered no apparent post-traumatic stress whatsoever, to the point where colleagues had begun to joke that I must have made the whole thing up. I was also travelling the world again, the only difference being that the foreign desk was now a little more cautious about where I went. Somalia, in particular, was out of bounds. Having a reporter kidnapped there once could be put down to misfortune. Twice would seem like carelessness. Hence my 'embed' on HMS *Cornwall*, a 5,500 tonne frigate patrolling with the international anti-piracy fleet off the Somali coast. It was a way of continuing to pursue the pirate story, but with the advantage that if we did come across any pirates, it would be them putting their hands up, not me. Even Jane had been won over when I'd explained how well-armed the *Cornwall* was.

'It has a 4.5 inch gun as its main weapon,' I'd told her.

'Only 4.5 inches?' she asked.

'Not 4.5 inches *long*. 4.5 inches *wide*. That's very big indeed.'

Cornwall was the lead vessel in the NATO-led operation 'Ocean Shield', a multi-national naval mission now tasked with stopping the Somali piracy problem. There were also missions led by the EU and the US, plus naval presences from nearly every other big shipping nation in the world. All had watched the explosion in piracy in 2008 with mounting alarm. Together they had now formed a loose confederacy of maritime policemen, temporarily burying a number of historic hatchets in pursuit of a common foe. Countries that could have fought half a dozen World War IIIs between them were now on joint patrol: Americans and Iranians, Indians and Pakistanis, Chinese and Taiwanese, Greeks and Turks, looking out not just for their own boats, but each other's.

Unfortunately, having widespread backing for the mission was no guarantee of success. For one thing, it was a dauntingly large area to patrol. A flotilla that numbered some 30 ships at best was having to cover the entire Gulf of Aden and part of Somalia's Indian Ocean coast, an area of at least two million square miles. And for another, the presence of vessels several hundred times bigger and better-armed than the pirate skiffs seemed to pose alarmingly little deterrent. If anyone had thought that the mere sight of huge frigates and battleships on the horizon would make the pirates think twice, they were wrong. From Eyl, Hobyo, Harardhere and dozens of other pirate enclaves, scruffy skiffs continued to venture forth in search of victims, content to take the not-particularly-wild-gamble that their chance of bumping into a naval vessel in an area the size of Western Europe was remote indeed.

At the time I went aboard HMS *Cornwall*, its commanders were bracing themselves for a seasonal surge in business. The summer monsoon period, which made the sea too choppy for even the most desperate buccaneers, was at an end, and attacks in the Gulf of Aden were starting up again. The pirates' previous hunting season had been highly profitable. Just the week before my visit, one gang picked up a $2 million ransom from the owners of the MV *Irena*, an oil tanker whose 21-strong Filipino crew had been held off the coast of Eyl for five months. That, though, was now the lower end of the scale in payout terms. Back in March, the *Sirius Star* had been freed for an estimated $4 million. Overall for 2008, the pirates were thought to have netted in the region of $150 million. All of which more than made up for the odd failed mission, or the odd one of their ranks shot dead or arrested by the likes of HMS *Cornwall*.

The outside world was only just waking up to the stakes involved. In April, shortly before the hijacking of the MV *Irena*, a group of pirates had taken the US-flagged *Maersk Alabama*, a container ship sailing to the Kenyan port of Mombasa and carrying, ironically enough, cargoes of food aid destined for Somalia. Unusually for a modern-day container ship, it was crewed not by Filipinos, Chinese or Eastern Europeans, but by 21 Americans. Aware of their potential value on the hostage market, the crew managed to overpower their captors, while three pirates who took the captain hostage separately were shot dead by snipers on a US naval boat. But what became a tale of all-American heroism could easily have been an all-American tragedy. Had the pirates got the crew to the Somali mainland, they could very easily have fallen into the hands of the Shabab. It would have given newly-elected President Barack Obama the worst hostage crisis since the storming of the American embassy in Iran in 1979.

On US network TV, pirates were now being talked up as big-time bogeymen, with questions being asked at high levels in Washington. Just where, exactly, was all that ransom cash going? And what if the pirates formed some unholy alliance with Al Qaeda? After all, if this much havoc could be caused just by a bunch of ransom-seekers, what might happen if a bunch of jihadists got the same idea? TV pundits described the Horn of Africa as a whole new region of instability for their viewers to worry about, this time not just one single bad apple like Iraq or Afghanistan, but a whole crop of failed and warring states: Somalia, Yemen, Ethiopia, Eritrea, plus a vast stretch of sea that was a spawning pool for all manner of criminality. There wasn't just piracy, but arms shipping, people trafficking and drug-smuggling. Yet it was through here that a large number of the ships that supplied the civilised world with its daily goods, be it cars, oil, cement, or food, had to pass. The piracy problem was now the world's problem, as Mr Obama had made clear after the *Maersk Alabama* incident.

'I want to be very clear that we are resolved to halt the rise of piracy in that region,' he declared. 'To achieve that goal we're going to have to continue to work with our partners to prevent future attacks.'

Objective number one of that partnership was marked out in a large naval chart that I'd picked up at the EU mission's HQ in Djibouti, where a skull and crossbones flag hung on the wall of the public affairs office. It was entitled *'Anti-Piracy planning chart for The Red Sea, Gulf of Aden and Arabian Sea'*. It had been printed just a few months before by the British Admiralty, presumably the first such chart they had done in 200 years. Etched out in blue ink through the narrow straights of the Gulf of Aden was a shipping route called the 'Internationally Recommended Transit Corridor'. It was a stretch of water about ten miles wide, running in a dead straight line for about 500 miles. The IRTC, as it was known, was the new designated safe route for shipping in the Gulf of Aden. Vessels passing through would sail to a given rendezvous point, and then join a convoy which would have a naval escort through the most dangerous stretches of water, avoiding the Somali coastline to the south and the Yemeni coastline to the north, where pirates also lurked inshore. Sailors with an eye for an ancient history likened it to the Greek myth of the straits of Scylla and Charybdis, with its deadly whirlpool on one side and man-eating monster on the other.

Those same classically-minded observers might have recalled, though, that many of the benighted crews that braved Scylla and Charybdis did not make it. In similar fashion, the IRTC had not stopped the pirates continuing to snare victims. About a quarter of ships chose not to use it, either because they were in too much of a hurry to wait for rendezvous instructions, or because they still weren't convinced there was much danger. Those who did, meanwhile, ran the same risks as a herd of wildebeest migrating through the Serengeti. Slower-moving craft, which strayed from the group or failed to keep up, were at risk of being picked off by the small, agile pirate skiffs. Being made of wood, small and low-slung, the skiffs were largely invisible to radar, and often a ship's watchman would fail to spot them until they were just a few hundred yards away. Armed with the element of surprise, they could swarm aboard and have the crew rounded up before any warship could intervene. According to one of HMS *Cornwall*'s senior officers, Lieutenant Commander Graham Bennett, they had on average just 15 minutes to act once a ship had raised the alarm.

'Our window of opportunity is very short,' he told me. 'As soon as the pirates are on board, we have lost control of the situation as they have control of the hostages.'

I raised this over dinner one night in the quarters of Commodore Steve Chick, the *Cornwall*'s most senior officer. Commanders took it as a personal failure whenever a ship got taken, he said, but once the pirates had their guns pointed at a captain's head, there was very little they could do.

'Why don't you just attack any vessel that gets hijacked?' I asked.

'You are into a hostage release situation,' Chick replied. 'For which you are talking about special forces-type operations, and the willingness from the flag state to accept that there may be casualties. You only have to look at how those situations can end – the French recently lost one of their hostages.'

He was referring to the *Tanit*, a yacht skippered by an idealistic young French couple, Chloé and Florent Lemaçon. Depending on your point of view, they'd embarked on what was either a free-spirited or reckless cruise through the Gulf of Aden back in April, and had been taken by pirates not far from where we were now. The French government had given the go-ahead for an armed operation, fearing the pirates were planning to get them ashore and spirit them away to the same mountains where José and I had been held. The French calculated that it would be easier to free them at sea than on land. But as commandos stormed the boat, killing two pirates, a stray French round hit and killed Florent Lemaçon. It showed how this kind of asymmetric conflict handed the Somalis the key advantage. While the pirates would see the death of a gang member as just a business overhead, Western governments did not want casualties at all, especially civilian ones. For Chloe Lemaçon, now a widow with two young children, a few months in a cave and a ransom payment would no doubt have been preferable.

All the same, unlike Britain's military campaigns in Iraq and Afghanistan, few on board HMS *Cornwall* questioned the point of being here. On the contrary, there seemed a certain relish in tangling with such an old adversary again – not least, perhaps, because other worthy opponents were thin on the horizon. At a time when the future of modern warfare appeared to be guerrilla conflicts waged in cities, deserts and mountains, the Navy was having to justify itself more than any other branch of the Armed Forces. Politicians on all sides were questioning the expense of battleships, submarines and aircraft carriers designed for a superpower war against the Soviet Union. What was the point, when what were now needed were foot patrols and school-building projects in Basra or Helmand? The pirates provided a useful answer. They were a timely reminder of something that Britain's political masters had gradually forgotten over the past two hundred years – that without properly-funded navies, the seas of the world could be just as troublesome as anywhere on land.

Certainly, stepping on board the *Cornwall* was in some ways like travelling back to a bygone era of war fighting. Work on the ship had started on the Clyde back in the early 1980s, when East-West tensions were still high. Yet by the time it was launched in 1985 by the Princess of Wales, whose portrait still hung in the corridor near the officers' mess, Mikhail Gorbachev was about to launch *perestroika* in the Soviet Union. The total war it had been built for had never happened, but it was still very much equipped to fight one. Its arsenal was awesomely powerful. As well as its main 4.5 inch gun, capable of obliterating somewhere like Bossaso from 20 miles away, it was equipped with Harpoon surface-to-surface missiles, which could deliver half a ton of high explosive as far as 150 miles. There was also a fearsome thing called Goalkeeper, a sort of super-Gatling gun designed to destroy incoming missiles by creating a hail of fire at 4,200 rounds a minute.

'The idea is that you fire so many bullets that one of them, at some point, will hit the missile before it hits you,' explained Lieutenant Commander Alex Kendrick. So far, nobody had ever had to test it out for real.

Against the *Cornwall*'s latest foe, however, none of that hardware was much use. Instead, its most effective weapon was a Lynx helicopter that flew daily sorties in search of pirate activity on both land and sea. While the NATO force was under strict orders never to land on Somali terrain, the Lynx could scour the coastline for pirate dens hidden among the cliffs, caves and sand dunes. The helicopter pilot, Lieutenant Commander Roger Wyness, was a suntanned, wiry Mancunian with a middle-distance stare that looked like he'd just walked off the set of *Apocalypse Now*. He'd previously done a stint chasing cocaine smugglers in the Caribbean, although from what he said, hunting pirates sounded a lot more dangerous. The only way to spot their dens was with the naked eye, which involved skimming along the beaches, coves and inlets at very low height. A mismanoeuvre, mechanical breakdown, or lucky burst of gunfire from a disturbed pirates' nest could drop him into their clutches, giving them either a chance for some on-the-spot justice, or a very valuable hostage cargo.

'When we first got here we didn't go within ten miles of the coast,' Wyness said, as his crew of two Marine snipers and a navigator prepared for another sortie. 'We first started it about a month ago, and it was very nerve-wracking – we briefed in very considerable detail for every conceivable scenario of what might go wrong. We know the implications if we get caught.'

In the event of a *Black Hawk Down* type-incident, Wyness and his crew had been put through full hostile environment training. Not the watered-down crash course of the kind that I'd done, but the sort taught to special forces soldiers, spies and others who might find themselves behind enemy lines. As well as being drilled in how to live rough and evade capture, each crew member carried a thick roll of $100 bills so that they could pay as well as shoot their way out of trouble. It was a modern-day version of the 'goolie chits' used by British pilots in Mesopotamia in World War I, which carried several gold sovereigns plus a message in Arabic promising further riches to anyone who helped them back to British lines. Wyness knew, though, that plenty of people on the mainland might be willing to double his money, especially given that *Cornwall*'s predecessor, HMS *Cumberland* had killed those two pirates down in Eyl. Had any local pirate gangs put up bounties for nosey helicopter pilots, I asked? He made no reply, but his gloved finger drew a brief slit mark across his throat.

Since the start of his sightseeing tours, Wyness had counted 15 separate pirate camps on the northern Puntland coastline. At each one, the Lynx would hover long just enough to snatch a few photographs, which went back to the *Cornwall*'s staff intelligence officer, Lieutenant Martin Tickle. Sat at a computer in a cramped, windowless room below deck, Tickle ran me through the slide show he'd compiled so far.

One photo, marked 'Pirate Camp 5', was at a place called Qoow, ten miles outside Bossaso. To the uneducated eye, it could have been just a fishermen's rest-stop: a few skiffs pulled up above the tidemark, and a brushwood bivouac nearby. But certain 'trip wires', as Tickle referred to them, told a different story. No ordinary fishermen would need skiffs with twin high-powered engines, or such a huge stash of reserve fuel barrels. One further item, half-hidden under a tarpaulin, gave the game away as clearly as hoisting the Jolly Roger. It was a grappling ladder, which the pirates would attach to their victim's ship before swarming aboard. There was no other good excuse for having one, although that hadn't stopped the pirates thinking a few up when caught. A public affairs officer in Djibouti had told me how one group, when arrested, had claimed they were just passing 'ladder salesmen'. When asked why they only had one ladder on board, they'd said they were running low on stock.

A second camp, hidden amid a stretch of crimson crags, reminded me of where I had been held. There were a few blankets stretched out in the shade of an overhang, the remains of a campfire, and clothes hung out to dry on the rocks. An elderly, grey-bearded man, clad, oddly enough, in an England football shirt, was staring up at the camera and waving his arms around. Another photo, labelled 'Camp Geesaley', showed three men in white vests lounging around under some beach palms, not looking the slightest bit concerned about the military helicopter eyeballing them. 'These chaps clearly appeared to have had a zero bothered factor about the helicopter being there,' said Tickle.

The sheer number of camps, and the fact that some of them were just a stone's throw from Bossaso, suggested that what little law and order there was in the port really did stop once you left town. Lt Commander Bennett, however, had a positive spin on this. Previously, he said, the pirates had not needed to hide out in remote spots. They'd operated openly from the towns along the coast, enjoying a certain status as local heroes. But a year on, public opinion was turning against them, as the influxes of ransom cash brought in problems with drugs, drink and prostitution. There'd been anti-pirate demonstrations in some villages, backed by clan elders who feared the wealthier pirates might soon challenge their own power. The pirates' gangsta-rap swagger, the feting of their get-rich-or-die-tryin' lifestyle, was no longer acceptable, or not in public at least.

'The big concern among the community leaders now is that piracy is eroding their traditional values,' Bennett said. 'The people who have got lots of ransom money can buy lots of weapons, drugs, and build power bases in their own right. At another level, traditional clan values are eroded by low-level crime, prostitution, drugs, and other bad things that are coming in. As a consequence, the pirates no longer operate in the towns. They have been hoofed out, and have to operate on these remote beaches.'

To what extent this was wishful thinking on the part of NATO high command, I wasn't sure. It was fair, though, to say that Bennett's ear was closer to the ground than most. NATO was mindful that as with Iraq and Afghanistan, the key to long-term success against piracy was not Western firepower at sea, but building up local security forces on land. Bennett, a bluff, jokey fellow in his early 50s, had been tasked with liaising with the Puntland authorities. To that end, he'd launched Operation Patch – 'Yes, as in pirate's eye patch' – a pioneering project to schmooze Puntland's various power-players, and persuade locals that piracy was not in their long-term interests. It was a role that had seen him take the concept of gunboat diplomacy into uncharted new waters, steering a tricky course between traditional naval power play and modern-day hearts-and-minds strategy. In a charm offensive via some Somali journalists he'd invited on board, he'd tried to recruit local clan chiefs to the anti-piracy cause, stressing that contrary to popular opinion, the NATO warships weren't just there to protect marauding foreign trawlers. In the same breath, however, he'd warned bluntly that if clan chiefs let the piracy continue, more of their young men were going to get shot.

Like the crisis team on the *Telegraph*, it had taken Bennett a while to work out who he could deal with on the land. He spoke warmly of his local contact on the Bossaso Coastguard, a Somali who spoke fluent English. But when I asked if he meant Abdiweli Ali Taar, the Coastguard man I'd met the year before, he shook his head. It transpired that there were not one, but two Coastguards in Bossaso, both running as rival operations, and each apparently claiming the other was a charlatan and fraud.

'We're still finding out who is really who, and we were wary at first of getting in with ex-pirates,' he admitted. 'But to be fair, everybody we have dealt so far seems determined to eradicate piracy, and we have to start somewhere. If we can engage, rather than just fighting the symptoms, that will be how we can sort this out.'

Already, the partnership seemed to be bearing fruit. Several of the camps that the Lynx had photographed were the result of tips passed to them via Bennett's Coastguard contact, who picked up occasional word of activity along the coast, but lacked the resources to search such a wide area. The Coastguard had also done a few raids themselves, despite not being particularly well-armed.

'They are brave, they go off and have firefights,' said Bennett. 'They raided a pirate camp about a month ago and four of them got killed. We say, "Why do you do it, when you're only on $150 a month?" They say, "It's because we don't want pirates to take over." True, we can't validate what they say, but they are either very good people or very good actors.'

It was for the latest stage in Operation Patch's charm offensive that *Cornwall* was within sight again of Bossaso. An invitation had gone out to the Coastguard to pay a visit, along with a few other selected local dignitaries and journalists. Their boat was due to sail out from the port later in the day, and I was curious to see who might be among the boarding party. If Ahmed and Mustapha were still out in Bossaso, touting themselves as local hacks, it would make for a very timely re-union indeed. I hadn't discussed with Bennett the possibility of chucking them in the ship's brig, but it would fascinating to observe their reactions if they saw me waiting to greet them.

Meanwhile, *Cornwall* remained on standby to answer any distress calls from ships about to receive a boarding party from any of the pirate camps. Wyness and his crew were on duty from dawn to dusk – the pirates didn't like working in the dark, apparently – and could scramble within minutes of any mayday call coming through. They would then race off in a bid to intercept the pirates before they got too close to the ship. A sustained burst from its belt-fed machine guns, which would churn up a spectacular spray of water, was normally enough to make any pirate craft that hadn't reached its target think twice. But if necessary, the two Royal Marine sharpshooters in the rear were both armed with super high-powered 0.50 calibre sniper rifles that could take out either a person or an outboard engine with a single shot.

'The helicopter can be as steady as a rock if we want it to be, and I have seen these guys fire 20 shots into a plastic bag at 300 or 400 yards,' said Wyness. 'As soon as the pirates get on to a ship's bridge with their guns they are in control, and you are into the realm of special forces stuff. But if we see someone climbing up a ship with a weapon, he will go for a swim with a bullet in the back of his head.'

So far – and somewhat, I sensed, to his disappointment – no pirate had taken the plunge. Not for lack of sightings of the enemy, but because of the rules of engagement laid down by the legal people at NATO HQ in Bahrain, who insisted on very clear evidence that an attack was about to take place. On several occasions, Wyness had spotted pirate skiffs full of armed men, yet unless they were actually about to board a ship, there wasn't much he was allowed to do.

'So far we have been denied permission every time when we have requested to either fire a warning burst or take out an engine,' he said, frustration in his voice. 'It is difficult when I am hovering over the boat from just feet away, looking at RPGs and AK-47s, but the legal people need to know if the intent is there.'

Some of the more experienced pirates seemed to have become aware of how tight the rules were, and just ignored the helicopters completely.

'We chased one bunch recently, they were old hands and clearly weren't going to stop for us,' Wyness said. 'We followed them, but then we ran low on fuel and had to return. It is massively frustrating when that happens, and I can tell you, it gets difficult for me to keep the morale up for my guys.'

It was a similar story for the *Cornwall*'s two Royal Marine boarding teams. Each eight man team had done a three-week course training at the naval base at Faslane in Scotland, practising their boarding techniques on old tugs. If a pirate boat was spotted, they would head out in a couple of rigid inflatable motorboats and apprehend them. But again, only if the pirates were actually in the act of attacking a ship would shots be fired or arrests made. Otherwise, the standard drill was simply to confiscate any weapons on board, and then let them go on their way. The cost, manpower and hassle involved in putting pirates before a court meant that in practice, it was only worth prosecuting the most open-and-shut cases. The nearest country willing to put them on trial was Kenya, a thousand miles away, where the court system was already log-jammed with pirate defendants. The only alternative was taking them back to be prosecuted in Britain, a prospect most Somali pirates would be overjoyed at. They'd do a few years in a comfortable British jail, and then have a good chance of claiming asylum, as the British government counted Somalia as too dangerous for deportation.

Instead, the *Cornwall* relied on a tactic known as 'disruption and harassment'. The Marines would confiscate the pirates' weapons, and destroy their skiffs' high-powered engines (although obligingly leaving one intact so the pirates could get back to shore). 'If we can disrupt their activities, they can always re-equip and come back, but we think they will eventually begin to lose heart,' reckoned Commodore Chick.

I wasn't so sure myself. The going rate for equipping a pirate skiff with crew, outboard engines and RPGs was only about $7,000, which was very small change out of the average ransom payment. The pirates who had taken Colin Darch's boat had not been the slightest bit bothered when their two skiffs had sunk during the hijack. Anyone deprived of their kit would not find it that hard to start up again. And besides, just what kind of a message did 'disruption and harassment' send out? The logistical difficulties of prosecutions were understandable, but it was still the equivalent of stopping a bunch of armed bank robbers in a high street, taking their weapons off them, and then letting them go. In effect, a blind eye worthy of Lord Nelson himself was being turned to the act of armed hostage taking, something normally viewed as a very serious offence indeed.

It was also a far cry from the way previous eras of Royal Navy commanders had dealt with pirates. Back in the 17th and 18th centuries, the authorities made it very clear that buccaneering was a mug's game. At the old Admiralty courts down at Execution Dock in Wapping, judges took the view that hanging was quite literally too good for them, ordering the gallows rope to be tied deliberately short so that the 'drop' that each convict made wasn't enough to break his neck outright. Instead, the condemned man would asphyxiate slowly, his thrashing feet performing a macabre sailor's jig known as the Marshal's Dance. Nor was dignity granted once death finally come.

Rather than being buried, pirates would routinely have their bodies displayed in a gibbet, as decaying, real-life examples of the folly of their lives. The gibbeted remains of the 17th century pirate William Kidd, who famously killed a crewman by hitting him with a bucket, swung in the sea breeze at Tilbury Point on the Thames for a full 20 years, there as a warning for all passing sailors to see.

Today, by contrast, the only courts that held out a noose for the Somali pirates were the ones in Bossaso. But even if the *Cornwall* arrested a bunch from the camp just ten miles outside the city, they would not be sent there for trial – not because they might bribe their way to freedom, but because of British government concerns for human rights.

'At the moment the United Kingdom has concerns about the reliability of the Puntland justice system, so we can't hand them over,' said Bennett. 'We need transparency to make sure that crimes are fairly tried regardless of what clan they are, and there is also an issue about the death penalty for pirates.'

I sensed that neither Bennett nor anybody else on HMS *Cornwall* was entirely happy with the range of options at their disposal. If nothing else, it gave the Navy little chance to prove themselves as warriors again in the eyes of the public back home. Yet this wasn't the only politically awkward aspect of the mission. The Nelsonian blind eye was also being turned the issue of ransom payments. The foreign naval presence was under instructions not to stop any of the millions of dollars being handed over by the shipping companies, which were being delivered under their noses at sea. A boat or plane would drop off a bag full of cash, upon receipt of which the pirates would then depart from the hijacked boat. The shipping industry had been doing this for years, but in the past, it had been in clandestine fashion, rather than with the world's navies and media watching. Now, though, politicians in Somalia, Britain and elsewhere were demanding to know why the shipping industry was coughing up so easily, and why navies weren't being instructed to get in the way.

*****

The people who masterminded the ransom payments on behalf of the shipping industry were not the shadowy figures one might expect. Movies usually portrayed such negotiations as taking place in seedy bars or hotel lobbies, with men in dark glasses handing suitcases of cash to one another. In reality, they operated out of smart boardroom offices in London's financial Square Mile, which has served as a hub for the global shipping insurance industry ever since Lloyd's Register started up in a local coffee house in the 17th century.

For any shipping line whose vessel came to grief at sea, one of the top people to turn to was Stephen Askins of Ince & Co, a City law firm based in St Katharine's Dock, just up from the old Admiralty Courts at Wapping. A former Royal Marine who had re-trained as a lawyer, Askins was living proof of the phrase 'worse things happen at sea'. He and his on-call team answered four or five mayday calls a week, be it a cargo freighter sinking, a tanker causing an oil slick, or a ferry going down with hundreds of passengers on board.

I first met him at his offices on a wet and bitterly cold day in February, not long after my release. As I waited for him at reception, I flicked through a copy of *Lloyd's List,* the daily shipping newspaper. On its front page was a story about the release of MV *Faina*, a Ukrainian freighter that had been one of Askins' higher-profile Somali piracy cases. It had had a plot twist worthy of a spy thriller. When the pirates had boarded it, they had found that what looked like an ordinary cargo ship was carrying a secret consignment of Soviet-made T-72 tanks, rockets and anti-aircraft guns. To add to the intrigue, documents discovered on board said the cache was bound for rebel movements in southern Sudan, in breach of an international arms embargo. The US navy had surrounded the craft to prevent the weapons being offloaded, but it was still confirmation of everybody's worst fears about the potential for a piracy case to suddenly escalate into something much more serious. Askins and his team spent the next five months negotiating with the pirates, who originally wanted a $35 million ransom, but settled for $3.2 million. From his point of view, it counted as a job well done.

'Is there a moral argument about paying ransoms?' he asked, rhetorically. 'Yes, of course there is. But there is also the question of how you get your ship's crew out by any other means. The people who want ransom payments to be banned don't go on to discuss how you otherwise free the people currently held hostage.'

Askins stressed that contrary to popular wisdom, it was not illegal to pay ransoms in Britain. The only exception was if there was a 'reasonable belief' that the hostage takers were terrorists. If the kidnap was purely criminal, and had taken place in some lawless foreign land where the local police were of little help, pragmatism generally prevailed. Western governments would not generally get involved in the actual handover of money, but they were prepared to look the other way while it was done as a private transaction. It wasn't just in failed states like Somalia. In countries like Nigeria, Colombia and Mexico, hundreds of ransoms were paid out every year to spring businessmen from the clutches of various kidnapping gangs. By mutual consent between gang and ransom payer, though, most such cases simply never made the news.

In Somalia, none of pirate gangs had been proved to have any connections to the Shabab or Al Qaeda, so the anti-terrorism clauses did not apply. The pirates were also – by global kidnapping standards at least – relatively easy people to do business with. That was the view, anyway, of Leslie Edwards, a professional hostage negotiation advisor recognised as one of the leading players in the field in Britain. A burly former Army officer who now ran his own firm, Compass Risk Management, he'd helped negotiate in some 45 kidnap cases over the years, from aid workers in Iraq through to oilmen in the Niger delta and the teenage daughters of wealthy landowners in Venezuela. Once, he'd even secured the return to the BBC of some tapes of a new dramatisation of *Robin Hood*, stolen from a film set in Hungary. Every case, he said, brought its own unique stresses. By the end of the tougher days, he'd go back to his hotel room soaked in sweat and exhausted, yet so wired he could barely sleep. On his very first piracy case, when the tug delivering the ransom broke down in the middle of the night 100 miles off the Somali coast, he found himself on the point of throwing up because he was so tense. But now, with six ship hijackings under his belt, he'd concluded that of all the different kidnappers he'd dealt with, the Somalis were not that bad.

'Piracy cases are stressful, sure,' he told me. 'On a hijacked ship you have got maybe 25 crew, which means also 25 wives, 50 parents, maybe 50 kids and 100 grandparents, so you feel a lot of responsibility. But the Somalis have got a brilliant business model. They seldom deliberately hurt or kill the crew. They never claim to be Islamic fundamentalists because they know that would make it illegal for the insurance companies and lawyers to pay them. And they normally have a code of conduct for how they treat the hostages. Sometimes they even put up lists of do's and don'ts in Somali around the ship, with fines for anyone who breaks them.'

'But the other golden rule they stick to is that once an agreement has been reached and payment has been made, they will release the hostages. There is seldom any messing about, no trying to keep maybe one or two people, or holding out for longer in the hope of getting more money. It might take 60 or 90 days to negotiate the agreed ransom, sure, but each ship owner knows that eventually, the Somalis will keep their word. As such, there is very little reason to want a navy to do an armed raid, when you have can a peaceful alternative for $1 or $2 million.'

True, Edwards said, some ship owners took a little time to come round to this way of thinking. Many was the time he'd arrived on a case to find some irate shipping magnate screaming abuse at the kidnappers down the phone, demanding to know why some navy wasn't steaming to the rescue.

'Often the real problems aren't the kidnappers, but the ship owners,' he said. 'They can't understand how a bunch of Somalis in sandals and shorts, from one of the poorest nations on earth, can make a laughing stock of the world's navies. There'll be a lot of shouting and swearing, calling the pirates bastards and all that, and quite often I will have to spend the first day or two repairing the damage.

'But then we point out to the owners what might happen if a navy ship carries out a raid. For one thing, some of their staff might die. And for another, the pirates might run the ship aground on the coast, which means it can probably never be recovered and will be a total loss. Just in terms of the value of the ship and the cargo alone, that could be $50 million or more. At that point they begin to see the logic of it. And the Somalis will generally make it an attractive option by sticking to their side of the bargain. They may be from a poor, desperate country, but they've got good business brains, and they're clever enough to see how to keep the money coming. And to be honest, I don't think the navies or governments want it done any way either. Raiding a ship is very risky for their reputations if it all goes wrong, and it just isn't worth it when there is a way of resolving the thing peacefully.'

He was sceptical of the talk from the anti-piracy fleet about the world's navies being united by the pirate threat. When push came to shove, he said, there was no such thing as collective responsibility.

'Take a hijack I dealt with last year. The ship was flagged in the Caribbean, but owned by a German company, which had an HQ in Holland. The crew were Filipinos, but with Russian officers. The firm that chartered the ship was Danish, and the cargo belonged to a South African outfit. Who is responsible for that in terms of the international community? Which country's navy is going to stick their neck out? Frankly, nobody wanted to get involved, so it ended up between us and the ship owners to sort it out. The pirates wanted $3 million and we got it down to $1 million in a couple of weeks. Job done.'

*****

In the end, I never did get to meet my old acquaintances from Bossaso again. The *Cornwall* hung around outside the port for a couple of hours, but no boarding party sailed out to meet them. Bennett was told that there was 'emergency cabinet meeting' going on which required the attendance of all senior players in the city. What it was about we never learned, only that it was a more pressing appointment than that with the 5,500 tonne frigate that had sailed all the way from

Djibouti to see them. Bearing in mind my previous experience of Puntland's cabinet ministers, I wondered whether it might just have been a particularly heavy qhat session the night before.

The local bigwigs weren't the only people ignoring the *Cornwall*'s imposing presence in the bay. As the ship turned round to head back to Djibouti, it spotted a large skiff about a mile away, gunwales low in the water. It was clearly carrying a heavy load, hidden under a tarpaulin. When the Marines were despatched to investigate, a man at the skiff's stern waved them away, as if to say there was nothing to worry about. Then the tarpaulin suddenly rippled, and a black Somali head poked out to see what was going on. Then another. And another. The skiff was a people trafficker, like the one my old friend Faisal had taken en route to Greece, and the 'cargo', on hearing another boat approaching, thought they were about to be rumbled. They needn't have worried. Once again, this was a crime where the Nelsonian blind eye was being turned. The *Cornwall* was under orders not to intercept people traffickers, partly because they had no proper facilities for accommodating refugees, and partly because the smugglers had a nasty habit of throwing their passengers into the water if they got chased. This wasn't to get rid of the evidence, just another cynical manipulation of the rules under which the foreign warships operated. If any navy saw a man overboard, they were obliged, on humanitarian grounds, to attend to the rescue before anything else. Had the Royal Marines tried to arrest the people smugglers, they would end up having to pull several dozen people out of the sea first. Instead, the *Cornwall* radioed the boat's position and direction to the Yemeni Coastguard. It would be their call whether they would be arrested.

Despite being hamstrung by rules of engagement, the multinational force did claim some progress in imposing law and order on the Gulf of Aden. Successful piracy attacks were well down on the numbers for the year before, although as time went on, the pirates had simply gone further in search of victims, pushing into the Indian Ocean. Rather than just going on one-day hunting sorties, they increased their use of so-called 'mother ships' – larger boats, often hijacked dhows or trawlers, that could put to sea for a month at a time. The mother ships would serve as floating operations centres, towing a few smaller skiffs with them and sailing hundreds of miles into the ocean, out of range of the helicopter patrols of the multinational naval fleet. Ships began to be attacked as far away as the Seychelles, 1,000 miles from the Somali coast. By increasing the size of their hunting ground, they reduced not only the chances of being caught, but also the chances of their victims being on the look-out.

Such had been the case with British yachting couple Paul and Rachel Chandler, who were hijacked in October 2009 as they sailed from the Seychelles towards Tanzania, a route they'd assumed was safe. The pair, from Tunbridge Wells in Kent, were eventually released some 13 months later, having spent much of their time in captivity separated from one another. Once again, their capture was an incident that painted the Royal Navy's pirate-fighting capabilities in less than flattering light. Three weeks after the hijacking, it emerged that a Royal Navy support ship, the *Wave Knight*, had apprehended the pirate skiff as it was taking the Chandlers towards a mother ship. But rather than intervening, the *Wave Knight* simply watched as the couple were put on board the mother ship. The Navy said that as the pirates already had their guns to the couples' heads, only a special forces operation could have freed them, and even then it would have been very risky. But once again, it generated the worst possible headlines back home. An innocent British couple, dragged away from the holiday of a lifetime by Somali thugs, and all the mighty Royal Navy could do was sit and watch. Combined with growing concern over the way so many 'ladder salesmen' were being let go, it led to fierce criticism of the Navy again. The sniping infuriated naval high command, so much so that its most senior officer, First Lord Sea Admiral Sir Mark Stanhope, abandoned the usual practice of not responding to press criticism. At a speech a month later at London's Chatham House think-tank, he set the record straight.

'Before anyone asks questions on the *Wave Knight*, I would like to make a statement,' he told the assembled company. '*Wave Knight* did exactly the right thing. She acted professionally and in accordance with her primary purpose, which was to assure the safety of the Chandlers. I take real issue with some of the emotional and scurrilous language being used to describe the actions of my sailors... They do not appreciate, and I do not like them, being branded cowards.'

He had a point. As with all its anti-piracy operations, the Navy was doing what it could within the rules that were laid down for it. It wasn't their fault if their political masters were reluctant to take the risk of casualties. Nor was it their fault if Britain refused to let its Navy deliver the kind of rough justice that it used to hand out in days of old. True, there was an arguable case for rather more prosecutions, and perhaps tougher sentences. But as Commodore Chick had pointed out to me, even long stints in jail wouldn't necessarily be that much of a deterrent. 'We could lock up several hundred of these pirates if we wanted to,' he said. 'But there is probably another 1,000 waiting to come.'

17: The Nation That Committed Suicide

LIKE A CROWD come to watch an up-and-coming local prize-fighter, the queue for the audience with Somalia's brightest political hope in years stretched all the way round the drab theatre building in East London. Watched over by a heavy police presence, hundreds of Somalis stood shivering in the cold March wind, wondering whether there was still room inside – and why the one white guy in the line had nearly got himself arrested.

I was wondering that too, given that it was me who was lying spread-eagled on the pavement, two policemen pinning my arms down and yelling in my face. My crime, such as it was, was to have been on the guest list for the evening, for which the instructions were to wait at the theatre's side door until a bouncer opened it to let a select few jump the queue. Alas, the moment he did so, a scrum of others tried to barge in too. To the passing constables, it looked like a mass break-in, with me at the front.

'Think you can just push your way in, do you?' snarled one of them, as he grabbed me from behind and dragged me down the road.

'No, I'm on the guest list. I was told to come to this door. I'm from the *Sunday Telegraph*, and...'

'Yeah, sure you are, mate. That how you get into all the events you cover, is it?'

Five minutes later, having scrutinised a press card and listened to what no doubt sounded like a tall tale about being kidnapped the year before, they let me go. *What is it about me and Somalis?*, I asked myself, as I swept the dust off my jacket and re-joined the queue. Whenever I went near them, I ended up being detained in some fashion.

The man everyone was so keen to get inside the theatre to see was Somalia's new president, Sheikh Sharif Ahmed, who was being cautiously hailed as his country's first chance of decent leadership in 20 years. Britain was rolling out the red carpet out for him, a courtesy not extended to the succession of warlords who had held the presidency before him. Sharif came to the theatre fresh from an audience with Gordon Brown, the first Somali head of state to meet a British prime minister since Siad Barre's day.

From his visit to Mr Brown he'd come away with £8 million in funding for his administration in Mogadishu, although it seemed the mandarins in Whitehall were wanting a very good return on their money. They were pinning their hopes on Sheikh Sharif as the man who would end the country's inter-clan violence, defeat the Shabab, and turn the tide on the pirate armadas, no small challenges by any means. Oh, and could he also fix a deal to free Paul and Rachel Chandler, the British yachting couple, who'd now been held for some six months? Rumour had it that some of the £8 million he'd been given was unofficially earmarked to buy their freedom.

Inside the theatre, after an hour of warm-up acts from leading lights in the Somali diaspora, he finally came on. Numerous Scotland Yard bodyguards flanked him, a reminder that friendship with the West made him a marked man

'Over the last 20 years, Somalia has been synonymous with war and displacement,' he said, to cheers and claps. 'Now terrorism and piracy have been added to this list – and they threaten death and destruction far beyond our borders.'

He spent much of his speech denouncing extremism, urging fellow Somalis in London, Manchester, Leicester and elsewhere to look out for radicals in their midst. No one wanted a Somali version of the July 7 bombings, he warned. His Foreign Office minders looked on approvingly. It was a very on-message speech – and all the more surprising given that the last time Sharif had held the reins of power in Somalia, the West had helped get rid of him.

Sharif had been one of the founding members of the Islamic Courts Union, the religious movement that had been running Mogadishu when I had visited in 2006. The story went that as a young schoolmaster, one of his own 12-year-old pupils had been snatched for ransom by a militia gang. Appalled by the fact that it had happened within his own clan's territory, Sheikh Sharif campaigned in his neighbourhood to set up an Islamic court, to which he was appointed leader. Having got his pupil and several other kidnap victims freed, he spread the court's jurisdiction to other neighbourhoods, inspiring similar outfits that eventually all joined forces.

From then on, Sharif had always remained at the more moderate end of the Courts movement. Unlike Sheikh Aweys, the chap I'd interviewed in Mogadishu, he wasn't on any UN or US 'wanted' list. However, the notion that the Courts might be a broad mosque politically-speaking had fallen on deaf ears in the administration of President George W Bush, to whom they were never anything but a prototype for an African Taliban. Having failed to dislodge the Courts through the warlords, the US had tacitly backed an invasion by Somalia's neighbour and long-term enemy, Ethiopia, ostensibly on the basis that the Courts provided a threat to regional security. In late December 2007, some three months after my own visit to Mogadishu, armoured columns from Ethiopia's US-subsidised army had rolled over the border towards the capital. The Islamists' technicals were no match for the Ethiopian tanks, and after a few one-sided skirmishes, the Courts' leadership scattered.

Like most invasions of Somalia, though, the Ethiopian victory had been short-lived. In place of the Courts, the Ethiopian forces installed the Transitional Federal Government (TFG), the fractious UN-backed body that until then had not dared set foot in Mogadishu. But within weeks, a fierce guerrilla war was being waged against both the occupying army and the TFG, who were widely denounced as quislings. After its brief window of peace under the Courts, Mogadishu echoed to the more familiar sound of battle as the Islamists deployed roadside bombs, mortar attacks and suicide bombers. Within the first three months, more than 1,000 people, mostly civilians, were killed. Hundreds of thousands more fled altogether.

The Ethiopian invasion also handed the initiative to the Courts' more hard-line factions. While Sheikh Sharif and other moderates fled abroad, the guerrilla campaign on the ground was a natural draw for the Courts' more radical affiliates, in particular the Shabab. A steady trickle of foreign jihadists, blooded by the campaigns in Iraq and Afghanistan, swelled their ranks, attracted by the chance to have a crack at what they saw as Western-backed crusade against a legitimate Islamist government.

Then, as the intensifying guerrilla campaign forced the Ethiopians to abandon many cities outside Mogadishu, Shabab militias began imposing exactly the kind of hard-line vision the outside world had always dreaded. By late 2008, they were issuing religious edicts as extreme as anything the Taliban ever dreamed up. Reports of stonings, amputations and beheadings became commonplace, while drinking and dancing were outlawed in favour of more wholesome forms of recreation, such as Koranic recital contests in which guns were dished out as prizes. Women were banned from wearing bras on the basis that they showcased the female form, with Shabab 'inspectors' pouncing on any female with a notably firm bust. In the summer of 2010, people were even forbidden from watching the World Cup. As a Shabab spokesman sternly put it, 'they will not get any benefit by watching madmen jumping up and down.'

In a bid to gain acceptance on the ground, the TFG invited the Courts' more moderate players to return from political exile and join its ranks, electing Sheikh Sharif as president in early 2009. He was, on paper, the ideal candidate – road-tested as a leader from his days with the Courts, but not so hard-line as to be unacceptable to the outside world. Yet the man now addressing the crowd in Whitechapel was increasingly a head of state in name only. In the past year, his grip on the country had grown ever weaker in the face of the Shabab's onslaught, and he now controlled little more than a few blocks of Mogadishu around the presidential compound. Among those attacking the government forces were fighters loyal to Sheikh Aweys, the Courts leader who I'd found so charming when I'd met him in Mogadishu. Now he had showed himself in rather different colours, throwing his lot in with the Shabab in a bid to topple Sheikh Sharif's administration entirely. Dependent for his survival on a detachment of African Union peacekeepers, today Sheikh Sharif spent almost as much time on foreign jaunts as he did at home. The joke was that he found it simply too tough to stay in

Mogadishu for months on end, not that anyone particularly blamed him.

Watching him address the crowd, it was easy to see why he might prefer the role of roving ambassador to holding court at home. The cheers in the audience came not just from his own supporters, but Somalis of all clans, creeds and political views, glad just to see someone, anyone, with a chance of fixing the mess back home.

'I really hope Sheikh Sharif can be the country's saviour,' said Abdiweli Abdullahi, a taxi driver who'd come from Cardiff to see him. 'He is the first person who seems acceptable to all sides.'

When I asked Abdullahi, though, if he might now think about returning to Somalia and help Sharif rebuild the nation, he shook his head. 'Not right now,' he said. I wasn't surprised. Britain, after all, was safe and comfortable, a promised land for any Somali lucky enough to get here.

Or so I assumed. It was estimated that there at least 100,000 Somalis now living in Britain, with nearly every big city in England hosting its own 'Little Mogadishu' district, complete with grocers' shops selling qhat flown in from Kenya. Some had first set foot here more than a century ago, as colonial-era seamen and dockhands who settled in the dock areas of Cardiff, Liverpool, and London's East End. Many more, though, had arrived in the wake of the collapse of Somalia's government in 1991. Yet despite being one of Britain's biggest – and oldest – diasporas, they were often described as an 'invisible' community, cut off from the society around them.

The lack of integration had started with the early generation of sailors, many of whom intended only to stay in Britain long enough to earn some money, and were therefore slow to learn English. But it had continued with the new arrivals, who often found themselves struggling with the transition from their war-torn homeland. For all the well-intentioned efforts of government policies promoting multiculturalism, Somalis played little part in British public life. Save for the BBC broadcaster Rageh Omar, there were few well-known Somali cultural figures or politicians; indeed, the only famous Somalis that the average Briton had heard of were the pirates.

Instead, the one area in which the Somali community performed notably was crime statistics, as the younger generation struggled to find its way in the new world their parents had escaped to. Growing up mainly in inner-city areas, Somali youths were prone to becoming involved with street gangs, swapping one kind of clan violence for another. In London, they were among the fastest growing groups in Feltham Young Offenders' Institute, graduates on the fast-track to a life of villainy. In criminal circles, they were also acquiring a reputation for being tough operators. Two Somali brothers, Yusuf and Mustaf Jama, were serving life in jail for the shooting of PC Sharon Beshenivsky during an armed robbery in Bradford in 2005, earning the dubious distinction of being the first people in Britain to be convicted of shooting dead a female police officer. And two other young Somalis, Yasin Omar and Ramzi Mohammed, had been among the four men convicted of the botched bombing of the London Underground on July 21, 2005. Among the law-abiding, respectable majority, the fear was that their community would become famous for all the wrong reasons.

The worries of the diaspora had been set out to me by Somalis I'd met through my unofficial role as their homeland's correspondent at the *Sunday Telegraph*. Whilst my recent experience of the country hadn't amounted to much beyond staring at the walls of a cave for six weeks, the paper still viewed me as its expert-in-residence, even though they had no intention of ever sending me there again. But it hadn't proved hard to cover the country's affairs from my own doorstep. London, I discovered, had dozens of Somali enclaves: Ealing and Hanwell in the west, Whitechapel and Wood Green in the east, Brixton and Peckham in the south, to name but a few. In Islington alone, there were said to be 33 different Somali community associations, all operating separately because each sub-clan wanted to be head of their own little organisation. Meeting people wasn't difficult. Most enjoyed the novelty of taking tea with a Westerner who'd visited their country, and were intrigued by my tale of being kidnapped, even if it was small beer compared to what they'd often fled themselves.

Among them was Fahad Mohammed, an articulate young man in his early 30s who was employed as a youth liaison worker across London. I met him at his office, where there hung a police-sponsored poster that read 'Don't let guns tear our community apart'. While that message might be too late for Somalis in Mogadishu, Mohammed hoped it was not too late for Somalis in London. He spent much of his time mentoring Somali teenagers, who ticked nearly every box in terms of social indicators that might lead them into trouble, although he seemed to be a lonely voice in raising such concerns. Politicians in Britain devoted much handwringing to why so many young Afro-Caribbean men ended up in jail, and why a few young Anglo-Pakistanis felt compelled to blow themselves up on Tube trains. Yet nobody talked in the same way about young Somalis, who were black, Muslim and from a country where violence was already a way of life.

'The best way to describe Somalia is as a country that committed suicide 20 years ago,' Mohammed told me. 'Those who have come here over the last decade or two have often seen a lot of dreadful things – their parents being killed in front of them, or the rape of their mother. In addition to all that psychological baggage, they have all the difficulties of adjusting to an entirely new country and culture. It has produced a community which is still not getting to grips with things properly even after ten years. Underachievement, unemployment and poverty are all there, and the number of Somalis in the criminal justice system is simply unbelievable.'

I was struck by his candour. Most the youth workers I'd ever interviewed tended to downplay their client group's problems, often to the point of defensiveness. Mohammed, by contrast, spoke of parts of his community being on the verge of imploding. One of the problems, he said, was the absence of the clan system, the very thing that caused so much difficulty back home. When a Somali stepped off a plane at Heathrow, he was no longer a noble Darod or a warlike Habr Gidr, instead he was just another man with a suitcase. In a big, sophisticated city like London, boasting that you were a clan big shot back in Bossaso didn't mean very much. But while it meant that the

Majerteen of Camden rarely went to war with the Darod of Islington, it also dissolved the social glue that had held people together through thick and thin for 40 generations. With it vanished a strong sense of identity, of inspirational forefathers, of values and principles tested over a millennium.

'We have a very rich culture, passed down through the oral tradition of a nomadic society,' Mohammed said. 'My father was killed in the civil war, so my own clan history I learned from my grandfather's lap. He told me about 16 generations of my family, how they went from being camel herders to middle-class businessmen, and the values of charity and being humble, honourable people, that life is not just about material gain. It gives you a sense of pride, that you have a legacy and character to uphold. Unfortunately, today all this tradition dies when people arrive at Heathrow. They see the bright lights after coming from a place that was perhaps just a village with no running water. They get a mobile phone and clean clothes, and all of a sudden, nobody can tell them anything. And because this is an oral history, if it isn't passed from generation to generation, it's lost for ever.'

Another problem was that fathers, whose role it was traditionally to pass such wisdom on, were often absent in the British Somali community. Some, like Mohammed's, had been killed in the civil war, others were still back home in Somalia, having despatched their kids abroad with a female relative in the hope that they would get a more sympathetic hearing from immigration officials. Mohammed felt that Britain's generous welfare system, with its housing allowances and child benefits, also encouraged paternal absence. It was all very well for the equality-minded British to argue that a woman should not have to be dependent on her partner for her upkeep. But in a traditional Somali culture, that robbed a man of his breadwinner identity. Mohammed knew many tales of family break-up that centred around this unexpected tilt in the power relationship.

'Our menfolk feel emasculated,' he said. 'The woman gets the house, the benefits, and the custodial rights, while the man finds it difficult to get work. Even if he was a teacher or a doctor back home, here he finds it hard to requalify, so he's just a useless guy on the streets of London. He starts chewing qhat, because it reminds him of how he once used to be somebody, then the wife gets fed up of that, realises that with the benefits she doesn't need him any more, and kicks him out. But then she's on her own, and while back home you can have the extended family look after the kids, here she's just got herself.'

A good case study of the problems Mohammed described was Mohammed Abdullahi, who'd moved to London from Somalia back in 1997. A quietly-spoken, earnest 31-year-old, today he was a community worker in Islington and a cultural advisor to Scotland Yard. As a teenager, though, he'd been a member of a Somali street gang.

'When I first came here I was living near the Odeon Cinema in Holloway,' Abdullahi told me. 'The weather was different, the people were different and the language was different, so I couldn't understand what was going on. It felt like being deaf the whole time. I ended up with this new group of Somali friends, who were the only people who could speak my language, and I didn't really have any choice but to hang around with them. But as I got to know them, I found they were into drugs, robbing and stealing.'

For a time, Abdullahi enjoyed himself. Gang membership brought the shy, skinny youngster things that were otherwise unavailable – money, girls, and respect, or at least fear, from others.

'You get to like the bling, the drugs, the power of people being afraid of you whenever you walk down the street or get on the bus,' he said. 'You can act how you like, shout in the street, have no respect for anybody at all.'

Gradually, though, his new lifestyle came to remind him of the militia thugs back home, the very people he'd come to Britain to escape.

'My picture of coming to the UK was wearing a suit, looking good, going to university, joining the army, not stealing or mugging in the street. In Kenya or Somalia you can understand people doing that, but not here.'

Abdullahi drifted away from the gang, doing his exams and going to college. Many of his pals from the old days, though, had not moved on. He told a poignant story about one gang friend from Holloway, Yusuf, whose younger brother, Ahmed, was still in Mogadishu, working as a shoe-shiner outside a government compound. The compound was good spot for business, but a frequent target of mortars. Two of Ahmed's colleagues had died in such attacks. Yet while Yusuf spend his days in London doing little but smoking weed, Ahmed was still trying to better himself, always asking his brother to send him school books.

'Yusuf used to be amazed by his brother's attitude,' Abdullahi said. 'He used to wonder how his brother still had the morale to go and study. Why didn't he just take a gun and rob people? Yusuf actually felt guilty about living in Britain where he had everything, yet choosing to be on the wrong side of life.'

For many Somali men in Britain, there were simple solutions to that sense of personal failure. Either turn over a new leaf, as Abdullahi had done, or blot it out altogether with another lungful of weed or mouthful of qhat. Some, though, were now finding the answer to their angsts in radical Islam. At certain mosques around London, there were imams who would give a familiar, reassuring patter: that the blame for their own fecklessness lay not in themselves, but on the moral decay of the Western culture around them, and the temptations it placed in a good Muslim's way. The Little Mogadishus around Britain were now home to a growing number of young men who had swapped their saggy jeans, baseball caps and spliffs for robes, skull caps and Korans, their self-doubts as street-slingers replaced by self-certainty as zealots.

Both Mohammed and Abdullahi stressed that the vast majority of self-professed 'radicals' were probably harmless. The most they might ever do would be to raise money for the Shabab, who had some sympathy among Somalis in Britain because of their struggle against the Ethiopians. To Mohammed, that was little different to Irish pubs in north London passing round a bucket for 'the cause' in the 1970s. Yet rumours persisted that a few young Somalis were actually going to train in the Shabab's ranks, just as young Pakistanis from northern England had gone to Al Qaeda camps in Afghanistan. Who they were, and how many, nobody really knew. Such people seldom broadcast their intentions. But Mohammed and Abdullahi would both hear the odd story second or third-hand. It usually involved a family fretting about their son, often a tearaway who'd recently become religious, and who'd now mysteriously disappeared abroad on a 'study break'.

Already, there was one documented case, that of Abu Ayyub al-Muhajir, the *nom de guerre* for a 21-year-old Somali student from Ealing. In 2007, after dropping out from Oxford Brookes University, he'd gone to Somalia as a volunteer for the Shabab, blowing himself up at an Ethiopian army checkpoint and killing 20 soldiers. In a video shot before his death, he urged fellow British Somalis to follow his example, talking in a soft, earnest English accent not unlike Mohammed's.

'I advise you to migrate to Somalia and wage war against your enemies,' he said, speaking against a backdrop of a black and white Shabab banner. 'Death in honour is better than life in humiliation.'

Despite his efforts, Abu Ayyub had not generated much publicity. The British media didn't care that much about Somalis killing themselves in their own country. But both Mohammed and Farad feared that one day, they would turn on the TV news and learn that some radicalised Somali had blown himself up on a bus or Tube train in London, killing dozens. That, they predicted, would cause a nationwide backlash against Somalis in general, just as it had done against the Pakistanis after July 7. Already fragile, dysfunctional and leaderless, the Somali community would be ill-equipped to cope.

'I am really scared that it will be people from our community who carry out the next big terrorist attack in Britain,' said Abdullahi. 'A lot of Somalis don't like to talk about this kind of thing, or they say I am exaggerating the threat and that it is only a tiny minority of people who get involved in radicalism. But you only need a tiny minority to do the damage.'

Mohammed was blunter still. Even if Britain's Somali community didn't stage its own version of July 7, it risked self-destructing of its own accord anyway, just like the old country had 20 years ago. 'I give us one more generation,' he said, shaking his head. 'We need to make the transition to living here properly. Otherwise we will exist as a people, but as a culture and a legacy we will become extinct.'

Afterword

AS I WRITE the last few pages of this book, a sleeping figure lies next to me under a blanket, now mercifully silent after yet another night of snoring and grunting. It is not, thank God, another kidnapped Spanish photographer, but my daughter Robyn, who was born to Jane and me six months ago. I am still in touch with my old bedfellow from the caves of Somalia, though, and I hope that in a few years' time, Robyn will get to meet Uncle José, and learn all about the strange adventure that we had together. It will make an interesting postscript to my battered 1965 copy of the *Ladybird Book of Pirates*, which my parents read to me as a child, and which I now intend to read to her one day.

Still, the unexpected new chapter in the age old tale of piracy is as yet unfinished. As of now, February 2011, more than 700 mariners are being held hostage on the Somali coast, with 67 ships hijacked in the last 12 months alone. Piracy now costs the world economy an estimated $12 billion a year, according to a recent report by London's Chatham House think-tank – and kidnapped sailors are sometimes paying the price in blood. This month four American yachters were killed by their hijackers during a stand-off with a US warship, one of a growing number of cases where pirates have turned to violence. Other tactics have included dragging hostages in the sea, locking them in freezers, and torturing them – all acts of brutality designed to make shipping firms pay ransoms more quickly. The anti-piracy task force, meanwhile, is now patrolling as far out as the Seychelles Islands, 1,000 miles east of the Somali coast, which served as pirate havens themselves back in the 1700s.

In those days of old, pirates often drew a symbol of an hourglass alongside their Jolly Roger flag. In an age before clocks and watches, its message to any would-be prey was just as bloodcurdlingly clear as the skull and crossbones – your time is running out. Today, the naval commanders are saying the same thing about the Somali pirates, insisting that sooner or later, the bonanza will end. Protection measures are more sophisticated, and ships more alert, making successful attacks harder. In the Seychelles, extra courts and prisons are being built, and elsewhere, new laws are being drafted to prosecute pirates for conspiracy rather than having to catch them in the act. Soon, the naval commanders claim, the risk-reward ratio will tilt to the point where buccaneering no longer seems an attractive career.

Or will it? Try telling that to Farah Ahmed Yusuf and his gang, who were seized by an anti-piracy patrol as they tried to hijack a freighter on January 5, 2009 – the day after I was released in Bossaso. The Dutch government decided to make an example of them by taking them back for prosecution in Holland, and 18 months later, I sat in a maximum security courtroom in Rotterdam as they became the first pirates to face trial in Europe in modern times. It quickly became clear, though, that getting caught might be the best thing that ever happened to them. Yusuf's defence lawyer, Willem-Jan Ausma, told me that the soft Dutch jail his client was being held in, complete with its TV and en-suite bathroom, was the most comfortable place he'd ever stayed in his life.

'When I first spoke to him, he said being here was like heaven,' he said. 'For the first time in his life he didn't feel he was in danger, and he was in a modern prison with the first modern toilet and shower that he'd ever had.'

Not that Yusuf was facing long inside. Having convicted him and his four cohorts of the obscure 17th century offence of 'sea robbery', the Dutch court sentenced them to just five years in prison each. Taking into account the 18 months already served on remand, and time off for good behaviour, they could expect to be free within less than a year – and then apply for asylum to remain in Holland permanently. As in Britain, the Dutch authorities deem Somalia too dangerous to repatriate people to, even convicts. 'When it is not possible to send them back to their own country, the judge will just have to set them free, like thousands of other Somalis who are here already,' Ausma said.

Thus, by committing an act of piracy, Yusuf had achieved the very goal dreamed of by my old friend Faisal and so many others who flocked to the people smugglers' boats in Bossaso. It can scarcely have been the message that the Dutch intended to send out. Yet with people for whom normal life is so grim that even jail can seem like paradise, it is hard to know what deterrent would really work. Just like the pyrates of old, they are desperate men, who will roll the dice of death-or-glory even when it is loaded against them. And as long as they have a safe haven from where they can hold hostages, negotiate ransoms, and, crucially, spend their ransom cash, passing ships will always be at risk. So too, will be aid workers, businessmen, journalists like me and any other foreign visitors to Somalia.

Despite this, there is no talk whatsoever of any new international effort to stabilise the country. The West has had enough on its plate over the past decade with Afghanistan and Iraq. It has no stomach to intervene in yet another volatile Muslim land, especially not one like Somalia, which has few strategic resources, and which has already demonstrated, back in the days of *Black Hawk Down*, just how savagely it can bite any hand that tries to feed it. As the Mad Mullah himself told the British a century ago: 'I have no cultivated fields, no silver, no gold for you to take. I have nothing... All you can get from me is war – nothing else.'

Instead, Somalia remains left to its own devices, the only officially failed state in the world, and one that has now been that way for 20 years. As many Somalis tell me, there is now an entire generation of youngsters there who have grown up without any idea of government at all, knowing only the law of the gun, or, in areas controlled by the Shabab, some extreme interpretation of the Koran. As Britain's M15 chief Jonathan Evans recently pointed out, that makes it a prime potential breeding ground for international terrorism, just as Afghanistan was when it hosted Al Qaeda and the 9/11 plotters.

True, there are those who doubt that claim. Even jihadists crave a little stability in their lives, and Somalia is so anarchic now that even Al Qaeda might find it hard to operate there reliably. But it is still civilisation in reverse, and with every year that passes, life in Somalia will become more nasty, brutish and short, and all the harder to get back into forward gear again. Ironically, when the piracy boom first started, many Somalis hoped that it might at least encourage the outside world to help them again, to give the land that committed suicide a chance to clamber out of the grave. Yet so far, despite the best efforts of the 'ladder salesmen', that hope has not come true. And until it does, I may never have the chance to return to that cave in those empty northern mountains, and see whether my initials are still on the wall.

Also from Monday Books

Generation F / Winston Smith

(ppbk, £8.99)

Youth worker Winston Smith - winner of the Orwell Prize for his edgy, controversial and passionate writing - opens a door on the murky, tragic world of children's care homes and supported housing schemes. Frightening, revealing and sometimes very funny, *Generation F* is his story.

'Winston Smith paints a terrifying picture'
- *The Daily Mail*

'What carried the day was his passion and conviction that we should know what wrongs had been done in our names' - *Orwell Prize judges*

From all good bookshops, online from www.mondaybooks.com or via 01455 221752.
All of our titles are also available as eBooks from amazon.co.uk

Sick Notes / Dr Tony Copperfield

(ppbk, £8.99)

Welcome to the bizarre world of Tony Copperfield, family doctor. He spends his days fending off anxious mums, elderly sex maniacs and hopeless hypochondriacs (with his eyes peeled for the odd serious symptom). The rest of his time is taken up sparring with colleagues, battling bureaucrats and banging his head against the brick walls of the NHS.

If you've ever wondered what your GP is really thinking - and what's actually going on behind the scenes at your surgery - *SICK NOTES* is for you.

'A wonderful book, funny and insightful in equal measure'
– Dr Phil Hammond (Private Eye's 'MD')

'Copperfield is simply fantastic, unbelievably funny and improbably wise... everything he writes is truer than fact'
– British Medical Journal

'Original, funny and an incredible read' – ***The Sun***

Tony Copperfield is a Medical Journalist of the Year, has been shortlisted for UK Columnist of the Year many times and writes regularly for *The Times* and other media.

From all good bookshops, online from www.mondaybooks.com or via 01455 221752.
All of our titles are also available as eBooks from amazon.co.uk

Perverting The Course Of Justice / Inspector Gadget

(ppbk, £7.99)

A senior serving policeman picks up where PC Copperfield left off and reveals how far the insanity extends – children arrested for stealing sweets from each other while serious criminals go about their business unmolested.

'Exposes the reality of life at the sharp end'
– *The Daily Telegraph*

'No wonder they call us Plods... A frustrated inspector speaks out on the madness of modern policing'
– *The Daily Mail*

'Staggering... exposes the bloated bureaucracy that is crushing Britain' – *The Daily Express*

'You must buy this book... it is a fascinating insight'
– *Kelvin MacKenzie, The Sun*

In April 2010, Inspector Gadget was named one of the country's 'best 40 bloggers' by *The Times*.

From all good bookshops, online from www.mondaybooks.com or via 01455 221752.
All of our titles are also available as eBooks from amazon.co.uk

Second Opinion: A Doctor's Dispatches from the Inner City

Theodore Dalrymple (hdbk, £14.99)

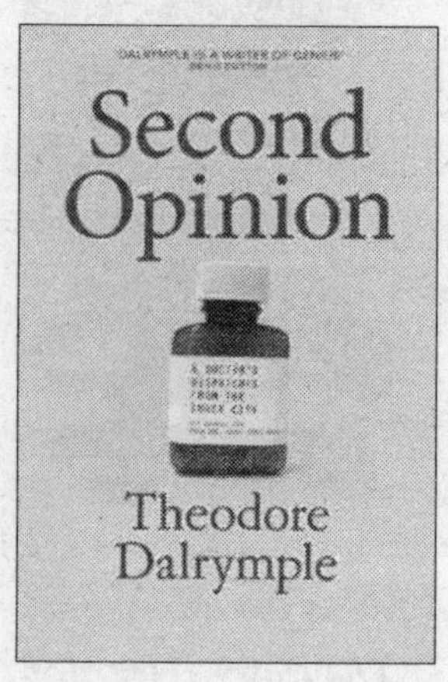

Theodore Dalrymple has spent much of his working life as a doctor in a grim inner city hospital and the nearby prison; his patients are drug addicts and drunks, violent men and battered women, suicidal teenagers and despairing elderly. For many years, Dalrymple - acknowledged as the world's leading doctor-writer - wrote a column in The Spectator in which he recounted his experiences. This collection of those shocking, amusing and elegant columns offers a window into a world many of us never see.

'Dalrymple's dispatches from the frontline have a tone and a quality entirely their own... their rarity makes you sit up and take notice'

– ***Marcus Berkmann, The Spectator***

'Dalrymple is a modern master'

– ***Stephen Poole, The Guardian***

'The George Orwell of our time... a writer of genius'

– ***Denis Dutton***

From all good bookshops, online from www.mondaybooks.com or via 01455 221752.

All of our titles are also available as eBooks from amazon.co.uk